Alexander
the
Great

The World Generals Series

"Palgrave's World Generals Series will feature great leaders whose reputations have transcended their own nations, whose bold characters led to new forms of combat, whose determination and courage gave shape to new dynasties and civilizations—men whose creativity and courage inspired multitudes. Beginning with illustrious World War II German Field Marshall Irwin Rommel, known as the Desert Fox, the series will shed new light on famous warrior-leaders like Napoleon, Frederick the Great, Alexander, Julius Caesar, Genghis Khan, drawing out the many important leadership lessons that are still relevant to our lives today."

—*Gen. Wesley K. Clark*

This distinguished new series will feature the lives of eminent military leaders from around the world who changed history. Top military historians will write concise but comprehensive biographies including the personal lives, battles, strategies and legacies of these great generals, with the aim to provide background and insight into contemporary armies and wars as well as to draw lessons for the leaders of today.

Rommel by Charles Messenger

Alexander the Great by Bill Yenne

Montgomery by Trevor Royle

Alexander
the
Great
Lessons from History's
Undefeated General

Bill Yenne

palgrave
macmillan

ALEXANDER THE GREAT
Copyright © Bill Yenne, 2010.

First published in 2010 by PALGRAVE MACMILLAN® in the U.S.—a
division of St. Martin's Press LLC, 175 Fifth Avenue, New York, NY
10010.

Where this book is distributed in the UK, Europe and the rest of the world,
this is by Palgrave Macmillan, a division of Macmillan Publishers Limited,
registered in England, company number 785998, of Houndmills,
Basingstoke, Hampshire RG21 6XS.

Palgrave Macmillan is the global academic imprint of the above companies
and has companies and representatives throughout the world.

Palgrave® and Macmillan® are registered trademarks in the United States,
the United Kingdom, Europe and other countries.

ISBN: 978-0-230-61915-9

Library of Congress Cataloging-in-Publication Data is available from the
Library of Congress.

A catalogue record of the book is available from the British Library.

Design by Letra Libre

First edition: April 2010
10 9 8 7 6 5 4 3 2 1
Printed in the United States of America.

Contents

Illustrations appear between pages 102 and 103.

Foreword

ALEXANDER THE GREAT WAS THE FIRST GREAT MILITARY COMMANDER OF the West. Before him were legends or mere mortals; after him, all were emulators. No one since has moved as far, as rapidly or as successfully given their respective technologies: not Julius Caesar, not Hannibal, not Genghis Khan, nor Gustavus Adolphus, not Napoleon, and not the armies of Hitler or Stalin.

Bill Yenne's fast moving and insightful biography of Alexander is the best yet at drawing out the lessons from history's first and greatest undefeated general. It is more than a record of battles and campaigns; rather, it is a remarkable and compelling life story.

Alexander's life was to fight and conquer, to craft and lead armies, to seek and solve complex tactical and strategic challenges, whether they were military, logistical or geographic. He sowed fear in the psyche of his enemies, and reached deeply into the hearts and minds of his followers to grasp the deepest wellsprings of motivation, courage and commitment. No one has ever done all this more successfully.

Alexander was, first and foremost, born into the role. Son of the most prominent and successful military leader of his day, Philip of Macedonia, Alexander was brought up in the company of warriors, weaponry, physical challenge, personal leadership, court intrigue, Greek city-state diplomacy and raw ambition.

His physical gifts were awesome. Strength, coordination, stamina, eyesight—even his physical appearance was impressive. By age 16 he was mature enough physically and emotionally to command a wing of an army.

And, at the same time, he was tutored by the best minds of contemporary civilization, including Aristotle. To put it in modern lexicon, he was a lot more than just a "warrior spirit," though he certainly had that. He was also an innovative problem-solver and a non-doctrinaire visionary who continued to push the boundaries of Western civilization technologically and intellectually.

Alexander was inordinately self-confident—but with good reason. He had proven himself from his earliest days. His extraordinary innate physical and mental qualities were trained, disciplined and hardened emotionally and physically in a way none of his adversaries—nor the over two thousand years of would-be emulators—could have ever replicated. He had seen battle, rivalries and war from his earliest experiences.

Leading from the front was Alexander's trademark. He was in the thick of the fight, and often in the front rank. He must have seen and smelled the fear and blood-lust of close battle, and thrust and swung his weapons with extraordinary effect. By his example he challenged others. And he must have learned and grown stronger with each bout and battle.

For there is this about combat—it is learned by experience. The lessons are not altogether transferrable in words or logic. And by having fought and survived time and again he must have built an enormous store of "battle-savvy," that killer instinct of when to thrust, when to pivot and when to parry. In modern lexicon, his skills and learning might be best understood as a professional athlete, say an NFL quarterback, who consistently delivers something beyond the playbook, whose instincts and on-the-field presence carry the team beyond the coach.

But to carry the analogy forward, most of his opponents were not even in the same league. They hadn't been schooled and hardened in the incessant conflict of Greece; they hadn't been coached and tutored by the best; and they hadn't been seasoned by so much leadership and responsibility from an early age.

At West Point, we studied his lessons tactically—all the principles of war that we study date back to Alexander. The principles of the objective, mass, maneuver, the offensive, economy of force, security, surprise and simplicity. He used maneuvers to break up the enemy's plans, and to seize and maintain the initiative. He was active—he imposed his plans on the enemy. He was adaptable, and relentless in pursuing decisive tactical advantage. In battle after battle, open battlefield, siege and pursuit as Alexander marched through Asia—feats wonderfully described by Yenne—these principles shine through. His legacy has thus formed the basis for over two thousand years of Western military thought.

No less remarkable were Alexander's strategy, logistics and communications. He kept his army focused on long range objectives. He periodically halted, refreshed and reorganized. He maintained contact with the reaches of his far-flung and growing empire by courier. His battles flowed into campaigns, his campaigns into seasons, and the seasons into more than a decade of systematic conquest. He didn't overcommit, outrun his logistics or collapse back on his line of communications—all of which are signs of strategic error.

Equally remarkable was his diplomacy and governance. He rewarded friends, formed governing structures and created loyalties even among those whom he defeated and who were of widely diverse cultures. He did everything but establish succession—but then, he hardly expected to die of disease at the age of 33 either.

Today, our battlefields are too lethal, and the scales too vast for the kind of up-front tactical leadership by the highest level commanders. Gunpowder, rifled weaponry, the machine gun and artillery all increased the lethal zone. Today, high powered optics, electronic intelligence collection and synthesis, satellites, aircraft and missiles have further extended the battlefield. What can be seen can be hit, and what can be hit can be killed—this is the mantra of modern precision weaponry. Command is exercised electronically, even in real-time. Top commanders seldom face their opponents physically and in-person, and rarely smell the fear of the impending clash of arms.

Still, the legacy of Alexander endures to inform and will inspire generations to come. He did it all, without defeat. He was in the cockpit of command earlier, longer, at greater personal risk and more successfully than any who have followed. May he be studied for the right purpose, and the lessons used for the right aims. This is what we must hope and strive to ensure.

—*General Wesley K. Clark (ret)*

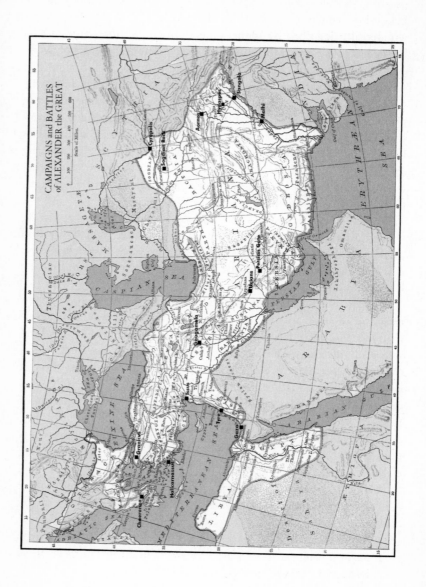

CAMPAIGNS and BATTLES
of ALEXANDER the GREAT

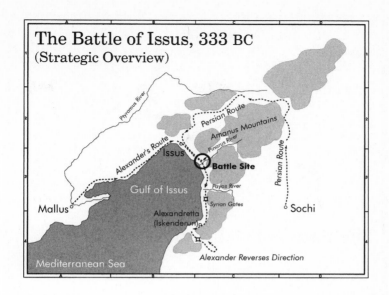

The Battle of Issus, 333 BC
(Strategic Overview)

Phyramus River

Persian Route

Amanus Mountains

Alexander's Route

Pinarus River

Issus

Persian Route

Battle Site

Gulf of Issus

Payas River

Mallus

Syrian Gates

Sochi

Alexandretta
(Iskenderun)

Mediterranean Sea

Alexander Reverses Direction

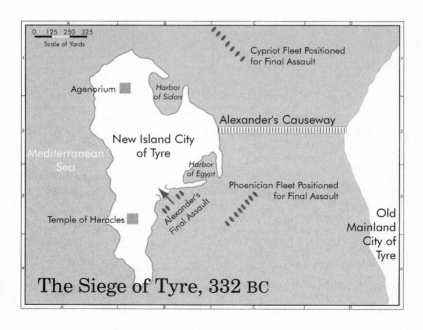

0 125 250 325
Scale of Yards

Cypriot Fleet Positioned
for Final Assault

Agenorium

Harbor
of Sidon

Alexander's Causeway

New Island City
of Tyre

Mediterranean
Sea

Harbor
of Egypt

Phoenician Fleet Positioned
for Final Assault

Temple of Heracles

Alexander's
Final Assault

Old
Mainland
City of
Tyre

The Siege of Tyre, 332 BC

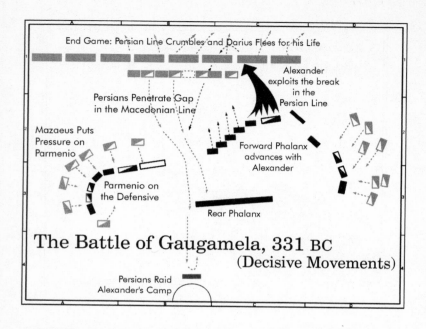

End Game: Persian Line Crumbles and Darius Flees for his Life

Alexander exploits the break in the Persian Line

Persians Penetrate Gap in the Macedonian Line

Mazaeus Puts Pressure on Parmenio

Parmenio on the Defensive

Forward Phalanx advances with Alexander

Rear Phalanx

The Battle of Gaugamela, 331 BC
(Decisive Movements)

Persians Raid Alexander's Camp

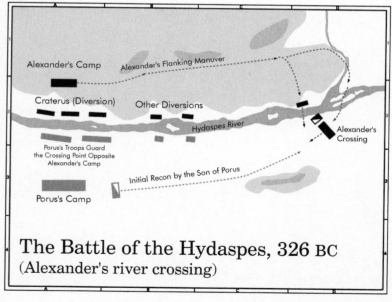

Alexander's Camp

Alexander's Flanking Manuver

Craterus (Diversion)

Other Diversions

Hydaspes River

Alexander's Crossing

Porus's Troops Guard the Crossing Point Opposite Alexander's Camp

Initial Recon by the Son of Porus

Porus's Camp

The Battle of the Hydaspes, 326 BC
(Alexander's river crossing)

Prologue

AROUND MIDNIGHT ON THE LAST DAY OF SEPTEMBER IN 331 BC, ON a mountain somewhere east of the modern Iraqi city of Mosul, a group of Macedonian officers took a walk. They went to the edge of a cliff to look out at the vast encampment of their enemy at a place called Gaugamela. What they saw made their blood run cold.

Writes Lucius Mestrius Plutarchus, better known as Plutarch (ca. AD 46–120), in his *Lives of Noble Greeks and Romans,* "When they saw the plain between the Niphates and the Gordyaean mountains all lighted up with the barbarian fires, while an indistinguishably mingled and tumultuous sound of voices arose from their camp as if from a vast ocean, they were astonished at their multitude and argued with one another that it was a great and grievous task to repel such a tide of war."

Before them lay the enormous army of Darius III, the monarch of the Achaemenid Persian Empire, the greatest empire yet seen in the history of the world. Observers reported, and historians long believed, that the Macedonian officers gazed that night upon the campfires of a million-man army.

Only eleven nights had passed since the Macedonians had looked into the sky and seen the most disturbing of omens. "First the moon lost its usual brightness, and then became suffused with a blood-red color which caused a general dimness in the light it shed," writes the first-century AD historian Curtius (Quintus Curtius Rufus) of this lunar eclipse in his *Historiae Alexandri Magni,* or *History of Alexander the Great.* "Right on the brink of a decisive battle [at Gaugamela] the men were already in a state of anxiety, and this now struck them with a deep religious awe which precipitated a kind of panic."

The Macedonian officers, though they were victorious veterans of two titanic field battles against the Persian army, thought that their time had run out. It was their belief that they were outnumbered by a factor of about 20 to 1, and that defeat awaited them in the coming battle.

They went to the tent where their commander was relaxing, and nervously proposed that the only viable tactic against such an immense foe would be a surprise attack under cover of darkness.

When their commander had heard them out, the 25-year-old Alexander of Macedonia looked up and replied. According to Plutarch, Alexander told them, "I will not steal my victory."

By this he meant that he wished the coming battle to be decisive and conclusive. Alexander wanted there to be no doubt that Darius had been beaten—fair and square, and in broad daylight for all to see.

That night in the light of his own fire, Alexander calmly projected the confidence of a man who had no doubt of his victory the following day.

Three years earlier, as he was preparing for his unprecedented campaign against the Persian Empire, the priestess at the oracle of Delphi had told him "Thou art invincible, my son!"

She was right. He was never defeated in battle.

He had beaten Darius's army at the Granicus River (now known as Biga Çayi or Kocabas Çayi) in 334 BC, and Darius himself at Issus in 333 BC. At Gaugamela, he would defeat the greatest empire in the history of the world, and bring into being a new one that was even greater.

His empire was almost of the same geographical scale as the Roman Empire, but the Romans had been empire-building for centuries by the time their dominion reached its greatest extent under Trajan. Alexander did it all in a dozen years.

Alexander's influence on the course of cultural and political history was felt in the fusion of Greek, Middle Eastern and Indian civilizations that is characterized as the Hellenistic Age, the period from 323 BC to AD 30, when Greek cultural influence and power were at their peak in Europe and Asia.

So highly regarded were Alexander's accomplishments in his lifetime and thereafter that there was a widely held belief that he was the son, not of a mortal father, but of Zeus, the king of the gods. Even four centuries after his death, his biographer Arrian (Lucius Flavius Arrianus; second century AD), wrote in *Anabasis Alexandri* or *The Campaigns of Alexander*, "it seems to me that a hero totally unlike any other human being could not have been born without the agency of the deity."

He was actually the son of Philip II of Macedonia, or Macedon, the warrior king who was the first ruler to unify Greece. Born in 356 BC, Alexander was educated personally by the great philosopher Aristotle, became a consummate horseman, and heroically commanded a wing of his father's army in the victory over the Thebans and Athenians at the Battle of Chaeronea—all while he was still a teenager.

Alexander's strategic vision is legendary. When he was still a boy, Philip once remarked that Alexander would need a great empire because Macedonia was too small for him. Philip was right. Of course, strategic vision is only one thing. Alexander also had both the skill to realize that vision by creating an empire of unprecedented scale *and* the shrewdness to manage this empire.

Conversely, he has been characterized as a megalomaniac whose delusions of grandeur were fed by his battlefield successes and by his coming to believe the stories that he was the son of Zeus. His great military campaign began with a widely supported mandate to crush the Persian Empire on behalf of Greece. However, he was widely criticized, in his own time and later, for continuing the campaign beyond Persia in order to fulfill his extravagant desire to rule the whole world.

Setting aside the motivations that drove him, Alexander conducted his campaigns with both military discipline and a strategic prescience that complemented his aspirations.

While many strategic visionaries lack tactical dexterity, Alexander had it in abundance. His battlefield victories were the building blocks of his campaigns, just as his campaigns brought him his empire. Repeatedly, we see Alexander's tactical brilliance manifesting itself in his being able to maneuver his way to victory despite being outnumbered by substantial margins.

At Gaugamela, he was almost certainly outnumbered by a narrower margin than 20 to 1, but he still faced an army more than twice the size of his own. Yet he soundly defeated this army. He did so by audaciously outflanking Darius with cavalry even before the battle began, by doubling his phalanx into two parts to prevent Darius from outflanking *him,* and by personally leading a fearless cavalry charge that caused a panicked Darius to abandon his chariot and flee the battlefield on a purloined horse.

Probably no more than a few days or weeks after Alexander's victory, a scribe in Babylon sat down to record the event in cuneiform on a clay tablet that today rests in a climate-controlled case in the British Museum in London. Having noted that "a heavy defeat was inflicted on the troops of Darius," this ancient historian noted that "on the twenty-fourth of the lunar month [October 1, 331 BC], in the morning, the King of the World erected his flag."

The military leader who exuded confidence in the flickering firelight on the last day of September was Alexander III of Macedonia. The man called the King of the World, who erected his flag on the battlefield about 12 hours later, was Alexander the Great.

Born into a State of War

DURING THE FOURTH AND FIFTH CENTURIES BC, A COLD WAR WAS BEING waged between the Persian Empire and the Greek city-states that defined the political history of what was, to them, the entire known world. Apart from several years of open conflict at the beginning of the fifth century BC and the much-heralded campaigns of 490 and 480–479 BC, this war was characterized by subterfuge and proxy warfare. It was an era of Persian backing of individual city-states in intra-Hellenic conflicts, as they sought to leverage one Greek faction against the other. By the time Alexander of Macedonia was born, this Greco-Persian state of war had been a reality for nearly 150 years.

Before the beginning of the fifth century BC, these two political and cultural poles had evolved separately. Greek, or Hellenic, culture spread from modern Greece throughout the northeastern Mediterranean. Hellenic influence was present from the shores of the Black Sea to present-day Italy and was particularly dominant within the rim of the Aegean Sea, including the west coast of what is now Turkey, then known as Asia Minor.

The Persian Empire grew outward from modern Iran, absorbing the Assyrian Empire to the west in the eighth century BC. The empire reached its greatest extent during the Achaemenid Dynasty, which began with Cyrus the Great in the sixth century BC and lasted for two centuries until it was crushed by Alexander himself.

Under Cyrus, the Persian Empire came to include present Afghanistan, Kazakhstan and Kyrgyzstan. He also brought Hellenic enclaves along the eastern shore of the Aegean, notably Ionia, under Persian rule. In the course of his empire building, Cyrus established a reputation for Persian armies being ruthlessly efficient—and unbeatable.

The Persian dominions were governed by satraps, puppet governors, who might be drawn from local populations but who answered to the Persian monarch. The term itself derives from the Persian word for "protector of the province," and is the equivalent of the later title "viceroy."

When he was killed in battle in 530 BC, Cyrus was succeeded briefly by a series of ineffective relatives, and finally, in 522 by a Zoroastrian Persian who would rule for 36 years as Darius I, or Darius the Great. Under Darius, the Persian Empire expanded northward into modern Ukraine and crossed the Bosporus, extending into Europe. He conquered eastern Thrace, including parts of what is now Bulgaria, and reached the Danube River. Though Hellenic culture still predominated in the regions of the Aegean rim, monolithic Persian rule brought a new political reality to the area.

While the Persians were unified under a single powerful emperor, the Greek city-states were independent political entities. Persian emperors ruled as absolute monarchs, while in Greece Athens was flirting with democracy by the beginning of the fifth century BC.

The clash between Hellenic and Persian civilizations boiled over into open conflict in 499 BC as the Persian-occupied Hellenic states of Asia Minor revolted. With the help of Athens and Eretria on the Greek mainland, the Ionian Revolt succeeded at first, but withered under a Persian counterattack.

Though he recovered the Greek cities that had briefly thrown off Persian rule, Darius saw the rebellion as both an affront and a genuine security threat. He therefore decided that the best defense against the Greeks was a good offense—so he decided to conquer all of Greece.

In 492 BC, Darius launched the first Persian invasion of the heart of Greece. He won early battlefield successes in Thrace, and coerced Macedonia into becoming a Persian vassal state.

In 490 Darius captured a number of Aegean islands and made an unopposed landing near Eretria on the Greek mainland north of Athens. With Eretria captured, the Persians moved south, intending to seize Athens. After a landing at Marathon, they were only about two dozen miles from the city.

Under the veteran commander Miltiades, the Athenians succeeded in bottling up the Persian army on the Plain of Marathon for nearly a week. To break the deadlock, the Persian leader Artaphernes decided on an end run. Since he couldn't get through the Athenian line, he pulled out a sizable force, including his cavalry, and embarked to sail around the Attic peninsula to attack Athens directly.

However, it was Miltiades who broke the stalemate. With the Persian force at Marathon depleted, the Athenian army launched a double envelopment, crushing the Persians from both sides. The battle is recognized as an important turning point in Western history for having saved the flowering of Athenian civilization from being nipped in the bud by Persian occupation.

Not until 480 BC did Persia, under Darius's son and heir, Xerxes I, renew the campaign against the Greeks. In the meantime, the principal Greek city-states, including notably both Athens and Sparta, had met near Corinth at the suggestion of the Athenian leader Themistocles and agreed to form a coalition to present a united front against the Persians.

Rather than repeating his father's 490 amphibious landings in central Greece, Xerxes traveled overland, as had Darius I in 492. His idea was to enter Greece with a force large enough to subdue all of Greece in one campaigning season.

The Greek coalition strategy, advanced by Themistocles, called for intercepting the superior number of Persians at the confined spaces of the pass through the mountains at Thermopylae. By hitting the Persians in a narrow choke-point, rather than on a broad battlefield such as Marathon, the defenders could neutralize the impact of the very large numbers of the Persian army.

As it had been the Athenians who met the Persians at Marathon, it was the Spartans who met the Persians at Thermopylae. Specifically, it was Sparta's King Leonidas I, the core of whose force included 300 men of his elite bodyguard.

The narrow pass at Thermopylae greatly benefited the defenders, and the Persian advance sputtered to a bloody halt. Only after a traitor showed the Persians a little-known path by which they could outflank the Spartans was Xerxes able to break the impasse. The Persian leader finally crushed Leonidas and his troops, but at immense cost.

Meanwhile, Greek naval forces successfully impeded the Persian fleet in the Straits of Artemisium, though it did not stop them.

In the wake of their defeat at Thermopylae, the Greek armies were unable to prevent the Persians from marching into Athens, though by the time they reached the city, most of the civilian population had been evacuated. It was rather like Napoleon's capture of Moscow in 1812. It was strong on symbolism, but an empty city is merely an empty city. In order to defeat the Greeks, Xerxes needed to destroy their military power, not merely capture symbolic targets. To consolidate Persian power in Greece, he needed to cross into the Peloponnesus, the peninsula south of the Gulf of Corinth that constitutes the southern part of modern Greece. He also needed to eliminate Athenian naval power. Fortunately for the Athenians and for Greece, however, Themistocles had realized after Marathon that an important prerequisite to Persian domination of Greece would be domination of the Aegean Sea. For this reason, he had built up the navy, even at the expense of Athenian land forces.

The milestone battle for the future of Greece was to occur at sea. It came in September 480, near the island of Salamis off the south coast of the Attic peninsula, not far from Athens. As had been the case at Thermopylae, the Straits of Salamis presented a very confined space, and one where the Persian numeric superiority would be less effective than it might have been in the open sea.

The Persian vessels fell into disarray as the Greeks maintained a disciplined battle line. Watching from a hilltop on the shore, Xerxes witnessed the decisive defeat of his fleet. Though the campaign continued into 479, Salamis marked the high-water point in the defeat of the Persian attempt to conquer Greece. Like Marathon, Salamis is seen as one of the turning-point battles of world history. Attempts by

Xerxes to recapture the initiative in the summer of 479 met with losses at Plataea and Mycale that marked the end of realistic Persian ambitions in Greece.

As the sun set on the great campaigns of 480–479, there was no adjournment of the cold war. Xerxes' son Artaxerxes I waged war indirectly against the Greeks, especially the Athenians, by financing proxy wars, or simply funneling cash and hardware to anti-Athenian elements among other Greek city-states.

As the direct Persian military threat abated, the rivalry between Athens and Sparta over political and military primacy within Greece came to the fore.

❖

Sparta's political sphere of influence centered on the Peloponnesus, where it controlled a military alliance of regional city-states, known as the Peloponnesian League. Northeast of the Peloponnesus in Attica, a peninsula extending into the Aegean Sea, Athens had evolved into a maritime power whose sphere of influence was the Aegean rim.

Militarily, the respective strengths of Athens and Sparta were roughly analogous to those of the British Empire and the German Empire prior to World War I. While Britain was the world's leading sea power, Germany possessed the most powerful land army in Europe.

Meanwhile, as Sparta evolved into a military society, Athens became a great center of scholarship, literature and the arts that would influence Western European civilization for centuries. As Athenian political power was reaching its peak, the city's great philosophers, such as Socrates and Plato, created the foundation of Western philosophy. Pericles, who had commanded the Athenians at Mycale, became the leader of Athens by way of the democratic process that flourished in the city, and he presided over what historians regard as a golden age of Athenian civilization.

As Sparta dominated the Peloponnesian League, Athens formed its own bloc, the Delian League, named for the island of Delos, where Athens and its allied city-states met to formalize their association. A recent analogy would be the rival Cold War alliances of NATO and the Warsaw Pact.

Athens and Sparta, along with their blocs, came to blows in a series of armed conflicts that reached their climax in the Peloponnesian

War, which began in 431 BC. As the two states battled, Persia backed Sparta with money and matériel, having deduced that more mileage was to be had on their road to keeping the Greeks off balance by taking the indirect approach than through a direct attack.

During the long conflict, both sides were able to thwart attempts by the other to invade their territory. However, the tide turned when Athens felt obliged to intervene in a conflict in Sicily between its allies and Sparta's allies. An unanticipated and disastrous defeat of the Athenian fleet in a series of naval battles marked the beginning of the end for Athens, which finally capitulated in 404.

Buoyed by their success in the Peloponnesian War, the Spartans undertook a somewhat successful campaign in Asia Minor aimed at liberating the Greek cities from their wartime allies, the Persians. With the Spartans thus overextended, a coalition including Athens, Corinth and Thebes attacked the Spartans in Greece in 395 BC. The Persians now switched sides, backing the anti-Sparta coalition in the ensuing Corinthian War. Sparta was unable to achieve a repeat of its triumphant campaigns of 406–404, and the war devolved into a stalemate. At sea, a revived Athenian navy was able to reassert Athenian dominance in many areas of the Aegean rim.

As Spartan luck waned, the pendulum swung back and the Persians closed their purse to the Athenians. It was Persia's King Artaxerxes II who engineered the truce that ended the Corinthian War. The Persian Empire had essentially won another Greek war by again tipping the balance between Athens and Sparta.

In this twilight of Athenian and Spartan power came the series of events that would set the stage onto which Alexander would step as he began his climb to greatness.

⊞

Alexander's doctrinal grandfather was the statesman and military leader Epaminondas of Thebes. As a young man, Alexander was greatly influenced militarily by his father, Philip II of Macedonia, whose tutor in such matters had been Epaminondas.

Persia had created a power vacuum by equalizing and neutralizing Athens and Sparta, and Thebes inserted itself into this space when Epaminondas achieved a shocking and unexpected victory over a Spartan-led force at Leuctra in 371 BC. It was traditional practice to organize soldiers into rectangular blocks called phalanxes, with each man on the front backed by a dozen others who would press forward if he fell. Also standard procedure was to put the strongest troops on the right wing of the formation.

At Leuctra, Epaminondas outfoxed Sparta's King Cleombrotus by putting his strength on the left and packing his left-wing phalanx 50-men deep. On his right, he arrayed his troops in an echelon formation, which allowed him to outflank the weakest part of the Spartan line.

Military historians have argued for centuries about whether Epaminondas's asymmetrical line was intentional tactical brilliance or mere expediency in the face of a larger force. All agree that it worked. Cleombrotus himself died on the field and the Spartans were decisively routed.

Thebes emerged as the major player among Greek city-states, but only briefly. Nine years later, in 362, there was a rematch at Mantinea, with Thebes supported by Athens. Epaminondas repeated the same basic tactics that had favored him at Leuctra, and again they worked. Thebes prevailed on the battlefield, but Epaminondas himself was killed in action.

Had the great leader survived to relish the victory, Thebes might have remained as it had become after Leuctra, but it would not. Meanwhile, however, neither Sparta nor Athens was strong enough to reassert itself as the dominant power in Greece. The Greek city-states had essentially defeated one another.

Into this vacuum of power stepped a young man from the far north who had learned the art of war from Epaminondas. This man was Philip of Macedonia. Philip turned 20 in the year of Mantinea. He was born in 382 at Pella in Macedonia, the youngest son of King Amyntas III and Queen Eurydice. His bothers, Alexander and Perdiccas, would each precede him as king.

Until the fourth century BC, Macedonia, also called Macedon, had remained a political backwater. In Athens, Corinth, Sparta and Thebes, Macedonians were considered crude barbarians, or at best, untutored country cousins. The flowering of the arts and literature that took place in Athens in the fifth century BC was a far cry from the tribal, hunter-gatherer culture of the Macedonians living in the rugged mountains far to the north.

As the city-states had their ongoing rivalry, Macedonia was in frequent conflict with its neighbors, such as Thrace to the east and Thessaly to the south. To the west were Epirus and Illyria.

When King Amyntas died in 370 BC, and Philip's oldest brother assumed the throne as Alexander II, the Illyrians promptly tested the young king by invading Macedonia. Alexander was able to defeat the Illyrians, but only with Athenian help. Shortly thereafter, Alexander became embroiled in a conflict with Thessaly that brought Thebes into the fight. At the time, Thebes was at its peak as a military power, and Macedonia was forced out of Thessaly. Among their concessions, Alexander was forced cancel his alliance with the Athenians, but he refused to surrender the throne to Ptolemy of Aloros, his mother's lover.

Ptolemy killed Alexander in 368 and served as regent because the middle brother, Perdiccas, was still underage. Three years later, however, Perdiccas killed Ptolemy and assumed the throne as Perdiccas III. To placate the Thebans, Perdiccas was forced to surrender his younger brother, Philip, as a hostage.

In Thebes, Philip grew to manhood close to the center of Theban power. He learned much about both political and military affairs from Epaminondas, and he became acquainted with Plato. His time spent in Thebes can be compared to the eye-opening time that Russia's Peter the Great spent in Western Europe in the 1690s.

Philip returned to Macedonia in 364, two years after Mantinea and well aware of the power vacuum that existed in the Hellenic world after the downfall of Thebes. He saw it as Macedonia's destiny to fill it. When Perdiccas was killed battling the Illyrians in 359, Philip became king.

Philip drew upon large resources of manpower to create a disciplined standing army. Applying what he had learned from Epaminondas and from studying his mentor's victories, Philip allowed more room to maneuver within the phalanx, backing them with mobile cavalry and teams of archers. He also equipped the men in his phalanx with a longer spear known as a sarissa. About 18 feet in length, it proved to be a formidable weapon in the hands of an infantryman strong enough to wield one.

Philip, like Alexander later, utilized the Macedonian cavalry as a shock force, a hammer pushing the enemy against the anvil of the phalanx. While the central phalanx held the enemy center—and held it well, given the length of the sarissa—rather than bashing at it, mobile forces, specifically cavalry, attacked the enemy flanks. The elite horsemen of the Macedonian army, the Companion Cavalry, were organized into eight squadrons averaging 250 men each.

The ultimate success of Philip's Macedonian legions was also attributable to his disciplined and astute subordinate commanders. Just as Napoleon had Louis-Nicolas Davout; just as Ulysses S. Grant had William Tecumseh Sherman; just as Dwight Eisenhower had George Patton, Philip's strategic vision benefitted from the tactical brilliance of a great battlefield commander. Parmenio, also known as Parmenion, helped perfect the tactics that Philip had learned from Epaminondas.

Philip then set about molding Macedonia into the dominant power in Greece, establishing a reputation for invincibility that had perhaps not been seen in Greece since the term had described Sparta at the end of the Peloponnesian War.

In 346 BC, Philip found an auspicious opportunity for his professional army in his successful intervention in the decade-long Third Sacred War, which began as a fight between Thebes and Phocis over who should control Delphi. With its great oracle and its Temple of Apollo, Delphi was a site sacred to all Greeks, so Philip was able to style himself as a defender of Apollo.

"Philip, as if he were the avenger of the sacrilege, not the defender of the Thebans, ordered all his soldiers to assume crowns of laurel, and proceeded to battle as if under the leadership of [Apollo]," writes Justinus (Marcus Junianius Justinus; second or third century AD). "This affair brought incredibly great glory to Philip in the opinion of all people," who, as Justinus phrased it, called him "the avenger of the god, and the defender of religion."

❖

It was now clear throughout Greece that the Macedonians were the single, unquestioned superpower in the Hellenic world. In Athens, the great center of art and literature, the intelligentsia bemoaned the surrender of Hellenic civilization to the "barbarians." It was rather like the way that the fall of Rome to the Germanic barbarians six centuries later would be perceived by devotees of Roman civilization.

However, the reality is always more complex than the stereotype, as Athenian culture and learning came to influence the Macedonian court when Philip later enlisted the great philosopher Aristotle as a tutor to his son, the young Alexander.

In addition to defeating his neighboring adversaries in tests of arms, Philip had sought to form more amicable relationships with rival kings in a manner that has often been practiced between monarchies through the years—by marrying their daughters. Philip married often. His first of seven wives was the Illyrian princess Audata. Philip's second and third wives were Phila of Elimiotis and Nicesipolis of Thessaly. According to Plutarch, both Audata and Phila were deceased by the time of Philip's fourth marriage, and none of his wives had yet borne a son.

His fourth wife, whom he married in 357, was Olympias, the daughter of the late King Neoptolemus of Epirus, and a woman of great beauty that was rivaled only by her mysterious charisma and by her wild abandon. Plutarch counted her among the women who were "addicted to the Orphic rites and the orgies of Dionysus from very ancient times." Plutarch adds that Olympias, "affected these divine possessions more zealously than other women, and carried out these divine inspirations in wilder fashion, used to provide the revelling companies with great tame serpents."

In Plutarch's words, "the night before that on which the marriage of Philip and Olympias was consummated, the bride dreamed that there was a peal of thunder and that a thunderbolt fell upon her womb, and that thereby much fire was kindled, which broke into flames that travelled all about, and then was extinguished."

Philip himself is said to have later dreamed that he had put a seal on his wife's womb, and on it was the figure of a lion. This was interpreted by Aristander, the court prognosticator, as meaning that her son would be bold, like a lion.

Plutarch reports the widely discussed alternate legend that the son born to Olympias had been fathered, not by Philip, but by Zeus in the form of a serpent. He tells that at the sight of a serpent lying by the side of Olympias as she slept, Philip "no longer came often to sleep by her side, either because he feared that some spells and enchantments might be practiced upon him by her, or because he shrank for her embraces in the conviction that she was the partner of a superior being."

A boy child was indeed coming, and soon the world would know what these omens meant.

CHAPTER 1

Auspicious Beginnings

IN JULY 356 BC, A HORSE OWNED BY PHILIP OF MACEDONIA WON ITS race at the Olympic Games. When the good news reached the monarch, it was just one element in a trifecta of glad tidings that arrived that day. Philip had also learned that his able commander Parmenio had triumphed in a great battle against the Illyrians, and that Olympias had finally borne him a son. This especially pleased him because his favorite soothsayer, Aristander of Telmessos, had earlier told him that the child within the womb of Olympias was a son who would be as bold as a lion.

Philip, who had just defeated the city of Potidaea, celebrated the good news that he had received, noting it was auspicious that there were three. "These things delighted him, of course," writes the Greek historian Plutarch in his *Lives of Noble Greeks and Romans*. "The seers raised his hopes still higher by declaring that the son whose birth coincided with three victories [including Potidaea] would be always victorious."

By the Athenian, or Attic, calendar, Philip's son, named Alexander, was born on the sixth day of the month Hekatombaion, or Hecatombaeon, which corresponds to July 21 on the modern calendar.

As Plutarch writes, Alexander was born "on the day the temple of Ephesian Artemis was burned." This particular temple of Artemis, the goddess known to the Romans as Diana, was located at Ephesus—near Selçuk in modern Turkey—and was no obscure religious site. It was one of the Seven Wonders of the Ancient World. The fire certainly got the attention of all present on that dark July 21. Plutarch writes that "all the Magi who were then at Ephesus, looking upon the temple's disaster as a sign of further disaster, ran about beating their faces and crying aloud that woe and great calamity for Asia had that day been born."

Writing with twenty-twenty hindsight, Plutarch certainly saw the boy child of Olympias as the future manifestation of "woe and great calamity" for the Persian Empire in Asia.

Hindsight colors much of what has been written about Alexander's youth. The stories that were handed down orally, and later penned by his biographers, tend to seem more like allegories that support the better-documented facts of his later life. They paint a portrait of a smart, skillful boy, the kind of person that we would expect to grow into the man that Alexander became. Conversely, one can conclude that many of the stories must have a basis in fact because Alexander did indeed become that sort of man.

Some stories show a boy so sure of himself that his confidence borders on arrogance. For instance, when invited to run in the Olympic Games as a teenager, he replied that he would do so only if the other runners on the track were kings.

To educate the young prince, Philip hired some of the best minds in Greece. The Macedonians had defeated Athens militarily, but remained in awe of Athenian arts and sciences. In 343, Philip brought Aristotle to Macedonia from Athens to educate Alexander. Philip was so pleased with the results of Aristotle's tutoring that, as part of his tuition payment, he restored the city of Stagira—Aristotle's hometown—which he had destroyed during one of his campaigns.

The distinguished philosopher instilled a love of learning and literature in the boy, instructing him in science and healing arts. He also gave Alexander a copy of Homer's *Iliad,* which he kept with him through his travels as an adult. Some claim that Alexander loved Aristotle more than he loved his father. Philip had given him life, but Aristotle "taught him a noble life."[*]

One of the best-known anecdotes of Alexander as a boy, and one that is considered to have a basis in fact, concerns the horse Bucephalas. This animal, who would be Alexander's favorite for most of his adult life, was brought to the court of King Philip when Alexander was about ten years old by a Thessalian named Philoneicus. Plutarch describes Bucephalas as "savage and altogether intractable, neither allowing any one to mount him, nor heeding the voice of any of Philip's attendants, but rearing up against all of them."

Considering the colt too wild to be of any use, Philip dismissed Philoneicus and told him to take Bucephalas away. According to Plutarch, at this point, Alexander piped up, observing "What a horse they are losing, because, for lack of skill and courage, they cannot manage him!"

Philip was naturally skeptical of the boy's impertinence, but Alexander proceeded to bet his father the sale price of the horse that he could ride him. Naturally, the story would not have been memorialized as part of the Alexander legend if Bucephalas had bucked him off. When Alexander dismounted after a successful ride, Plutarch tells that Philip told him "My son, seek thee out a kingdom equal to thyself; Macedonia has not room for thee."

As with the wails of the magi at Ephesus ten years earlier, it is a prophetic statement that may or may not have been spoken, but that illustrates the direction that young Alexander was headed.

✛

Whatever notional kingdom Philip may have imagined for Alexander on that day in 346 BC, it is certainly true that Philip was still imagining a bigger kingdom for himself. It was in the same year that he successfully subdued the Phocians and that Athens finally succumbed to Philip. He was also consolidating his control over the regions to the north from Illyria to Thrace, planning attacks still farther afield

---

[*]George Willis Botsford and Charles Alexander Robinson, *Hellenic History*. 3rd ed. (New York: Macmillan, 1948), Chapter 18).

against the ancient Greek city of Byzantium, and dreaming of eventually attacking the Persian Empire.

Later the center of the great Byzantine Empire, Byzantium, now Istanbul, is located on the Bosporus, which, along with the Dardanelles (known as the Hellespont in the ancient world), is one of the crossing points between Europe and Asia Minor, and a gateway on the water route between the Black Sea and the Mediterranean. As Justinus writes in his *Epitoma Historiarum Philippicarum,* or *Epitome of Philippic History,* this "noble city and seaport . . . would be a station for his forces by land and sea."

In the same paragraph, Justinus adds that the ambitious Philip "made an expedition, too, into Scythia, to get plunder, that, after the practice of traders, he might make up for the expenses of one war by the profits of another." Scythia was the umbrella term used by the Greeks to describe the lands across the vast region of steppes north and east of the Hellenic enclaves on the Black Sea that stretches into Central Asia.

Having failed in his initial forays against Byzantium, Philip tried again in 339. While the Macedonian army may have been invincible on the battlefield, besieging fixed targets, such as fortified cities, were still a challenge. Though this Byzantine venture disappointed Philip in 339, his son was taking note of the need for a functional siege strategy. Alexander would never fail in a siege.

While Philip was away, Alexander had an opportunity to prove himself. As Plutarch writes, "Alexander, though only sixteen years of age, was left behind as regent in Macedonia and keeper of the royal seal, and during this time he subdued the rebellious Maedi [in southwestern Thrace], and after taking their city, drove out the Barbarians, settled there a mixed population, and named the city Alexandropolis."

It was also during the absence of Philip that Alexander, as regent, entertained envoys from the Persian king Artaxerxes. Plutarch, always keen to cite incidents from Alexander's early life that predicted future greatness, relates that Alexander "won upon them by his friendliness, and by asking no childish or trivial questions, but by enquiring about the length of the roads and the character of the journey into the interior, about the king himself, what sort of a warrior he was, and what the prowess and might of the Persians. The envoys were therefore astonished and regarded the much-talked-of ability of Philip as nothing compared with his son's eager disposition to do great things."

In any case, the highly regarded abilities of Philip had been successfully challenged at Byzantium, and this got the attention of the city-states, who began to conspire against him. They had submitted to the barbarian from Macedonia when he was powerful, but they saw his troubles in the north as an opportunity. It was a typical case of initially submitting to strength, but rebelling against the first perceived sign of weakness.

In August 338, the battle lines were drawn at Chaeronea in Boeotia, with Athens and Thebes joining forces against the Macedonian king and his Thessalian allies. Neither side wanted the other to be the power that defeated Philip, so they went in together. As Justinus writes, "The Thebans espoused their cause, fearing that if the Athenians were conquered, the war, like a fire in the neighborhood, would spread to them. An alliance being accordingly made between the two cities, which were just before at violent enmity with each other, they wearied Greece with embassies, stating that 'they thought the common enemy should be repelled by their common strength, for that Philip would not rest, if his first attempts succeeded, until he had subjugated all Greece.'"

If Chaeronea was make or break time for Philip and Macedonia, it was the coming of age moment for young Alexander, who had just turned 18 and was about to be tested in his first major battle.

❖

Apparently impressed with his son's potential, Philip placed the teenager in command of the Companion Cavalry on the left flank of the Macedonian line, while Philip himself took charge of the right flank. As such, Philip faced the Athenians, while Alexander was opposite the more capable army of Thebes. Among the latter troops were the Sacred Band, the most recent incarnation of the elite force that had played a pivotal role in routing the Spartans at Leuctra in 371 BC.

Tactically, Philip lured the Athenians out of a defensive posture, making them more vulnerable and pulling them away from the Theban positions to their left. This in turn provided an opening for Alexander and the Companions to drive a wedge between the enemy contingents.

As Alexander attacked, the Theban forces collapsed into disarray—except for the Sacred Band, who held their ground. Nevertheless, the boy general attacked and pummeled them, killing more than three quarters of the Sacred Band before they were finally battered into submission. With this, Alexander and the Companions turned on the Athenian center, just as Philip finished off the Athenian cavalry.

Most ancient accounts agree that the Battle of Chaeronea was long and bloody, and that when it was over, any question regarding the primacy of the Macedonians was laid to rest. As for Philip's primacy, the only star that shone as bright over Greece that night was Alexander's.

Chaeronea confirmed what should have been understood throughout Greece at the end of the Third Sacred War eight years earlier. The old days were gone forever, and the new days were ruled by Macedonia.

With this, Philip began to make plans for a major campaign against the Persians in Asia Minor.

❖

However, even as Philip was now Greece's unquestioned king, he was about to have his share of trouble within his own house. As Plutarch writes, "the disorders in [Philip's] household, due to the fact that his marriages and amours carried into the kingdom the infection, as it were, which reigned in the women's apartments, produced many grounds of offence and great quarrels between father and son, and these the bad temper of Olympias, who was a jealous and sullen woman, made still greater, since she spurred Alexander on. The most open quarrel was brought on by Attalus [a member of Philip's court and an officer in his army] at the marriage of Cleopatra [Attalus's niece], a maiden whom Philip was taking to wife, having fallen in love with the girl when he was past the age for it."

Olympias had known that Philip was a polygamist when she married him, and she probably would have acquiesced to his marrying Cleopatra as a second wife had Philip not had the audacity to repudiate Olympias at the same time. In so doing, Philip would also have to repudiate the legitimacy of Olympias's son, Alexander, as his heir.

As Justinus writes, an understandably spiteful Olympias taunted Philip with the well-known, albeit mythical, story of Zeus having been Alexander's true father, but that she had actually conceived Alexander, not by Philip, but "by a serpent of extraordinary size."

Philip turned the taut back on Olympias, using it as an excuse to accuse her of adultery, which gave him grounds for the divorce that he sought. If they had ever been a happy family, those days were over. Philip's repudiation of Olympias had the presumably unintended consequence of his also repudiating Alexander.

"But what of me, base wretch?" Alexander asked Philip, according to Plutarch, during a drunken argument. "Dost thou take me for a bastard?"

At this point, Plutarch reports that Philip rose up against his son with drawn sword, but, fortunately for both, his anger and his wine made him trip and fall. Mocking him, Alexander said, "Look now, men! Here is one who was preparing to cross from Europe into Asia; and he is upset in trying to cross from couch to couch."

The most powerful leader in Greek history and the sovereign of the peninsula, Philip had lost the respect and allegiance of his son and protégé. After the angry exchange, Alexander took Olympias to Epirus, where her brother Alexander I was now ruling as a sort of vassal king under Philip. About a year later, Philip and Olympias apparently reconciled—up to a point—and she moved back to Pella, the capital city of Macedonia. Her relations with Philip remained strained, as she continued to insist that his famous son had actually been fathered by Zeus.

By the time of his marriage to Cleopatra and his repudiation of Olympias in 337 BC, Philip was preoccupied professionally with preparations for his ultimate military campaign against Persia. It is unclear whether he intended to conquer all of the Persian Empire or merely that part of it in Asia Minor, but having united Greece, Philip was ready to launch what was probably the biggest operation against the Persians in their longstanding state of war with the Greeks. Philip had even sent Parmenio with an advance contingent to cross the Hellespont and hold the crossing point from Europe into Asia Minor.

In October 336, Philip threw a party for the wedding of his daughter by Olympias, Alexander's sister Cleopatra. The bridegroom in this marriage was her uncle—Alexander I of Epirus. It was at the wedding banquet that Philip was knifed by one of his own personal bodyguards, a youth named Pausanias of Orestis.

There are various theories as to motive. Although both had their motives, most historians agree that Alexander was not among the conspirators, and that Olympias was probably not involved in plotting the assassination either. Parenthetically, Olympias later did engineer the murders of Europa and Caranus, the infant children of Philip by his young wife Cleopatra—and thus potential rivals for Alexander's throne.

In a further search for motives, the first-century BC Greek historian Diodorus Siculus (Diodorus of Sicily) reports that Pausanias was one of Philip's former male lovers and killed him in a fit of jealousy. Aristotle, in a contemporary account, says that followers of Attalus, the uncle of Cleopatra, had offended Pausanias. Justinus agrees that Pausanias had "suffered gross violence at the hands of Attalus [and that Attalus had] rendered him the laughing-stock of those of his own age."

In any case, the assassin was caught and killed before he reached his horse. Alexander had the body of Philip's killer staked out on public display and later cremated along with that of his victim. Young Alexander also made quick work of any and all who were said to have aided or abetted Pausanias and his scheme.

As Justinus writes, "Philip died at the age of 47, after having reigned 25 years. . . . As a king, he was more inclined to display in war, than in entertainments; and his greatest riches were means for military operations."

With Philip's death, Alexander took the throne. The nineteenth-century historian John Clark Ridpath writes that Alexander addressed the nobility of Macedonia, telling them that "the king's name has changed, but the king you shall find remains the same."

✦

The two kings were, of course, not the same. Justinus states that "To Philip succeeded his son Alexander, a prince greater than his father, both in his virtues and his vices. Each of the two had a different mode of conquering; the one prosecuted his wars with open force, the other with subtlety. . . . The father had more cunning, the son more honour. Philip was more staid in his words, Alexander in his actions. The son felt readier and nobler impulses to spare the conquered; the father showed no mercy even to his allies. The father was more inclined to frugality, the son to luxury. By the same course by which the father laid the foundations of the empire of the world, the son consummated the glory of conquering the whole world."

CHAPTER 2

Long Live the King

THE NEW KING OF MACEDONIA, REIGNING AS ALEXANDER III, inherited a troubled empire. "At the age of twenty years Alexander received the kingdom, which was exposed to great jealousies, dire hatreds, and dangers on every hand," wrote Plutarch. "The neighboring tribes of Barbarians would not tolerate their servitude, and longed for their hereditary kingdoms; and as for Greece, although Philip had conquered her in the field, he had not had time enough to make her tame under his yoke, but had merely disturbed and changed the condition of affairs there, and then left them in a great surge and commotion."

Alexander's first military campaigns as king in early 335 BC were aimed at preserving the empire that he had inherited from Philip. He marched north to the Danube and into what is now Serbia to subdue the Triballi, a Thracian people who had earlier been a painful thorn in Philip's side.

Meanwhile, the Thebans and Athenians interpreted Philip's death as the end of Macedonian primacy. They were encouraged by rumors that Alexander had been killed by the Triballi during operations in the north, and that the Macedonian command structure was in disarray. One can imagine their surprise when Alexander himself arrived at Thebes leading an intact and disciplined army.

Rather than simply engaging and defeating the Theban army—as he and Philip had done at Chaeronea in August 338—Alexander also destroyed the city, obliterating what had been one of the most powerful of all the Greek cities. He spared only the temples and the former home of the poet Pindar. The Theban death toll was in the thousands, and the survivors were sold as slaves.

This devastation, with its take-no-prisoners doctrine, both shocked and awed the Athenians, who sensed that their city was next. Athens capitulated immediately, groveling for mercy, congratulating Alexander on his victories since becoming king, and promising to silence and reprimand those Athenians who had spoken against him. Just a fortnight earlier, Athenians had rejoiced at the unfounded rumor that Alexander was dead. Now, all they could do was murmur "long live the king." Alexander chose to leave Athens intact, letting Thebes be his lesson to the city-states that Chaeronea had indeed irrevocably changed the balance of power within Greece.

His empire under control, Alexander now prepared to continue what Philip had barely started: to take the long-simmering cold war decisively to the Achaemenid Persian Empire, now ruled by Darius III, the 45-year-old great-grandson of Darius II, who had come to the throne the year before.

To rule Greece as regent in his absence, Alexander chose Antipater, or Antipatros, a 62-year-old Macedonian general and diplomat, whose loyalty to both Philip and Alexander was well established. He had served as Philip's ambassador to Athens after Chaeronea, and had served previously as Alexander's regent in the Macedonian capital of Pella during the 336–335 campaigns against the Triballi and the Thebans.

As Justinus writes, Alexander "divided all his private property, which he had in Macedonia and the rest of Europe, among his friends, saying, 'that for himself Asia was sufficient.'"

He also killed all of the relatives of his stepmother Cleopatra, including Attalus, so that there would be no pretenders to his throne to cause trouble in his absence. He made sacrifices to the gods in accordance with custom, and he went to Delphi. Here, as interpreted by the Pythian priestess, the oracle told him that he was invincible. That was all he needed to hear.

Alexander headed for the Hellespont, where Parmenio had already seized a bridgehead between Sestus on the European side and the old Thracian city of Abydos in Asia Minor. It was here that Xerxes had crossed in the opposite direction when he invaded Greece in 480 BC.

As Justinus writes, there was a "general assembly of the Greeks" held at Sestus, where "a vote was passed to make an expedition against Persia with Alexander, and he was proclaimed their leader. Thereupon many statesmen and philosophers came to him with their congratulations."

Justinus says that the people had given Alexander the mandate as the chosen "avenger of Greece so often assailed by the Persians."

Alexander's field commanders, Parmenio, Craterus, Coenus and Cleitus the Black were Macedonian, but his army consisted of troops drawn from throughout Greece. They included troops, especially Thessalians, who would fight under Macedonian command because Alexander was seen as the avenger of all Greece who would lead them to exact the long-desired vengeance against the hated Persians—who nearly everyone agreed were the enemy.

Notable among the international troops serving in Alexander's army—because of their reputation as warriors and because Alexander's biographers would refer to them repeatedly in accounts of his military exploits in Asia—was a large contingent of Agrianian javelin throwers. The Agrianians were a Thracian people from the area that is now southern Serbia. Alexander would use them consistently in his upcoming operations in Asia, frequently attaching them to units that he led into battle personally.

Estimates of the exact size of Alexander's Greco-Macedonian army vary, though not widely. Justinus reports 32,000 infantry, and 4,500 cavalry. Citing various ancient sources, Plutarch gives a range of between 30,000 and 43,000 infantry, and between 4,000 and 5,000 cavalry. These figures apparently do not account for logistical and support personnel, camp followers and auxiliaries, which would have included Alexander's engineers, who would play a vital role in future operations.

Meanwhile, Alexander's offensive naval strength was proportionally smaller than his land strength. His navy consisted of just 160–180 triremes, which would explain why he would pursue a land, rather than naval, strategy. The trireme, so named for its having three rows of oars on each side, was the standard Mediterranean warship of the fifth and fourth centuries BC. Though triremes were the most common warship of the day, larger vessels called quadriremes and quinqueremes were also used by various navies during this period. While Alexander emphasized land power over naval power in his military doctrine, he occasionally deployed a fleet comprised mainly of allied naval forces, and all three types of vessels were included.

Though the numbers in Alexander's army were relatively small, roughly the size of a modern corps, their training, discipline and experience—dating back to their battles under Philip—made them perhaps the best field army the world had yet seen. As Justinus wrote, "when [Alexander] selected his troops for so hazardous a warfare, he did not choose robust young men, or men in the flower of their age, but veterans, most of whom had even passed their term of service, and who had fought under his father and his uncles; so that he might be thought to have chosen, not soldiers, but masters in war. No one was made an officer who was not 60 years of age; so that he who saw the captains assembled at headquarters, would have declared that he saw the senate of some ancient republic. None, on the field of battle, thought of flight, but every one of victory; none trusted in his feet, but every one in his arms."

Strategically, Alexander's first "victory" in his Persian campaign was getting his army across the Hellespont intact in the spring of 334 BC. For Darius, this was a major missed opportunity. As the Allies discovered at nearby Gallipoli in 1915–1916, troops engaged in such operations are extremely vulnerable. Troops crossing a waterway are nearly always dangerously exposed. In the case of amphibious operations on a river or a sea, they are at the mercy of currents, crashing waves and underwater obstacles. In the case of crossing a pontoon bridge, such as Alexander's men were able to do, they are exposed in single file with no cover and no ability to disperse or take evasive action. In short, in ether case, they are sitting ducks for a well-entrenched defender. Darius, who reportedly had a 20,000-man cavalry force in Asia Minor, forfeited the easiest opportunity that he would ever have to defeat Alexander.

Justinus tells us that Darius, "from confidence in his strength, abstained from all artifice in his operations; observing that 'clandestine measures were fit only for a stolen victory;' he did not attempt to repel the enemy from his frontiers, but admitted them into the heart of his kingdom, thinking it more honorable to drive war out of his kingdom than not to give it entrance."

Reportedly, Alexander stepped ashore on the Asian continent in full armor, ready to do battle, and threw his spear into the sand on the beach at Abydos. He offered sacrifices to the gods, asking that the lands he encountered would willingly accept him as their king.

Traveling eastward from Abydos, into what is now Çanakkale Province of northwestern Turkey, Alexander's army marched toward Dascylium, a city near present-day Ergili, which had been the site of important battles in earlier Greek forays into Asia Minor. Agesilaus of Sparta had captured the city in 395, but less than a decade later it had been recaptured by the Persians. Alexander probably saw it as the essential first objective in any Asia Minor campaign. In 334, it was the capital of the Persian province of Phrygia.

As his army marched into Asia Minor, Alexander approached the river now known in Turkish as Biga Çayi or Kocabas Çayi, but then known as the Granicus. Slow moving except when choked with the spring run-off from Mount Ida, the Biga Çayi meanders in a northeasterly direction toward the Sea of Marmara. Like that small stream in Virginia known as Bull Run, the Granicus appears inconsequential if one bothers to notice it at all.

However, like Bull Run, the Granicus would give its name to a momentous battle that was the opening salvo in several years of warfare that would alter the course of history.

CHAPTER 3

From Granicus to Gordium

THOUGH HE WAS FAR AWAY IN HIS PALACE IN SUSA, NOW THE SOUTH-western Iranian city of Shush, Darius III, monarch of the Achaemenid Persian Empire, knew that Alexander was coming, and he knew what he was planning. One does not cross the Hellespont with an army of nearly 50,000 without its being noticed, and the news had reached Darius quickly. The Persian emperor assumed that decimating the upstart Macedonian and his army would be a routine matter for his Persian legions. As Justinus observes, Darius had "confidence in his strength."

The exact number of Persian combat troops is not known, and modern estimates vary widely from about 20,000 to nearly 50,000. Two of the principal Persian field commanders were Spithridates, the Persian satrap of Lydia and Ionia, and Mithridates, the son-in-law of Darius. The Persian force also included a substantial number of Greek mercenaries. At the Granicus, they were led by Memnon of Rhodes, reportedly a favorite of Darius.

The battle lines were drawn on opposite sides of the river, with Alexander to the north and west, and the Persians to the south and east. This being early May, 334 BC, the river was running high, and the Persians probably saw it as a decisive natural barrier. They could wait on their side and pick off Alexander's troops as they struggled ashore.

Alexander's plan of attack against the Persian defenses is described by Arrian of Nicomedia (Lucius Flavius Arrianus) in his *Anabasis Alexandri,* or *The Campaigns of Alexander.* A military leader himself, he had a good understanding of the tactical situation. According to Arrian, Parmenio proposed a flanking maneuver early the next day, but Alexander countered that they should not wait, but attack immediately. His rationale was that this would take the Persians off guard and give the Greco-Macedonian troops the instant gratification of getting into the fight straight away.

Alexander's confidence was also buoyed that day by a good interpretation of omens by Aristander of Telmessos, once his father's favorite soothsayer, who was now part of Alexander's entourage. The old fortune teller, who had once told Philip II that his son would be bold as a lion, now predicted a victory for that son.

The opening gambit was a fake attack by Parmenio on the left, against the Persian right. As the Persians moved their forces to cover this possible attempt to ford the Granicus, Alexander struck the true opening blow.

Alexander, like his father and like so many of history's greatest generals, led from the front. He went wide to his right, taking the Companion Cavalry across the Granicus and circling behind the Persian left flank. Here he engaged the cavalry led by Mithridates and Spithridates, who were apparently stunned to find Macedonians outflanking them from their rear so early in the battle.

It hadn't exactly been easy for Alexander, though. As Plutarch writes in his *Life of Alexander the Great,* Alexander "gained the opposite banks with difficulty and much ado, though they were moist and slippery with mud, and was at once compelled to fight pell-mell and engage his assailants man by man, before his troops who were crossing could form into any order. For the enemy pressed upon them with loud shouts, and matching horse with horse, plied their lances, and their swords when their lances were shattered. Many rushed upon Alexander, for he was conspicuous by his buckler and by his helmet's crest, on either side of which was fixed a plume of wonderful size and whiteness. But although a javelin pierced the joint of his breastplate, he was not wounded."

Indeed, in the hand-to-hand combat, Alexander is said to have broken two spears fighting the Persians at close range. He also lost the horse that he was riding that day—he had chosen for some reason not to use Bucephalas—to a Persian spear.

Meanwhile, as the Persian left and right were dashing to meet attacks both real and perceived, Alexander's phalanx forced its way across the Granicus to strike the Persian center, which now had no support from its flanking cavalry.

The fight in the center began with the difficult struggle by Alexander's men to get across the river. Once joined on the other side, the battle must have been vicious, but the Persians with their shorter spears would have been no match for the men with the 18-foot sarissa, the fearsome Macedonian spear.

As the Greco-Macedonian spearmen sliced through the Persian phalanx, they threatened the rear of the Persian cavalry that had turned 180 degrees to face Alexander and the Companion Cavalry. By this time, Parmenio, having faked the earlier attack on the Persian right, actually did cross the Granicus.

As for Alexander himself, he soon found himself facing the Persian cavalry commanders man to man. Mithridates, also leading from the front, was well ahead of his troops, presenting Alexander with an opportunity. This he took, ramming his spear straight into the Persian general's head, and knocking his lifeless body from his horse.

At this point, Spithridates and his brother Rhoesaces turned to attack Alexander. As Plutarch describes it, Alexander avoided Spithridates, but "smote Rhoesaces, who wore a breastplate, with his spear; and when this weapon snapped in two with the blow, he took to his sword. While he was thus engaged with Rhoesaces, Spithridates rode up from one side, raised himself up on his horse, and with all his might came down with a barbarian battle-axe upon Alexander's head. The helmet's crest was broken off, together with one of its plumes, and barely resisted the blow, so that the edge of the battle-axe touched the topmost hair of his head. But while Spithridates was raising his arm again for another stroke, Cleitus, 'Black Cleitus,' got the start of him and ran him through the body with his spear. At the same time Rhoesaces also fell, smitten by Alexander's sword."

Writing in his *Bibliotheca Historica,* or *Historical Library,* Diodorus Siculus tells a slightly different story, explaining that Alexander killed Spithridates first, and was then attacked by Rhoesaces, who "galloped up and brought his sword down on Alexander's head so hard that he split his helmet and wounded his scalp. As Rhoesaces aimed another blow at the same break in the helmet, Cleitus, known as 'the Black,' dashed up and cut off the Persian's arm."

With the entire Greco-Macedonian force across the river, the Persians were outflanked on all sides. As the tactical situation deteriorated, many of the Persians fled, although Memnon's Greek mercenaries, being veteran professional soldiers, stayed in the fight and were the last of the Persian force still fighting. They too, were finally defeated, although Memnon himself got away. Those mercenaries captured were considered Greek traitors and were sent back to Greece in chains. Perhaps their anticipation of such a fate was what kept them in the fight until the bitter end.

✣

The Battle of Granicus was a triumph both for Alexander personally and for his army. The actual casualty figures are unknown, but were probably lopsided in favor of Alexander—although it is likely that the historians exaggerated them. Plutarch repeats the story he was told that the Persians lost 20,000 infantry and 2,500 cavalry.

He then quotes Aristobulus of Cassandreia, who tells that Alexander's total losses numbered just 34. Aristobulus was an architect and military engineer who accompanied Alexander on the campaign and wrote an account that served as one of Arrian's primary sources. Continuing to reference Aristobulus, Arrian adds that Alexander ordered bronze equestrian statues to be cast by the sculptor Lysippus, who did a great deal of work for Alexander though the years, including statues of the young king himself. Justinus reports that Alexander lost nine infantrymen and 120 cavalry, while Arrian is somewhat more realistic, estimating losses at around 400 for the Greco-Macedonian army and ten times that number for the Persians.

The nineteenth- and twentieth-century writers who retold Alexander's story and repeated these figures usually did so adding the grain of salt that they are probably exaggerations. Equally probable is that they are based on numbers that were deliberately concocted at the time for domestic consumption. The first- and second-century writers upon whom we rely for most of our information about Alexander depended in turn on contemporary Greek sources, who likely repeated data that was deliberately skewed to let the folks back home believe Alexander was winning great battles against immense opposition, and that he was doing so with minimal losses.

It is too bad that more accurate figures were not recorded, for Alexander truly was winning major victories against a great foe. Granicus really was a serious defeat for the Persians in Asia Minor.

Like the battle that occurred in 1861 on that other small river, Bull Run of Virginia, the contest that took place on the Granicus did not have the outcome that the defender assumed. Just as the United States imagined in 1861 that General Irvin McDowell's army would easily rout the rebel army of General P. G. T. Beauregard, the Persians had all confidence that they would decimate the Greeks. Had the assumptions been correct, both battles would have been anomalous incidents, not the opening events of campaigns that would change history.

Like Bull Run, Granicus was a monumental defeat for the defender, both tactically and in terms of morale and public opinion within the region. Unlike 1861, however, the victor chose to exploit his victory politically and militarily. Unlike the Confederate army of 1861, which chose not to press on toward a defenseless Washington, D.C., Alexander kept up his momentum, and reaped the rewards.

❖

Throughout the summer of 334 BC, Persian satraps switched sides, and the Greek population welcomed Alexander as a liberator. Wealthy Sardis, the major city in Lydia, gave up without a fight, opening its gates to Alexander. So too did Ephesus.

Whether it was out of fear, intimidation or simply wanting to side with a winner, Alexander's reputation after Granicus opened many doors. As Justinus observes, "After this victory [at Granicus] the greater part of Asia [Minor] came over to his side. He had also several encounters with Darius's lieutenants, whom he conquered, not so much by his arms, as by the terror of his name." By establishing himself as an opponent to be feared, Alexander convinced many a would-be foe that resistance was counterproductive. Potential adversaries decided that there was more to gain by surrendering and taking their chances than by putting up a fight they were sure to lose.

The Ionian port city of Miletus, with about 400 ships of the Persian fleet close at hand, chose to resist. Alexander, whose fleet was much smaller, avoided a naval contest and besieged Miletus by land. He gambled correctly that the Persians would not attempt to challenge him ashore, and troops under Parmenio's son Nicanor made quick work of taking the city. As at Granicus, the last holdouts were Greek mercenaries who fought bravely. Unlike at Granicus, however, Alexander did not single them out for punishment. Rather, respecting their bravery and tenacity, he invited them to join his army.

According to Arrian, Alexander now adopted a radical maritime strategy in the face of the superior Persian navy. Indeed, it was radical to the point of recklessness, but it was certainly an example of Alexander's ability to think outside the box. "Alexander now resolved to disband his fleet," Arrian writes. "Partly from lack of money at the time, and partly because he saw that his own fleet was not a match in battle for that of the Persians. On this account he was unwilling to run the risk of losing even a part of his armament. Besides, he considered, now that he was occupying Asia with his land force, he would no longer be in need of a fleet; and that he would be able to break up that of the Persians, if he captured the maritime cities; since they would neither have any ports from which they could recruit their crews, nor any harbor in Asia to which they could bring their ships."

It was a classic instance of avoiding an enemy at his strongest and exploiting his weakness. Alexander responded to the situation by doing something that was very far beyond the parameters of what the Persians expected. The lesson that can be learned from this audacious move is not so much one of simply thinking far outside the box, but one of looking for unexpected solutions that actually show the promise of working.

Like his decision to attack across the Granicus without pause, this decision manifested a brashness that could easily have backfired, but that can be considered brilliant in retrospect by measuring its eventual success. To undertake a comprehensive war against a major maritime power without a navy is counterintuitive, but his decision illustrates Alexander's ability to understand the broad strategic scope of the campaign. Strategically, Alexander's land-war plan called for an advance into Asia Minor on a broad front. Sending Parmenio with one contingent into the interior, he himself worked his way around the west and south coasts of what is now Turkey, capturing port cities.

With Miletus now in Alexander's hands, the Persian fleet sailed down the coast to the old Dorian Greek port city of Halicarnassus. Now the Turkish city of Bodrum, in 334 BC it was the principal city of the Persian satrapy of Caria. Here Alexander faced Orontobates, Caria's satrap, who was supported by Memnon of Rhodes, the mercenary commander against whom he had done battle at Granicus.

In turn, Alexander formed an alliance with Ada, the daughter of a former satrap, Hacatomnus. Having married her brother Idrieus when he became the ruler, Ada became satrap herself when he died. She was then deposed by another brother, whose son-in-law, Orontobates, took over from him. Ada was still in possession of the nearby hilltop fortress of Alinda, and this she surrendered to Alexander.

Young Alexander and the 43-year-old former queen became close friends, and she went so far as to adopt him as a son not long after meeting him. She then lined Alexander up with some of the best chefs in Asia Minor, and these became part of his entourage as he campaigned onward.

* * *

Alexander proceeded to besiege Halicarnassus, proving himself a better master of siege tactics than his father had been. Alexander approached the siege as an engineering project. He made his initial attack using infantry under cover of darkness without bringing up ladders or siege engines. His plan was to use his phalanx troops to undermine the city wall. According to Arrian, they brought down one of the towers in the wall, which, however, "in its fall did not make a breach in the wall."

Next, Alexander had his men back fill the trench that the defenders had dug around the wall, so that he could bring up his siege towers. The defenders, however, launched a counterattack outside the walls, torching the towers and attacking the Macedonian troops. Over the next several days, the two sides battled, with Alexander's engineers continuing to undermine the walls, collapsing both wall sections and a second tower, and with the Persians continuing to set fire to the siege engines.

The Persian construction battalions were also hard at work, constructing new inner walls to replace sections of the city wall that the miners had managed to collapse. All of this was interspersed with bloody hand-to-hand skirmishes that took place as one side or the other took advantage of a situation by attacking, then quickly withdrawing.

At one point, a large number of defenders were killed in a bridge collapse. Arrian recalls that these troops, "in their retreat were fleeing over a narrow bridge which had been made over the ditch, [but] they had the misfortune to break it down by the weight of their multitude. Many of them fell into the ditch, some of whom were trampled to death by their own comrades, and others were struck by the Macedonians from above. A very great slaughter was also made at the very gates, because they were shut before the proper time from a feeling of terror. For the enemy, being afraid that the Macedonians, who were close upon the fugitives, would rush in with them, shut many of their friends out, who were slain by the Macedonians near the very walls."

When at last Orontobates and Memnon decided that their position was untenable and that "they could not hold out long against the siege, seeing that part of the wall had already fallen down and part had been battered and weakened, and that many of their soldiers had either perished in the sorties or been wounded and disabled," a decision was made to simply torch the city.

In the final push, Alexander's army prevailed. Orontobates was killed, but once again, as at Granicus, Memnon got away. Alexander rewarded Ada for her kindness and friendship by restoring her to the throne at Halicarnassus, where she reigned until her death in 326 BC.

Installing Ada to rule Halicarnassus was a template for the way that Alexander would rule the areas that he was conquering from the Persian Empire. Though he did not go so far as to accept other former Persian satraps as surrogate parents, he did adopt the Persian practice of satrapies, setting up subservient locals to rule the cities and states that he conquered. Often he reappointed former Persian satraps who switched sides. As skilled as Alexander was as a military leader, it is worth noting that he also had a keen understanding of politics. He knew that his satrapies were best ruled by someone who understood the complexities and nuances of local politics rather than by someone whom Alexander imposed from the outside. Like any good chief executive, Alexander operated under the principle that so long as his satraps were loyal to him and were competent managers, they were allowed to keep and execute their jobs.

⬚

Darius, who was impressed with Memnon's success in eluding Alexander twice, decided to make the Greek turncoat the centerpiece of a grand scheme of counterattack into Alexander's rear. As Arrian describes, the Persian monarch appointed Memnon, the leader of the Greek mercenaries fighting for the Persians, as "commander of the whole fleet and of the entire seacoast, with the design of moving the seat of war into Macedonia and Greece."

Using what Arrian calls "treachery," Memnon took control of the Aegean islands of Chios and most of Lesbos. The only stumbling block was the city of Mytilene on the latter island, which resisted Memnon's siege just as he became mortally ill. Mytilene eventually capitulated to Memnon's successor, Autophradates, but with Memnon's death in 333 BC, the Persian offensive ran out of steam. Antipater, Alexander's regent in Greece, organized a naval force that successfully blunted the Persian initiative.

Marching down the western coast of Asia Minor with his army, Alexander welcomed the news from the Aegean. As Plutarch relates, "on hearing of the death of Memnon on the seaboard, who was thought likely to give Alexander abundant trouble and infinite annoyance, he was all the more encouraged for his expedition into the interior."

If Memnon had lived and been successful in using captured Aegean islands as stepping-stones for an assault against Greece, Alexander's campaign in Asia Minor would have sputtered to a halt, as he would have had to backtrack to protect his rear.

Persian aspirations in the Aegean had been stymied, but the Persian fleet had by no means been eliminated as a challenge. Alexander's army may have been unstoppable ashore, but his deliberate decision not to develop an equally formidable navy meant that the Persian fleet under Autophradates retained a presence in the Aegean and eastern Mediterranean.

Pursuing the campaigning season into the winter, and into the early months of 333, Alexander continued to add new satrapies to his crown. Plutarch casually relates that he "subdued Paphlagonia and

Cappadocia," as easily as mentioning that he saddled Bucephalas. Many satrapies, like Sardis and Ephesus, were only too happy to welcome him as a liberator. Some resisted, but none presented the same challenge to the Macedonian siege engines as had Halicarnassus. As Arrian records in his *Anabasis Alexandri,* almost in checklist fashion, the former Greek colonies were restored to Hellenic rule one by one. There were the coastal cities of Lycia and Pamphylia, and Hyparna, which resisted in vain. Next came "Pinara, Xanthus, Patara, and about thirty other smaller towns [that] were surrendered to him."

After Granicus, Halicarnassus and the death of Memnon, Darius had to have perceived Alexander as the greatest threat ever faced by the Achaemenid Persian Empire. The Persian monarch, who had chosen not to attack Alexander's army at the Hellespont because he considered it not to be chivalrous, now resorted to subterfuge involving a paid turncoat. The man in question was Alexander, the son of Aeropus, who was one of Alexander's trusted officers, and a commander of Thessalian cavalry. His brothers had been involved in the assassination of Philip II.

Alexander III learned from an informer that Darius had made Alexander, the son of Aeropus, an offer to reward him with the monarchy of Macedonia if he would kill the king. Having discovered the plot, Alexander had the would-be assassin arrested.

✠

Early in 333 BC, Alexander linked up once again with Parmenio, this time in the ancient Greek state of Phrygia in central Asia Minor, the land once ruled by the mythical King Midas of the "golden touch." Specifically, Alexander's objective here was the Phrygian capital of Gordium. Located about 50 miles southwest the modern city of Ankara, the capital of Turkey, Gordium itself was the centerpiece of one of antiquity's great legends.

The founder of Gordium was said to have been a peasant farmer turned king named Gordias, who may have been the father of Midas. An artifact, thought to be from his ancient rule, still survived in Alexander's time. According to historians, a story well known throughout the known world told of an ox-cart that had been owned by Gordias that was still on display in the city. Located in either a palace or a temple—there are variations on the story—the cart was attached to its yoke by an elaborate knot of twine made from the bark of a cornel, or dogwood, tree. The legend held that whoever could figure out how to untie the Gordian Knot would, as Justinus tells, be "destined to become king of the whole world." Through the centuries, many had tried, but all had failed, owing to the complexity of the knot and the fact that neither end of the twine was visible.

As Plutarch writes, Alexander was at a loss how to proceed, but "finally loosened the knot by cutting it through with his sword, and that when it was thus smitten many ends were to be seen."

Arrian agrees, stating that Alexander "was unwilling to allow it to remain unloosened, lest this should exercise some disturbing influence upon the multitude, [so] he struck it with his sword and cutting it through, said that it had been loosened."

The knot was not actually untied, but Arrian notes that Alexander "departed from the wagon as if the oracular prediction concerning the loosening of the cord had been fulfilled."

The first year of Alexander's campaign against the Achaemenid Persian Empire had been an extraordinary one. On its eve, the oracle of Delphi had promised that he was invincible. Now, his smiting of the Gordian Knot confirmed, at least in his self-perception and the perception of those around him, that his destiny was to rule the world.

CHAPTER 4

Turning Point at Issus

By the summer of 333 BC, the Asia Minor campaign was essentially won. Persian hegemony over that region, which had prevailed since the days of Cyrus the Great, was over. Strategically, Alexander's next move was to continue south along the Mediterranean shore, through Syria and toward Egypt. For Darius III, the next move was to muster an unbeatable army and confront Alexander in a decisive battle. After that, he could roll back the Greco-Macedonian invaders—all the way to Greece itself.

When Alexander had crossed the Hellespont, the Persian king had laughed the haughty laugh of arrogance. As Justinus observed, Darius had "confidence in his strength." A year later, after seeing so much of Asia Minor slip away, Darius should not have been laughing, but he was.

In the early stages of Alexander's offensive campaign, Darius chose to let his satraps, the subservient potentates of the constituent states of his empire, take the lead in thwarting the young Macedonian. However, if you want something done right, the adage goes, you must do it yourself. This thought must have been on Darius's mind as he rode out of Susa in the fall of 333. Spithridates and Mithridates had failed to defeat Alexander at the Granicus River and had paid with their lives. This year, Darius would do it himself, and he would do it right.

Darius departed Susa, seat of his imperial administration, with a vast army, supported by an equally impressive logistical train and any number of camp followers. He even brought his own household on this expedition, including his mother, Sisygambis, and his wife, who was also his sister. Named Stateira, she was described by ancient historians as either the most beautiful woman in Asia, or with greater hyperbole, as the most beautiful woman in the world. Also present were the daughters of Darius and Stateira. Both under the age of 10, the younger one was named Drypteis, and the older one was known in most accounts as Stateira, like her mother, although Arrian calls her Barsine.

The exact size of the Persian army with which these women traveled is open to speculation. As Plutarch describes it, Darius was "coming down to the coast from Susa, exalted in spirit by the magnitude of his forces, for he was leading an army of 600,000 men."

In fact, the Persian force was probably significantly smaller than the second-century reports indicate.* Modern estimates suggest a force of around 100,000 troops, still a vast multitude that outnumbered Alexander by better than two-to-one. Among these were at least 10,000 highly trained Greek mercenaries and the "10,000 Immortals," an elite force of highly trained and fiercely loyal Persian troops who constituted both Darius's palace guard and the core of his standing army. The rest of the infantry would have included both Persians and troops drawn from Persian dominions in central Asia.

Justinus, whose estimate of the Persian manpower outnumbering Alexander was 400,000 infantry and 100,000 cavalry, wrote "So vast a multitude of enemies caused some distrust in Alexander, when he contemplated the smallness of his own army."

However, Alexander's strategic doctrine was based not on the application of overwhelming force but on molding an army of moderate

---

*John Clark Ridpath in *History of the World* (New York: Philips and Hunt, 1885), volume 1, chapter 47, calculates that there were 140,000 troops in the Persian army that marched out of Susa in 333 BC.

size into a fighting machine whose skill overcame its smallness. As such, it was not unlike the war plans adopted by NATO during the Cold War to address the alliance's numerical inferiority to Warsaw Pact forces.

It was now, after one year in the field, that Alexander's intuitive understanding of the demands of leadership was increasingly important. This was manifest in the way that he treated his troops. In an era when the notion of granting a leave from the front was an alien concept, Alexander sent troops back to Macedonia and Greece for R&R. When they returned, they brought new recruits. Alexander's generosity proved to be a recruiting tool. This is another example of Alexander's being ahead of his time and of his thinking outside the confines of the box of traditional practices.

Arguably, the most important of Alexander's leadership traits was his ability to inspire. Arrian writes of other interactions between Alexander and his men as they too contemplated the smallness of their army. He tells us that "lest dismay should fall upon his men, he rode round among his troops, and addressed those of each nation in an appropriate speech. He excited the Illyrians and Thracians by describing the enemy's wealth and treasures, and the Greeks by putting them in mind of their wars of old, and their deadly hatred towards the Persians. He reminded the Macedonians at one time of their conquests in Europe, and at another of their desire to subdue Asia, boasting that no troops in the world had been found a match for them, and assuring them that this battle would put an end to their labors and crown their glory."

As such, he made the campaign personal, stressing and appealing to the motives and aspirations of each group under his command, whether that be a desire for revenge, for glory, or for proving that they were the best of the best. Today, a commander might do the same thing by appealing to a soldier's patriotism, or to a person's role as a member of an elite group, as is the case within the U.S. Marine Corps.

❖

Darius studied his map for a place to stop the advance of Alexander's army, and he found it. In order to march his troops to the Mediterranean coastline from the Anatolian Plateau of central Asia Minor, Alexander needed to cross the Taurus Mountains, and there was essentially only one place to do this efficiently. Darius noted that Alexander would have to pass through what was known in antiquity as the Cilician Gates. Now known as Gülek Pass, the 3,400-foot pass is traversed by the six-lane E90 superhighway. In October 333 BC, it was traversed by the equivalent—an important and much-used caravan highway.

The Cilician Gates presented Darius with unique opportunities. Often a commander does not know where an enemy will be next. This time Darius knew. Alexander would have to go this way. A narrow pass also presents multiple opportunities for a defender, as high ground can be fortified before the battle and narrowness takes away room in which an attacker can maneuver. It was a battle that Darius should have won.

But by having arrived at the gates after Alexander had passed, Darius lost. Alexander knew that Darius was coming—it was hardly a secret that the vast Greco-Macedonian army was moving across Asia Minor—so he force-marched his troops to get through before the huge, unwieldy Persian army arrived. A small Persian advance guard was on hand to challenge Alexander, but he cut through easily under cover of darkness, and the skirmish was a mere whisper of what could have been a decisive battle.

Alexander was out of the mountains and had occupied the city of Tarsus before Darius could comprehend the magnitude of another missed opportunity.

Located near the Mediterranean, Tarsus was an important crossroads and trading city with a history that already spanned more than 6,000 years. Parenthetically, it would later be important as the birthplace of Saint Paul, and as the place where Marc Antony and Cleopatra first met. The town might have been just another tiny footnote to Alexander's story had it not been for a microbe that almost did what Darius had failed to do.

Upon reaching Tarsus, Alexander decided to take a dip in the Cydnus River (now Tarsus Çay). Aristobulus reports that it was very hot, and "in profuse perspiration [Alexander] leaped into the river Cydnus and swam, being eager to bathe in its water [but that afterward] Alexander was seized with convulsions, accompanied with high fever and continuous sleeplessness."

Contemporary accounts blame the cold water—it was November—but a bacterial infection seems more likely. Arrian adds that "none of the physicians thought he was likely to survive, except Philip, an Acarnanian, a physician in attendance on the king, and very much trusted by him in medical matters, who also enjoyed a great reputation in the army in general affairs."

Apparently, this reputation was not embraced by Parmenio. Alexander's biographers mention that when Philip prescribed an herbal potion, Parmenio passed a note to the young king cautioning him that Philip might have been bribed by Darius to poison him. Alexander ignored Parmenio, drank the medicine and collapsed. As Plutarch writes, "at first the medicine mastered the patient, and as it were drove back and buried deep his bodily powers, so that his voice failed, he fell into a swoon, and became almost wholly unconscious." However, Alexander soon recovered his strength, and "showed himself to the Macedonians, who refused to be comforted until they had seen Alexander."

⊡

By the time Alexander had marched to Mallus on the Mediterranean coast, he had word that the Persian army was two days away, due east, across the Gulf of Issus (now Gulf of Iskenderun) and across the Amanus (now Nur) Mountains, at Sochoi (or Sochi) in the Syrian plains. Parmenio, with an advance guard, was already part way around the gulf and camped near the village of Issus.

To get a sense of the geography, imagine the Gulf of Issus as a clockface. Mallus was at the nine o'clock position, and Issus was at one o'clock. Sochoi was due east of the three o'clock position. Near the two o'clock position, the gulf was fed by a stream then known as the Pinarus River, whose precise modern equivalent is subject to debate.

As at the Cilician Gates, terrain around the Gulf of Issus was destined to be an important factor when the two sides met. The coastal plain in the area was relatively narrow, just a few miles wide, and crowded between the Mediterranean and the steep Amanus Mountains. We should add that the coastal plain was itself not flat, but consisted of rolling hills that would complicate troop movements and visibility.

Alexander quickly moved the bulk of his force to Issus, established a base camp and continued clockwise around the Gulf of Issus to the town of Myriandros (later named for Alexander as Alexandretta, and now known in Turkish as Iskenderun) at the five o'clock position, probing toward the Persians, who were across the mountains.

Darius, meanwhile, decided to remain on the far side of the mountains and move counterclockwise from three o'clock to one, toward a place where he could cross the mountains above Issus and position himself in Alexander's rear, cutting him off from his base camp.

Had Darius remained on the open plains near Sochoi, Alexander probably would have attacked him there. Darius would have had room to maneuver and utilize his superior numbers more easily than he could on the cramped coastal plain around Issus. As it was, Darius was probably able to get just a portion of his 100,000 or so troops into position.

As Arrian writes, Amyntas, a deserter from Alexander's army, "advised him not to abandon this position [at Sochoi], because the open country was favorable to the great multitude of the Persians and the vast quantity of their baggage." However, like George Armstrong Custer at the Little Bighorn, Darius feared that his foe would slip away and avoid a decisive battle, so he moved to attack.

When he got word of Darius's movements, Alexander reversed himself at Myriandros, heading back counterclockwise, retracing his steps toward Issus. He had no intention of avoiding a fight. Knowing that Darius himself was present that day was an important driving force, causing Alexander to look forward to the coming battle.

As Arrian writes, Alexander called together his generals and cavalry commanders, exhorting them "to take courage from the dangers which they had already surmounted, asserting that the struggle would be between themselves who had been previously victorious and a foe who had already been beaten; and that the deity was acting the part of general on their behalf better than himself, by putting it into the mind of Darius to move his forces from the spacious plain and shut them up in a narrow place, where there was sufficient room for themselves to deepen their phalanx by marching from front to rear, but where their vast multitude would be useless to the enemy in the battle. He added that their foes were similar to them neither in strength nor in courage."

Unlike the situation at the Cilician Gates, this time Darius managed to arrive first, accomplishing his goal of getting between Alexander and his camp at Issus. The Persians even managed to dig in and construct some defensive positions along the Pinarus River. Since it was November, the river was at its lowest and was therefore less of a terrain factor than the Granicus had been 18 months earlier. However, as Arrian writes, probably quoting Aristobulus or Callisthenes, the Greek chroniclers who accompanied Alexander and upon whose accounts the later biographers relied, many parts of the river bank were steep and precipitous.

Darius positioned himself in his chariot at the center of his command, as was standard Persian practice. The bulk of his cavalry was on his right wing, on flatter ground near the Gulf of Issus. He had some cavalry on his left, but he considered it a waste of resources to put too many horses into the steep foothills where it was harder to maneuver.

In the center, the Greek mercenaries faced the Macedonian phalanx, including troops led by Coenus and Craterus, Alexander's veteran infantry commanders.

The Greco-Macedonian order of battle had the cavalry equally divided, with Parmenio on the left, near the gulf, in command of a force that included Peloponnesian cavalry. Also on the left wing were Cretan archers with Thracians under the command of Sitalces in front. Parmenio's mandate was to hold the seacoast and not allow the Persians to outflank him and cut him off from the sea.

Alexander himself commanded his elite Companion Cavalry, as well as the Thessalian horsemen that were on the right wing, at the base of the mountains. In turn, these troops were augmented by an infantry guard under the command of Nicanor, a son of Parmenio. The Greek mercenaries who had defected from the Persians the previous year in Asia Minor formed Alexander's reserve.

As Alexander approached, Darius sent his cavalry forward across the river. When Alexander saw that Darius had concentrated his cavalry on the seaward wing of his formation, he shifted the Thessalian cavalry from right to left.

Meanwhile, the Persian left wing curved so much into the mountains that part of it actually circled behind Alexander's right wing as he advanced. To address this, he moved two squadrons of the Companion Cavalry, under Peroedas and Pantordanus, from the center to the right wing.

According to Arrian, Alexander also placed some of the cavalry and archers "so as to form an angle with the centre towards the mountain which was in the rear; so that on the right, his phalanx had been drawn up separated into two wings, the one fronting Darius and the main body of Persians beyond the river, and the other facing those who had been posted at the mountain in their rear."

Darius had done everything right. He had organized his superior forces logically, and he had constructed defensive positions to stymie a counterattack even if his own attack failed. He had troops on the high ground above Alexander's right flank. The Persians waited as the Greco-Macedonian army advanced slowly. When the arrows began to fly, Alexander himself led a lightning charge across the river against the Persian left wing, surprising them with his speed.

"As Alexander had conjectured," says Arrian, "as soon as the battle became a hand-to-hand one, the part of the Persian army stationed on the left wing was put to rout; and here Alexander and his men won a brilliant victory."

However, the Greek mercenaries in the Persian center attacked the Greco-Macedonian phalanx, who had lost touch with their own right wing. This was because Alexander had penetrated deeply into the enemy lines, and his phalanx had not kept pace.

Ideally, the Persian phalanx should have closed behind Alexander's cavalry as they ran deep behind Persian lines, surrounding them. Fortunately, Alexander's quick early success had unbalanced the Persians. They became too busy fighting the Greco-Macedonian center to worry about their own left flank—to their own peril.

Darius had lightly packed his cavalry on his left in the foothills because he didn't expect a cavalry fight in that sector. Therefore, Alexander's Companions were able to rout them and send them running. This meant that the Companions were now able to outflank the Persian center.

It was a classic Macedonian maneuver. Alexander led a hammer that slammed the Persian phalanx against the anvil of his own phalanx. Meanwhile, the Persians who were in the hills above Alexander's far right failed to attack.

On the wing adjacent to the Gulf of Issus, where the Persian right faced Parmenio and the Greco-Macedonian left, the Persian cavalry took the offensive and crossed the river. Unlike the other wing, where Alexander's charge had quickly unsettled the Persians, the seaward Persian wing held its ground.

Darius may have done everything right in his preparation, but everything on his left and center had now gone wrong. His left collapsed under the force of Alexander's personal charge, and his center, which might have outflanked Alexander, was now being flanked by him. His left wing had crumbled. However, his right held, although it was cut off from his center.

Darius had expected to stand in his chariot, high above the fray, watching as his powerful superior numbers cut the Greco-Macedonians to ribbons. Now, the battle swirled around him, as did Alexander's horsemen.

Darius should have stood fast, urging his men to resist, rally and counterattack, but he panicked. Fearing for his own safety, he turned his chariot around and retreated. Arrian gives an almost comical description of Darius trying to get away in his wheeled vehicle, "conveyed safely in the chariot as long as he met with level ground in his flight; but when he lighted upon ravines and other rough ground, he left the chariot there, divesting himself both of his shield and Median mantle. He even left his bow in the chariot; and mounting a horse continued his flight."

Ironically, it was only when Darius made his cowardly dash that his strong right wing collapsed. As Arrian tells us, "the Persians did not give way until they perceived that Darius had fled and the Grecian mercenaries had been cut up by the phalanx and severed from them."

The retreat of the entire Persian army can best be described as chaos. Again, perhaps relying on the eyewitness accounts of Aristobulus and Callisthenes, the later biographers tell of panic as both infantry and cavalry retreated in disorder along narrow roads. Even though the Macedonians gave chase, killing as many of the retreating Persians as they could, more injuries may have been inflicted on the Persians by their trampling on one another.

Reportedly, Alexander himself pursued the retreating Darius until nightfall but failed to catch him. The Persian king got away along with 4,000 of his troops, forced marching all the way to the Euphrates. Other Persians who escaped made their way to Tripoli in Phoenicia (now Lebanon) and got away by sea to Chios, the Persian stronghold in the Aegean, a reminder that the Persian fleet remained a power at sea even as Alexander was victorious ashore.

There is no reliable estimate of the casualties at the Battle of Issus. Arrian gives the number of Persian dead as 100,000, but it is hard to imagine that Darius had many more than that in total on the battlefield. He also points out that among the losses were Arsames, Atizyes, and Rheomithres, three Persian cavalry commanders who were veterans of the Battle of Granicus. Justinus is more specific with his numbers, though he is probably still exaggerating when he states that 61,000 Persian infantrymen and 10,000 cavalry died, and that 40,000 Persians were captured. Justinus tallies Alexander's losses as a mere 130 infantrymen and 150 cavalry troops.[*]

Personally, Darius felt the sting of humiliation for the dishonorable way that he had escaped from the battlefield. Perhaps the worst part of this was that in his hasty retreat, he had deserted his mother, his wife and his daughters. Imagine Alexander's surprise when he rode into the abandoned Persian camp and found the royal women huddled in their tent.

"When Alexander came to see and console them, they threw themselves, at the sight of his armed attendants, into one another's arms, and uttered mournful cries, as if expecting to die immediately," writes Justinus. "Afterwards, falling at the feet of Alexander, they begged, not that they might live, but that their death might be delayed till they should bury the body of Darius. Alexander, touched with the respectful concern of the princesses for Darius, assured them that the king was still alive, and removed their apprehensions of death; directing, at the same time, that they should be treated as royal personages, and giving the daughters hopes of husbands suitable to the dignity of their father."

---

[*]John Clark Ridpath in *History of the World* (New York: Philips and Hunt, 1885. Volume 1, Chapter 47) notes that numbers vary widely among early accounts, and reports that the lowest number he found was 70,000 slain Persians, and 40,000 captured. George Willis Botsford and Charles Alexander Robinson in *Hellenic History,* 3rd ed. (New York: Macmillan, 1948), chapter 18, venture no guess as to Persian losses, but mention that Alexander's losses were "only 450 in number."

Alexander made good on his promise, extending it to all the Persian women who were captured at Issus, and later when Alexander occupied Damascus. Hearing that some of his men had raped some other women found at the Persian camp, Alexander ordered them tried and executed. Perhaps Alexander did this out of a sense of chivalry, or perhaps it was his savvy understanding of politics. In any case, his being magnanimous in victory could not help but enhance Alexander's reputation across the empire that he sought to rule.

Quoting Aristobulus, Arrian writes that Alexander allowed Darius's mother, wife and daughters to "retain the state and retinue befitting their royal rank, as well as the title of queens; for he had not undertaken the war against Darius from a feeling of hatred, but he had conducted it in a legitimate manner for the empire of Asia."

For many of the Greco-Macedonian officers and soldiers, what they discovered in the abandoned Persian encampment verged on culture shock. Darius was certainly a king, but to say that he "lived like a king" while on a campaign was an understatement. He traveled with a glittering portable palace, with all of the gold and jewelry which, as Arrian puts it, "the Great King was in the habit of taking with him as necessary for his luxurious mode of living, even though he was going on a military expedition." Arrian also mentions that Alexander's men discovered 3,000 talents ($46 million) in cash in Darius's camp, and even more in Damascus at Darius's headquarters there.

The splendor of Persian courtly life was beyond the imaginations of many, but it certainly got their attention and whetted their appetites for further plunder that would await them as Alexander's campaign pressed on into the heart of Persia. As Plutarch writes, "for the first time the Macedonians got a taste of gold and silver and women and barbaric luxury of life, and now that they had struck the trail, they were like dogs in their eagerness to pursue and track down the wealth of the Persians."

Darius subsequently sent Alexander a letter begging him to release his womenfolk. According to Arrian, he wrote that the battle had been decided "as seemed good to some one of the gods. And now he, a king, begged his captured wife, mother, and children from a king; and he wished to form a friendship with him and become his ally."

To the humiliation of the Persian king, Alexander declined his entreaty. Alexander replied that didn't want Darius's friendship, he wanted his empire.

According to Arrian, Alexander wrote back, telling Darius, "Your ancestors came into Macedonia and the rest of Greece and treated us ill, without any previous injury from us. I, having been appointed commander in chief of the Greeks, and wishing to take revenge on the Persians, crossed over into Asia, hostilities being begun by you. . . . I took the field against you, because you were the party who commenced the hostility. Since I have vanquished your generals and [satraps] in the previous battle, and now yourself and your forces in like manner, I am, by the gift of the gods, in possession of your land."

He then taunted Darius, telling him—with more than a little exaggeration—that he was already master of Asia. The Battle of Issus was the turning point that confirmed the decline of the Persian Empire as irrevocable. After Granicus, Darius might have regained the initiative and reversed Alexander's progress. After Issus, Darius had been reduced to begging. Taking this as a sign of weakness, Alexander taunted him by telling him that his requests could be met only by conceding his empire to Alexander.

"I am lord of all Asia," Alexander told Darius. "Ask for your mother, wife, and children, and anything else you wish. For whatever you ask for you will receive; and nothing shall be denied you. But for the future, whenever you send to me, send to me as the king of Asia, and do not address to me your wishes as to an equal; but if you are in need of anything, speak to me as to the man who is lord of all your territories."

Alexander was obviously teasing Darius when he said "whatever you ask for you will receive," because he knew full well that Darius would *never* address him as the king of Asia—even to get his family back.

CHAPTER 5

The Takedown of Tyre

IN HIS CAMPAIGN AGAINST THE ACHAEMENID PERSIAN EMPIRE—OF
which he intended to be master—Alexander's battles alternated between field battles and sieges of fixed locations. Twice in as many years
the Persians had put a great army into the field against him, and twice
they had lost. For the most part, though, the campaign during these
years was characterized by his methodical take down of one city after
another as he cut through the Persian dominions like a sword.

As had been the case after Granicus in May 334 BC, Alexander
followed the November 333 victory at Issus by continuing his relentless march. He headed southward along the Mediterranean shore,
from what is now Turkey, through modern Syria and into present-day
Lebanon. Strategically, it was his intention to march all the way to
Egypt, thus securing all of the ports in the eastern Mediterranean. As
Plutarch describes the strategy, Alexander was determined to eliminate Persian naval power by making himself "master of the seacoasts."

Many places submitted to Alexander willingly—or at least com-
pliantly. The people of the Phoenician enclaves of Byblos and Sidon
(now in Lebanon) handed over the keys to their cities. "As for
Cyprus," Plutarch relates, "its kings came at once and put the island
in his hands, together with Phoenicia, with the exception of Tyre."

Tyre, in what is now Lebanon, was the holdout. It had a unique place as the largest and most important Phoenician port in the eastern Mediterranean, and as an important Persian naval base. Tyre had been a prominent city for centuries by the time that Alexander arrived. The Phoenician merchants from Tyre had been among the first people to send their trading ships throughout the Mediterranean. The city grew rich and powerful and was coveted by its neighbors. King Nebuchadnezzar II, known as "the Great," who built the Hanging Gardens of Babylon, had unsuccessfully besieged the city for 13 years in the sixth century BC. Eventually, the Tyrians threw in their lot with the Persians.

To secure their metropolis, the Tyrians built a new city on an island a half mile offshore from the old city on the mainland. This new Tyre was now an impregnable fortress surrounded by two miles of stone walls that were reportedly as high as 150 feet. The island had two ship harbors, the northern one named for Sidon, the southern one named for Egypt. Through these harbors, Tyre could be supplied from the sea, regardless of who controlled the adjacent mainland.

Alexander had hoped to avoid the necessity of a siege entirely. He was optimistic when his army was met on the coast road by ambassadors from Tyre, who told him, according to Arrian, that the city "had decided to do whatever he might command."

Alexander said he would like to enter their city and offer a sacrifice to Heracles—known to the Tyrians as Melqart—at the temple that had been erected to him in the southern part of their island city-state. He explained that he was descended from Heracles, as were all of the kings of Macedonia. Their response was not what he expected. The Tyrians, then ruled by King Azemilcus, told him he was welcome at another temple of Heracles located on the mainland, but he could not enter the island.

With this, the die was cast. Tyre must be taken. Thus began an epic siege that took place over the spring and summer of 332.

In a speech possibly transcribed by Aristobulus or Callisthenes, and passed down by Arrian, Alexander told his officers of his strategic view of the eastern Mediterranean, explaining why Tyre was so important:

"I see that an expedition to Egypt will not be safe for us, so long as the Persians retain the sovereignty of the sea; nor is it a safe course, both for other reasons, and especially looking at the state of matters in Greece, for us to pursue Darius, leaving in our rear the city of Tyre itself in doubtful allegiance. . . . I am apprehensive lest while we advance with our forces toward Babylon and in pursuit of Darius, the Persians should again conquer the maritime districts, and transfer the war into Greece with a larger army."

The conventional wisdom held that Tyre could be assaulted only from the sea, and its huge, solid walls would protect it from that. Besieging Tyre presented a dilemma, given that the Tyrian fleet and the allied Persian fleet under Autophradates had naval superiority in the eastern Mediterranean, while Alexander had deliberately undercut his own navy.

According to folklore, readily retold by Arrian as fact, the solution came to Alexander in a dream. He dreamed that Heracles took him by the right hand and led him up into the city, walking on dry land. Though the dream needed little in the way of interpretation, it was declared to be a good sign by Aristander, the seer who had once told Philip II that his son within the womb of Olympias would be as bold as a lion. Alexander had relied on his prognostications more than ever after he correctly predicted the victory at Granicus.

If Tyre was separated from dry land by a half mile of water, he would just take the dry land to the city. Alexander decided to solve the problem at hand by turning Tyre from an island into the tip of a peninsula by building a causeway to it from the mainland.

The portion of the channel closest to the shore was a gently sloping tidal plain. There was an abundance of rock and other construction material nearby, so getting started on this project would be relatively easy. Closer to the island fortress city, however, the channel was 18 feet deep, so it would be more challenging. A difficult task under any circumstances, building a causeway here beneath hostile walls was a serious problem for work crews with Tyrian archers raining projectiles down upon them.

However, morale inside the walls was shaky as well. The Tyrians too, had a dream. They dreamed that Apollo told them he was, as Plutarch paraphrases it, "going away to Alexander, since he was displeased at what was going on in the city."

The project began with wooden pilings being driven into the mud with a roadway constructed on top. The work proceeded rapidly at first, but as the Macedonians got into the channel, the crews came under fire from Tyrian warships. To stave off this harassment, Alexander had two tall siege towers constructed at the end of the causeway from which his troops could return fire against the ships. Their elevated position meant that the men in the towers could see farther, and their projectiles had greater range, than they would from near sea level.

The Tyrians struck back using a transport barge as an incendiary device. They piled it high with wood scraps and other flammable material, including pitch and brimstone. To its masts they fitted long double yardarms, attaching caldrons containing additional flammable material. They towed the barge near the causeway towers using triremes, setting it on fire as it neared the towers at the end of the causeway. The yardarms were long enough to cantilever over the causeway and strike the towers, which were soon engulfed in flames.

Attempts by Alexander's personnel to fight the fires were met by archers aboard the triremes. The Tyrians also landed troops on the causeway who burned catapults and other equipment before withdrawing. After a stroke of engineering brilliance in his causeway idea, Alexander had been halted rather ignominiously.

However, it was merely round one. Alexander promptly ordered the causeway to be widened and new towers to be built. Meanwhile, he decided to acquire additional warships of his own, having realized that defeating Tyre would require sea power after all.

❖

Expanding his navy was actually easier for Alexander than might have been expected. Because most of his recent conquests and alliances had involved maritime powers, his new friends were willing to contribute to his fleet-building efforts. According to Arrian, Cyprus sent 120 warships to Alexander, while both Sidon and Rhodes contributed some triremes, and "about 80 Phoenician ships joined him."

Both Gerostratus and Enylus, the kings respectively of Aradus and Byblos, "ascertaining that their cities were in the possession of Alexander, deserted Autophradates and the fleet under his command, and came to Alexander with their naval force."

Alexander also personally joined the naval attack on Tyre, sailing with the fleet as it embarked from Sidon. His own position was at the right wing of the armada, farthest from the coast. His initial strategy had been to lure the Tyrians into a battle in the open sea.

The Tyrians had been looking forward to such a fight on the basis of Alexander's perceived naval inferiority, but when they observed Alexander's fleet most remained in port rather than accepting the challenge. Alexander's flotilla managed to sink three vessels, but aside from that they were at a stalemate.

Alexander for once had the superior numbers in a naval battle, but he could not lure out his enemy. If a fight took place, it would have to be in the tight confines of one of the island's two harbors. It was like Issus, only on water—and at Issus, it was Darius who was in too tight a space to make full use of his superior numbers.

Alexander decided to blockade Tyre and wait. He assigned the Cypriot triremes to block the northern Tyrian port and dispatched the Phoenician fleet to block the southern port.

He then turned back to his land strategy, ordering the rapid construction of catapults and siege engines, including battering rams and protected towers for the transfer of troops. These were placed on ships for the final assault against Tyre's fortifications. The Tyrians countered by building towers of their own in order to be higher than the Greco-Macedonian besiegers. It became a battle of fiery projectiles launched from higher and higher elevations.

Eventually feeling the pressure of the naval blockade, the Tyrians made an attempt to break out of the northern port using a force of seven triremes, three quadriremes and three quinqueremes. The ships moved silently so as not to alert the Cypriot blockade ships, but it would not have been necessary. The Cypriots were asleep at the tiller. Indeed, each ship was manned by a mere skeleton crew, with most hands having been quartered ashore. Catching the Cypriot fleet off guard, the Tyrians managed to sink or damage a number of vessels.

Roused from his tent—all of this happened in the heat of the summer afternoon as the officers were resting—Alexander ordered all available ships in the port on the mainland side of the channel to put to sea to prevent any additional Tyrian ships from reaching open seas. Alexander boarded a ship himself, intending as usual to lead from the front.

Despite calls from Tyrian lookouts that Alexander's ships were pulling out from their moorings, ships continued to leave the port. Alexander's fleet rallied, ramming and sinking a number of vessels, and capturing others.

Finally, Alexander developed a tactical plan that called for a complex amphibious landing under fire that would be considered ambitious even by a modern combat force. In the northern part of the island, where the causeway had been built, Tyre's walls were the most formidable and best defended, so Alexander moved to execute an unanticipated flanking maneuver by hitting a less well defended point in the southern end.

The attack would entail breaching the wall above sea level from the sea using siege engines aboard ships, and then using a portable bridge to push troops through this breach. Indeed, attacking a vertical wall above sea level is always much more difficult than putting troops across a sea-level beach using landing craft. With Tyrian defenses pierced, Alexander's fleet would attack the two Tyrian ports simultaneously.

When his first attempt to execute the plan was quickly repulsed, Alexander withdrew, postponing a renewed attempt until a patch of stormy weather had blown through. On the third day following, the seas were quieter and Alexander resumed the assault.

After seven months, the siege finally reached its climax on the last day of the month of Hekatombaion, the same month that Alexander celebrated his twenty-fourth birthday (July 20, 332 BC). Plutarch tells that after consulting some omens, Aristander had declared confidently "that the city would certainly be captured during that month." Because it was the last day of the month, and Tyre had held out for 200 days already, Aristander's words "produced laughter and jesting."

Arrian says that Alexander "led the ships containing the military engines up to the city. In the first place he shook down a large piece of the wall; and when the breach appeared to be sufficiently wide, he ordered the vessels conveying the military engines to retire, and brought up two others, which carried the bridges, which he intended to throw upon the breach in the wall. The shield bearing guards occupied one of these vessels, which he had put under the command of Admetus; and the other was occupied by the regiment of Coenus, called the foot Companions."

When the siege engines pulled back, Alexander sent in triremes with archers and catapults to get as close as possible, even if it meant running aground, to support the infantry assault.

Again leading from the front, Alexander himself headed the assault force that went ashore. Admetus's contingent was the first over the wall, but he was killed in action, struck by a spear. Alexander then led the Companion infantry in securing a section of wall and several towers. With Greco-Macedonian troops taking and holding a rapidly expanding beachhead, the defensive advantages of the fortified city began to evaporate.

Unfortunately for the Tyrians, their royal palace was in the southern part of the city, and it was one of the first major objectives to fall to Alexander's invading troops. King Azemilcus, his senior bureaucrats and a delegation of Carthaginian dignitaries, who had been trapped in Tyre when Alexander's fleet sealed the ports, were there but escaped to take refuge in the temple to Heracles. Ironically, this was the same temple at which Alexander had originally asked to be allowed to worship.

At the same time, Alexander's fleet forced its way into the two harbors. Phoenician ships entered the southern harbor, the Port of Egypt, and the Cypriot ships breached the entrance to Tyre's northern harbor, the Port of Sidon. Here at the Port of Sidon, the larger of he two anchorages, troops were able to get ashore inside the harbor. The defenders fell back to defensive positions at the Agenoreum, a temple to the mythical King Agenor, but were quickly routed. Alexander now had beachheads on either end of Tyre and the Tyrian defenders in a pincer.

Within a matter of hours, after a bloody siege of seven months, troops from both landings linked up in the northern part of the city. All of the defenses that had been erected on the causeway side were for naught.

❖

According to Diodorus, immediately after his victory Alexander ordered the causeway broadened to an average width of nearly 200 feet and made permanent, using material from the damaged city walls as fill.

The causeway is still there, although it if you visited it, you would not notice it. Over the past 2,300 years, wave action and drifting sand have caused it to grow into a broad isthmus about a quarter of a mile wide. The part of Tyre that was an island in 332 BC has been connected to the mainland ever since Alexander's day.*

Alexander gave no quarter to those he captured, killing them on the spot or eventually selling them into slavery. According to Arrian, the defenders suffered about 8,000 killed or executed and 30,000 made slaves, while the Greco-Macedonian force lost 400 killed in action during the entire siege. Curtius reports 6,000 Tyrian troops killed inside the city walls, and 2,000 executed in the aftermath. While these numbers were probably stretched in favor of Alexander, many later scholars, including Botsford and Robinson, repeat them. There is no way of knowing for sure.

In any case, Alexander walked into the Temple of Heracles around sundown that day to make his long-postponed sacrifice. It was the afternoon of the last day of Hekatombaion. Of all those who had laughed at Aristander for his outlandish prediction, none were laughing now.

Alexander spared King Azemilcus and gave amnesty to all those hiding in the temple when it was captured. The sight of his city's resounding defeat, and of Alexander standing in the temple that he had once asked to visit peacefully, was probably punishment enough for the king.

After the Battle of Issus and the siege of Tyre, Persia was no longer a Mediterranean superpower. Having had the heart ripped out of his army, and the bases ripped away from his navy, Darius would be unable to challenge Alexander significantly again until his army was deep inside the interior of the Persian Empire.

---

*Proceedings of the National Academy of Sciences, "Holocene Morphogenesis of Alexander the Great's Isthmus at Tyre in Lebanon," May 29, 2007. In this article, the causeway is described by Nick Marriner and his colleagues Christophe Morhange and Samuel Meulé of the Centre National de la Recherche Scientifique, Centre Européen de Recherche et d'Enseignement des Géosciences de l'Environnement in France. Using sediment core samples and computer modeling, they reconstructed the geological history of Tyre. They not only show how the causeway became permanent, but they discovered how Alexander's engineers made use of an existing submerged sandbar in their work.

CHAPTER 6

From Gaza to Alexandria

AFTER THE CAMPAIGN AT TYRE, WHICH CONSUMED THE FIRST HALF OF 332 BC, Alexander's army moved south toward Egypt, their way blocked by another "impregnable" fortress at Gaza. Still the scene of serious armed conflict in the twenty-first century, Gaza has been the crossroads of both major military campaigns and important trading routes for nearly 4,000 years. It was the site of both Egyptian and Canaanite settlements in the Bronze Age, and passed from the Egyptians to the Philistines 800 years before Alexander's time. According to the Old Testament, Samson pulled down the pillars of the temple here.

By the fourth century BC, Gaza was a well-established Persian city superimposed upon an Arab land and populated largely by Arabs. It was the last major city on the Mediterranean coastal road before one crossed the Sinai Desert into Egypt. Ruled by a Persian satrap named Batis (or Betis), Gaza was heavily fortified and defended by an army of Arab mercenaries.

Like Tyre, Gaza was surrounded by high walls. Unlike Tyre, it was not surrounded by water, but the fortified part of Gaza was situated high on a hilltop.

As at Tyre, Alexander initially considered the conquest of Gaza to be an engineering problem. However, according to Arrian, his officers "expressed the opinion that it was not possible to capture the wall by force, on account of the height of the mound" on which the city was constructed. However, as Arrian adds, "the more impracticable it seemed to be, the more resolutely Alexander determined that it must be captured. For he said that the action would strike the enemy with great alarm from its being contrary to their expectation."

The audacity of Alexander's engineering vision is amazing. At Tyre, he had turned an island into a peninsula to get his way. At Gaza, he proposed defeating the high-ground defensive advantage of a hilltop fortress by constructing a higher hill on the south side of the city wall. When it was completed, this hill would allow Alexander to bring up a siege engine to begin battering the wall. Meanwhile, Alexander also undertook to excavate beneath the Gazan walls to collapse them.

When the initial assault on the south side failed to produce the desired results, Alexander ordered his engineers to build a berm, or a wall of earth, around the entire circumference of the city. Arrian describes it as being the equivalent of 250 feet high and 1,200 feet wide, making it a construction chore of gargantuan proportions. Even with modern earthmoving equipment and without people shooting arrows at you, such a task would easily take a few months—which is about the length of time that Alexander's diggers spent in the fall of 332. This may be what happened to the 30,000 Tyrians who had become slaves over the summer.

While Alexander was supervising this project, an event occurred that Aristander interpreted as an omen. Plutarch writes that "a clod of earth, which had been dropped from on high by a bird, struck [Alexander] on the shoulder. The bird alighted on one of the battering-engines, and was at once caught in the network of sinews which were used to give a twist to the ropes."

Aristander told Alexander that there was good news and bad news in the omen. The old seer believed that Alexander would defeat Gaza, but that he was at serious personal risk.

By November, the digging was finished and the battle began. With the walls collapsing from beneath and from the battering rams against the outside, it is amazing that the defenders of Gaza managed to repulse three Greco-Macedonian attempts to get inside, but they did.

For Alexander, the fourth time was the charm, however. Arrian relates that a Companion named Neoptolemus was the first to get across the wall and into Gaza. He was quickly followed by a mass of phalanx troops, who fanned out and opened the city gates from the inside.

Remembering Aristander's prediction, Alexander initially kept out of the line of fire, but when some of his troops were in danger of being overrun by some counterattacking Arab mercenaries during one of the assaults, he personally led an attack. According to Arrian, Alexander was "wounded by a bolt from a catapult, right though the shield and breastplate into the shoulder. When he perceived that Aristander had spoken the truth about the wound, he rejoiced, because he thought he should also capture the city. . . . [though] he was not easily cured of the wound."

The wound is notable for having occurred to Alexander's shoulder, just as the object dropped by the bird had struck his shoulder.

As for the battle, Arrian tells that the defenders of Gaza fought to the last man, "all slain fighting there, as each man had been stationed." Curtius mentions that "some 10,000 Persians and Arabs fell at Gaza, but for the Macedonians too it was no bloodless victory."

In the account of the battle in his biography of Alexander, Curtius relates that Alexander singled out Batis for "special" treatment, specifically by copying what happened to Hector at the hands of Achilles in the *Iliad*. Curtius explains that as Batis was brought before him, Alexander said "You shall not have the death you wanted. Instead you can expect to suffer whatever torment can be devised against a prisoner."

As Curtius explains, Batis then gave Alexander a look that "was not just fearless, but downright defiant, and uttered not a word in reply to his threats."

"Do you see his obstinate silence?" said Alexander. "Has he knelt to me? Has he uttered one word of entreaty? But I shall overcome his silence; at the very least I shall punctuate it with groans." Thongs were then passed through the holes punched in the man's ankles and he was tied to a chariot. He met his death being dragged through his defeated city.

Both Arrian and Plutarch make a point of reporting that Alexander sold Gazan women and children into slavery, repopulated Gaza with people from adjacent cities and used the fortifications that had survived the attacks as a fortress to protect his own growing Mediterranean dominions.

✦

With Tyre and Gaza mercilessly subdued, Alexander marched across the hot, dusty Sinai Desert toward the ancient land of the pharaohs. He found a cordial welcome in Egypt, where the Persian rulers were strongly disliked for being, in the words of Curtius, "avaricious and arrogant."

After three millennia as an independent entity, most of the time as one of the leading civilizations on earth, Egypt had come under Persian rule in the sixth century BC. Inspired by Greek resistance in the fifth century BC, Egypt had thrown out the Persians, but had again become a Persian dominion just a dozen years before Alexander's arrival. In 343 BC, Pharaoh Nectanebo II, the third king of the Thirtieth Dynasty and the last native monarch of Egypt, was defeated by the Persian King Artaxerxes III, who preceded Alexander's nemesis Darius III. It was the end of an era, and the beginning of another. The latter was short-lived, as it ended the moment that Alexander reached the Nile in the late autumn of 332. Mazaces, the Persian satrap of Egypt, opened the doors and handed Alexander the keys. Without a battle, Egypt was now part of Alexander's growing empire. Though the Persians still held some island outposts, essentially everything on the rim of the Mediterranean that had been Persian now belonged to Alexander.

Even as Alexander first saw the Nile, vessels of his fleet were already moored at their new base at Pelusium on the eastern edge of the Nile Delta, having sailed there from Tyre. Alexander then directed his fleet to sail up the Nile to Memphis. Located about a dozen miles south of modern Cairo, Memphis was the ancient capital and longtime administrative metropolis of Lower Egypt.

As the ships sailed, Alexander led his troops overland to Memphis, marching south along the eastern bank of the river. On the way, Alexander was greeted with open arms. The Egyptians were only too happy to back a winner, especially one who would deliver them from the Persians. In Memphis, he was greeted as a hero with an enormous festival of music and feasting. The Egyptians wanted to put on a good show for their new Macedonian pharaoh.

Despite such a welcome, Alexander's stay in Egypt would be brief. He had bigger fish to fry. Since Issus, he was determined to pursue Darius, defeat him decisively, and possess his empire. Egypt was just a detour in Alexander's grand strategy. Because he would not be remaining in Egypt to rule his new dominion, Alexander needed to appoint a governor. Rather than installing a Greek or Macedonian, he picked Doloaspis, an Egyptian. According to Arrian and other early sources, he originally planned to split Egypt into two sections, governed by Doloaspis and Petisis, but the latter declined the offer, or quit soon after taking the job, leaving Doloaspis in charge of the whole country.

To command the military garrison that he left behind in Egypt, Alexander assigned the generals Peucestas and Balacrus, whom Alexander had appointed as satrap of Cilicia after the Battle of Issus.

From ancient Memphis, Alexander sailed north to found a new city, which he ambitiously envisioned as the new great metropolis of the eastern Mediterranean, superseding Tyre as a port and Memphis as an administrative center. Locating it on a site on the western edge of the Nile Delta, he named it for himself, calling it Alexandria.

❖

Having seen Alexander as a successful military engineer at Tyre and Gaza, we now become acquainted with Alexander the architect and city planner. As Arrian says, "he was seized by an ardent desire to undertake the enterprise, and he marked out the boundaries for the city himself, pointing out the place where the marketplace was to be constructed, where the temples were to be built, stating how many there were to be, and to what Grecian gods they were to be dedicated, and specially marking a spot for a temple to the Egyptian Isis."

Because he had no chalk at hand, Alexander and his helpers used grains of barley to delineate the outlines of buildings against the dark delta soil. However, as Plutarch tells it, "suddenly birds from the river and the lagoon, infinite in number and of every sort and size, settled down upon the place like clouds and devoured every particle of the barley-meal, so that even Alexander was greatly disturbed at the omen."

Alexander no doubt saw his city disappearing before his eyes, but Aristander and the court seers were quick to spin this turn of events in the opposite direction. They told Alexander that, again quoting Plutarch, the city would "have most abundant and helpful resources and be a nursing mother for men of every nation." If that was what they actually said, they were right. Certainly by Plutarch's time, this had come to pass.

Over the course of the coming years, Alexander would establish about a dozen other Alexandrias, but this one did in fact go on to be what Alexander had planned, becoming one of the most important cities of the world, and remaining as such for many centuries. Its lighthouse, the Pharos of Alexandria, would be included as one of the Seven Wonders of the Ancient World, while the Library of Alexandria is still remembered as probably the greatest to have existed in the ancient world. Constructed under the patronage of Ptolemy, one of Alexander's generals, who ruled Egypt after Alexander's death as Ptolemy Soter or Ptolemy I, this library itself ranks as a legendary wonder of civilization. It flourished in the centuries following Alexander's rule and survived until the first century BC, when it burned. Today, Egypt's second largest city after Cairo, Alexandria remains one of the most important ports in North Africa. The Bibliotheca Alexandrina, a much smaller library built to commemorate the lost original, opened in the city in 2002.

Having founded his city, Alexander made good on his desire to ride four days into the desert to Siwa Oasis to visit the legendary oracle of the Egyptian deity Amun, whom the Greeks called Ammon. Just as Arrian described it, Siwa is entirely surrounded by "a desert of far stretching sand." An isolated 600-square-mile forested area with springs and standing water in the middle of the desert near the Libyan border, Siwa is today an archeological site and tourist destination. It was more or less the same in 331 BC, with Alexander as one of the tourists.

Adding a bit of color to the story of Alexander's journey, Ptolemy tells that two serpents capable of speaking Greek served to guide Alexander to the Siwa Oasis. However, both Arrian and Plutarch disparage this account, agreeing with the account by Aristobulus that it was actually a pair of ravens that guided Alexander. The story also tells that Alexander's men never ran out of water in the desert because of several rare rain showers.

✦

As we have seen, Alexander was a great believer in prognostication. The oracle of Delphi had assured Alexander of his invincibility, and he was naturally anxious to consult the equally prestigious and well-known oracle of Amun.

Both Perseus and Heracles, great heroes of Greek mythology, had come here—and Alexander fancied himself a descendant of both. Moreover, Amun was seen as the Egyptian deity who was parallel to Zeus in the Greek pantheon as the king of gods, and Alexander also considered himself descended from Zeus—even without the claim of Olympias that Alexander had been fathered by Zeus in the form of a snake. Alexander wished to consult the oracle as to whether this story of his paternity was true.

Plutarch tells that at Siwa, the oracle "gave him salutation from the god as from a father."

At this point, Alexander posed a trick question, asking whether "any of the murderers of his father" had escaped his efforts to kill all of the conspirators in the death of Philip II. The trick in the question was that Alexander wished to deduce whether Philip was his true father, or whether it was Zeus, as his mother insisted.

"The prophet answered by bidding him be guarded in his speech, since his was not a mortal father," reports Plutarch. "Alexander therefore changed the form of his question, and asked whether the murderers of Philip had all been punished; and then, regarding his own empire, he asked whether it was given to him to become lord and master of all mankind."

Plutarch goes on to say that in one of his many letters home to Olympias, Alexander confided that the oracle—speaking through a priest, of course—had greeted Alexander with the phrase "Oh, pai dios," meaning "Oh, son of Zeus, or "Oh, son of god." Plutarch and others have suggested that the priest meant to use the polite greeting "Oh, pai dion," meaning "Oh, my son," but had mispronounced one letter, mixing up two Greek words. Either way, the story illustrates Alexander's self-perception. It is uncertain whether he truly believed himself the son of Zeus before 332 BC, or whether he still took the idea as symbolic. It is reasonably certain, though, that if not this year, he eventually did come around to believe in his divine paternity. After all, he was a big believer in oracles.

Having heard—or thought he heard—what he wanted from the oracle, Alexander made offerings to Amun and gave gifts in the form of cash to his priests. He then returned to his conquest of the Achaemenid Persian Empire.

CHAPTER 7

Decision at Gaugamela

HAVING WINTERED IN EGYPT, ALEXANDER DEPARTED FROM THAT country in the early spring of 331 BC. Three years had passed since he had crossed into Asia Minor and defeated the Persian army at Granicus. Passing through Tyre, Alexander had no trouble paying his respects at the Temple of Heracles. While in the city, he also took care of various administrative tasks related to rule over his dominions and the collection of taxes, also dispatching some of his naval assets to side with factions in the Peloponnesus that supported the war with Persia. Here, as often in the accounts penned by Alexander's various biographers, we see the skilled military leader in his other role, that of an administrator. Had he not been equal to this task, his growing empire would have collapsed behind him as he moved forward with his campaign.

Alexander then turned to the primary goal of his campaign, his showdown with Darius III, now in residence in the splendid ancient metropolis of Babylon, just south of modern day Baghdad.

Alexander left the Mediterranean coast in the month of Hekatombaion, one year after his defeat of Tyre, leading his army east by northeast into the Persian Empire, generally in the direction of the Euphrates River near where it crosses the modern border between Syria and Turkey.

In defensive wars, such as the one in which Darius now found himself, commanders look for natural terrain features into which to incorporate their defensive line. Darius saw the Euphrates as such a feature. The great, broad river was an ideal place to halt the advance of the Greco-Macedonian forces, and the Persian king sent Mazaeus with 3,000 cavalry troops to guard against a crossing. Formerly the Persian satrap of Cilicia, Mazaeus was now Darius's satrap for Mesopotamia, the vast plain that lies between the Euphrates and its sister river, the Tigris (now central Iraq).

Meanwhile, Alexander had sent an advance guard to begin building a pontoon bridge across the river at a place known in antiquity as Thapsacus, whose exact location today is not known. Under the watchful eye of the Persians, the Greek bridge builders went to work. Mazaeus watched and waited, probably intending to let his enemy do all the work, then send his cavalry across their own bridge to attack the small advance guard. For this reason, the Greeks deliberately stopped work on the bridge. They realized that if they completed the bridge before reinforcements arrived, Mazaeus could use their own bridge to attack them. When he got word that Alexander was approaching with his main force, Mazaeus pulled out, and the bridging moved to completion. So much for a terrain feature to anchor the Persian defense.

After crossing, Alexander might have turned his armies south, heading directly toward Babylon, the ancient Sumerian metropolis, to which Darius had earlier retreated. Instead, he turned north into the cooler climate of the eastern foothills of the Taurus Mountains, now named, in Turkish, Güneydoğu Toroslar. It was the hottest part of the summer, and as we have seen with twenty-first century armies operating in the vicinity of Baghdad, summer is not a good time for military operations in the region. Traveling by this route, Alexander reached the Tigris in September 331 BC.

Darius sent out reconnaissance teams—some of whom were captured by Alexander's men—to monitor the progress of the Greco-Macedonian army, but the Persians made no attempt to engage them in battle. This was a lucky thing for Alexander, for his troops had a great deal of difficulty getting across the Tigris, which was flowing fast and chest-deep on the horses as the cavalry crossed.

Darius was preparing for a decisive battle on more level terrain, where he could effectively employ his sizable army. As had been the case all along in this campaign, the Persians outnumbered the Greco-Macedonians, and Darius intended to use this to his advantage as he had been unable to do two years earlier at Issus.

Once across the river, Alexander rested his troops, and as they were camped, they observed a near-total lunar eclipse on the evening of September 20, 332 BC.*

"First the moon lost its usual brightness, and then became suffused with a blood-red color which caused a general dimness in the light it shed," writes Curtius. "Right on the brink of a decisive battle the men were already in a state of anxiety, and this now struck them with a deep religious awe which precipitated a kind of panic. They complained that the gods opposed their being taken to the ends of the earth, that now rivers forbade them access, heavenly bodies did not maintain their erstwhile brightness, and they were met everywhere by desolation and desert."

Egyptian astronomers traveling with Alexander confirmed to him that the eclipse was a natural phenomenon. Rather than explaining this to the mass of troops, they—as well as the typically optimistic and apparently infallible Aristander—declared the eclipse to be a bad omen for the Persians.

A day or so after that auspicious night, as his army marched south on the east side of the Tigris, about 1,000 Persian cavalrymen challenged Alexander. Many perceived them as the vanguard of Darius's army, but they were actually just stragglers on a recon patrol, and they were easily routed by a small cavalry counterforce led by Alexander personally. This probably played a role in restoring lost confidence among the Greco-Macedonian troops.

By this time, Darius had picked his battlefield, and here he camped to await Alexander. The place was a flat plain called Gaugamela, possi-

---

*Professor F. Richard Stephenson in *Historical Eclipses and Earth's Rotation* (Cambridge University Press, 1997, page 372) dates the eclipse to the night of September 20–21, 331 BC. Quintus Curtius Rufus in his *History of Alexander the Great* mentions that it was observed by Alexander's troops at first watch, therefore the evening of September 20.

bly named for a nearby hill called Tel Gomel (Camel's Hump). The exact location of Gaugamela is not known, but many archaeologists have identified it as being east of Mosul, a modern Iraqi city mainly on the west bank of the Tigris, across the river from the ruins of the ancient city of Nineveh. Some ancient writers suggest that the battle took place near Arbela (now Arbil or Irbil), about 50 miles east of the Tigris. Others, including Arrian, mention the site as being a half day's ride west of Arbela.

Plutarch and Diodorus mention that Darius was able to field a million-man army, while Curtius says it was half again larger than his army at Issus, or 900,000. Arrian is a bit more specific, identifying an infantry force of a million, plus 40,000 cavalry and 200 chariots with scythes extending from their axles. He also adds that Darius had 15 elephants that had been brought in from India.[*]

Arrian does go into some detail about the composition of Darius's grand coalition at Gaugamela. Representing many of the satrapies from throughout the Persian Empire, it embodied the multiethnic reality of a vast domain that had existed as such for two centuries. According to his detailed checklist, the Persian forces were augmented by more than a dozen allied commands. Based no doubt on the first-hand accounts of Aristobulus or Callisthenes, he itemized these as including Albanians; Arabs commanded by Ocondobates and Otanes; Arians led by Satibarzanes; Armenians commanded by Orontes and Mithraustes; Babylonians and Sittacenians led by Boupares; Bactrians and Sogdians, both under the command of Bessus, the satrap of Bactria; Cadusians; Cappadocians commanded by Ariaces; troops from India including "mountaineer Indians" commanded by Barsaentes,

---

[*] More recent scholars are divided between using the ancient estimates as fact and doing their own independent analysis, insisting that Darius could not have logistically supported a million-man field army in the Iraqi desert. In *History of the Art of War* (University of Nebraska Press, 1920, reprinted 1990) the German military historian Hans Delbrück, a pioneer in using demographics and economics to analyze ancient data, calculated a mere 52,000, which is at the low end of modern estimates. In his 1998 book, *Warfare in the Ancient World* (University of Oklahoma Press), John Gibson Warry suggests 91,000, and most modern analysts agree that it could not have been more than 100,000. There probably could have been around 200 chariots, as well as elephants, in the Persian order of battle.

the satrap of Arachotia; Medians led by Atropates; Parthian, Hyrcan-ian, and Tapurian cavalry commanded by Phrataphernes; Sacesinians; Sacian horse-bowmen; and Uxians and Susianians led by Oxathres. Finally, there were the Syrians under the command of Mazaeus, the satrap of Babylon, who had failed to challenge Alexander at the Eu-phrates. Also commanding troops on the field at Gaugamela that day was Ariobarzan, the satrap of Persis, who was to play a key role in an-other pivotal battle against Alexander three months later. Many of these ethnic groups represented lands into which Alexander would march during the coming years, and people who Alexander would come to rule.

Reports that reached Darius after Alexander crossed the Tigris in-dicated that the latter's army was larger now than it had been at Issus, and this was accurate. Probably relying on first-hand accounts, Arrian gives Alexander's troop strength at Gaugamela as 7,000 cavalry and 40,000 infantry, a number that is considered by modern historians as being within the realm of probability. Because modern estimates have placed the Persian strength at or below 100,000 rather than a million, Darius is likely to have had a numeric advantage, although it was prob-ably closer to 2–1 than the 20–1 ratio suggested romantically in the early accounts. Perhaps it might have looked as if Darius had a million-man army when the troops were beheld by their campfires by night.

❖

The night before the battle, identified by Plutarch as the eleventh since the eclipse, Alexander "passed the night in front of his tent with his seer Aristander, celebrating certain mysterious sacred rites and sac-rificing to the god of fear [Phobos]." Parmenio and some of the Com-panion officers climbed a nearby hill to take a look at the opposition.

At that moment, Darius was reviewing his command by torch-light. As Plutarch tells it, "When they saw the plain between the Niphates and the Gordyaean mountains all lighted up with the bar-barian fires, while an indistinguishably mingled and tumultuous sound of voices arose from their camp as if from a vast ocean, they were astonished at their multitude and argued with one another that it was a great and grievous task to repel such a tide of war by engaging in broad daylight." They then approached their king, proposing that they attack Darius under cover of darkness.

"I will not steal my victory," Alexander replied in a famous quote attributed to him by Plutarch.

Plutarch interprets this not as arrogance, but as Alexander's knowing that if Darius lost such a battle, he would blame it on a sneak attack. Alexander reasoned that if he beat Darius in broad daylight, the Persians would have no excuse but to accept a defeat as total and final. As Plutarch interprets his motives, Alexander did not want "an excuse to pluck up courage for another attempt, by laying the blame this time upon darkness and night, as he had before upon mountains, defiles, and sea."

While accounts say that a nervous Darius was up all night, Alexander made a brief mounted reconnaissance of the opposing lines and went to bed. He slept so soundly that Parmenio had a hard time waking him up. In so doing, Parmenio chided him that he had been sleeping as though he was already victorious.

Plutarch writes that Alexander replied, "Dost thou not think that we are already victorious, now that we are relieved from wandering about in a vast and desolate country in pursuit of a Darius who avoids a battle?"

With Alexander rising well after sunrise, the battle was slow to start. Darius could have, and probably should have, struck first, rather than waiting for Alexander's troops to assemble on the battlefield. Just as Alexander had used his engineers to great utility in his sieges, Darius had used his engineers to clear and level the terrain on which he intended to do battle. There would be no disadvantage to the use of chariots as there had been in the hills and ravines at Issus. Darius assumed that fighting his enemy on a battlefield of his own choosing— and of his own making—trumped any advantage to be had by an early unexpected attack.

Historians give the date as October 1, 331 BC, correlating it to the twenty-sixth day of the month of Boedromion in the Athenian calendar. By now, the heat of summer had long faded.

As at Issus, the Greco-Macedonian order of battle had Parmenio in command of the left (eastern) wing, with Thracian, Thessalian and other cavalry units. Alexander was in command of the opposite wing, including experienced mercenary cavalry commanded by Cleander and the Companion Cavalry under the direct command of Parmenio's son, Philotas. Also on the right were contingents of archers and javelin-throwers under Balacrus and Brison. Additional detached cavalry under Aretas and Menidas rode at some distance to the right of Alexander. This force was being arranged for Alexander's opening attack.

Anticipating a battle in which his own cavalry might become so fully engaged with the enemy cavalry that it would detach from his phalanx, Alexander decided to break the phalanx in two. There would be a rear, auxiliary phalanx as back-up for the primary phalanx in case the primary found itself outflanked.

To inspire his men, Alexander gave a speech in which he told them that they were not merely after limited objectives such as Phoenicia or Egypt, but were fighting for dominance of all Asia. Of course, Alexander had no comprehension of the true size of the continent. It was perceived at the time that the ends of the earth were not much farther ahead than the Greco-Macedonian army had already traveled.

As he prepared to go into battle, Alexander mounted his favorite steed, the aging Bucephalas. Presumably quoting eyewitnesses, Plutarch describes Alexander's accoutrements that day. He wore a Sicilian-made vest, a breastplate of "two-ply linen from the spoils taken at Issus," an iron helmet crafted by Theophilus that "gleamed like polished silver, an iron gorget set with precious stones." Plutarch went on to say that his belt, "too elaborate for the rest of his armor," but which he liked to wear into battle, was made by Helicon of Rhodes. Alexander's sword, was "of astonishing temper and lightness, a gift from the king of the Citieans, and he had trained himself to use a sword for the most part in his battles."

Darius had organized his own formation three lines deep, with his infantry phalanx in the rear, and a mixed main line of infantry and cavalry ahead. Darius himself was at the center of his main line, with Mazaeus commanding cavalry on the right (eastern) wing opposite Parmenio. On the Persian left, facing Alexander, was a cavalry force that included Satibarzanes and his troops from Aria, as well as Bessus with his Bactrian and Sogdian cavalry and Mardian archers.

Ahead of the Persian main line were the chariots, along with the Indians and their elephants. These were flanked on the right, opposite Parmenio, by the Armenian and Cappadocian cavalry. On the left, opposing Alexander, were Bactrian and Scythian cavalry. Eyewitness accounts quoted by second-century writers specifically mention that the Scythian cavalry troops and their horses were well armored.

As Plutarch describes him, Darius could probably be seen in the distance by Alexander, "through the deep ranks of the royal squadron of horse drawn up in front of him, towering conspicuous, a fine-looking man and tall, standing on a lofty chariot, fenced about by a numerous and brilliant array of horsemen, who were densely massed around the chariot and drawn up to receive the enemy."

Separated by more than seven miles as they formed up, the two masses of troops moved slowly, with the contingents led by Alexander, Aretas and Menidas all riding ahead. This had the effect of pushing the right wing far forward of the main line and the left wing, and po-sitioning the overall Greco-Macedonian line at a 45-degree angle to the Persian line. As Arrian describes it, Alexander led his right almost entirely beyond the ground that had been cleared and leveled by the Persians. In a sense, the Persian formation had been outflanked before the battle even started.

On Alexander's orders, Aretas and Menidas struck, engaging Scythian and Bactrian cavalry on the Persian left wing. The Persians pushed the attackers away, but in so doing, they moved left and sepa-rated themselves from the rest of the Persian force. There then ensued a ferocious cavalry battle, in which the Scythian armor was an advan-tage. Nevertheless, the zealous Greeks fought tenaciously.

With the battle joined, Darius sent his chariots forward as shock troops to attack the right wing of the Greco-Macedonian lines. They must have been frightening vehicles, with scythes on their wheel hubs like swords, slashing anyone who dared approach them from the sides. Alexander's men fought back with arrows and javelins rather than swords, but mainly they parted and allowed the chariots to pass through the lines so that they could be surrounded and at-tacked from behind. As the horses slowed to a stop when confronted by lances, Macedonian troops grabbed their reins and pulled them to a halt, and the small number of charioteers, now reduced to fighting as infantry, didn't last long. The Persian chariots lay useless like ex-pended projectiles.

By this time, the initial attacks by Aretas and Menidas had com-pletely severed the Persian left-wing cavalry from the Persian center, and they were ripe for a full-on assault. Alexander and his own cavalry from the Greco-Macedonian right, backed by light infantry, poured through the gap in the Persian line like a flood. This flood of flesh and iron, following an initial attack at 45-degrees, slammed into the Persian center at an angle.

As things were looking good for Alexander on his right, things were not going so well on his left wing, where Parmenio was in command. While Alexander's having outflanked the Persian left embodies the brilliance of a great field commander, he was losing his own left to another flanking maneuver. Mazaeus's Persian cavalry, supported by the Indians with their elephants, had managed to punch a hole in Parmenio's line. The Persian cavalry apparently broke through with such momentum that a contingent penetrated as far as the Greco-Macedonian rear, where they captured Alexander's supply dump and camp, killed a number of rear-echelon personnel and liberated some Persian prisoners. As Arrian describes it, "the Persians fell boldly on the men, who were most of them unarmed, and never expected that any men would cut through the double phalanx and break through upon them."

It was here that Alexander's decision to break his phalanx into two lines was validated. As the Persians had completely outflanked Alexander's left, they could theoretically now attack his phalanx from behind, forcing them to turn away from offensive operations in the main attack. However, because there were two, the rear phalanx could turn to defend the rear, while the forward phalanx could remain engaged.

Back on the central part of the battlefield, Darius was probably unaware that Mazaeus and his own right wing were seriously threatening Parmenio, or that Persians were in the Greco-Macedonian rear. He was focused on the center. After all of his careful preparation, things were not happening as planned. Darius found his phalanx attacked from the side as well as the center. Had he been so fixated on his preconception of how the battle would be fought that he had not noticed that Alexander was outflanking him before the fight started?

Alexander himself charged into the Persian center, leading his cavalry and making straight for Darius himself, while Aretas intercepted Bessus and the Persian cavalry trying to get back around to intervene in the center, where Alexander now threatened Darius personally.

Arrian describes the scene as one of bloody hand-to-hand combat, with Alexander leading the cavalry inward from the Persian left, while the Greco-Macedonian forward phalanx, with their 18-foot sarissas, slammed into the Persian center from the other side. As Arrian writes, "when the Macedonian phalanx in dense array and bristling with long pikes had also made an attack upon them, all things together appeared full of terror to Darius."

◈

To analyze the battle at its midpoint, the Greco-Macedonian army had fought a difficult battle on its right wing, successfully severing Bessus and the Persian left, and defeating him. In turn, Alexander had exploited this with his cavalry to hammer the Persian center against the anvil of his forward phalanx. Meanwhile, the double phalanx formation had precluded the Persians from outflanking the Greco-Macedonian center.

However, on the Greco-Macedonian left, the line had been penetrated—all the way to the Greco-Macedonian rear. Mazaeus had done to Parmenio what Aretas, Menidas and Alexander had done to Bessus—they had cut him off and were beating him up. As Plutarch writes, "the left wing under Parmenio was thrown back and in distress, when the Bactrian cavalry fell upon the Macedonians with great impetuosity and violence."

Somehow, Parmenio managed to get word to Alexander, explaining the situation, and asking for help in the form of reinforcements sent to the rear to immediately recapture the Greco-Macedonian camp. In reply, Plutarch relates that Alexander sent a message suggesting that Parmenio had "lost the use of his reason, and had forgotten in his distress that victors add the baggage of the enemy to their own, and that those who are vanquished must not think about their wealth or their slaves, but only how they may fight gloriously and die with honor."

Fighting gloriously was an option that Darius abandoned, and as he did, the battle changed. Although Mazaeus controlled the eastern third of the battlefield, Darius saw himself personally threatened as the resolve of those around him began to falter. "When they saw Alexander close at hand and terrible, and driving those who fled before him upon those who held their ground, they were smitten with fear and scattered," writes Plutarch.

As Diodorus Siculus describes in *Bibliotheca Historica,* Darius "received the Macedonian attack and fighting from a chariot hurled javelins against his opponents, and many supported him. As the kings approached each other, Alexander flung a javelin at Darius and missed him, but struck the driver standing behind him and knocked him to the ground. A shout went up at this from the Persians around Darius, and those at a greater distance thought that the king had fallen. They were the first to take flight, and they were followed by those next to them, and steadily, little by little, the solid ranks of Darius' guard disintegrated. As both flanks became exposed, the king himself was alarmed and retreated."

For Darius, as Plutarch tells it, "all the terrors of the struggle were before his eyes, and now that the forces drawn up to protect him were crowded back upon him, since it was not an easy matter to turn his chariot about and drive it away, seeing that the wheels were obstructed and entangled in the great numbers of the fallen, while the horses, surrounded and hidden away by the multitude of dead bodies, were rearing up and frightening the charioteer."

Darius, the frightened charioteer, panicked and ran, just as he had done at Issus. He abandoned his chariot, stripped off his heavy armor and mounted the nearest horse. Alexander might have given chase immediately, but as at Issus, Parmenio and the embattled Greco-Macedonian left wing were in need of his aid, so again he let the Persian king run. With the battle won in the center and on his right, Alexander decided to go pick up the pieces for Parmenio on the left.

A lot has been written about Parmenio's poor performance that day. Was it that he was outfought and outmaneuvered by Mazaeus? Had not the Persian center collapsed when it did, would Parmenio have been totally defeated?

The voices of criticism began with Alexander, who said that Parmenio had lost his mind, and continued with the historian Callisthenes, who was also present that day. As Curtius says, "there is general complaint that in that battle Parmenio was sluggish and inefficient, either because old age was now impairing somewhat his courage, or because he was made envious and resentful by the arrogance and pomp, to use the words of Callisthenes, of Alexander's power."

By the time Alexander reached the eastern part of the battlefield where Parmenio was, however, the tide had already turned. When Mazaeus had heard the news of Darius abandoning his position, he had backed off. As Curtius writes, "in his alarm at his side's reverse of fortune, [Mazaeus] began to relax his pressure on the dispirited Macedonians despite his superior strength. Although ignorant of why the attack had lost its impetus, Parmenion quickly seized the chance of victory."

Parmenio had rallied and counterattacked, and as Curtius reports, he optimistically observed to a Thessalian cavalry commander, "Do you see how after making a furious attack on us a moment ago those men are retreating in sudden panic? It must be that our king's good fortune has brought victory for us too. The battlefield is completely covered with Persian dead. What are you waiting for?"

Another factor in the collapse of the Persians and their allies was probably communication. There had to have been a dozen or so languages represented in the coalition, and perhaps only a handful of officers conversant in more than two or three of these. When Darius was seen retreating, the troops interpreted this as meaning the battle was lost, and there was no way to communicate fresh orders or organize a stabilization of the line. Coalition warfare has always been, and continues to be, dependent on there being a lingua franca, or common language agreed upon for specific communications. For example, in World War II, the Anglo-American Allies succeeded for many reasons, but a common language made their successes easier to achieve.

As he retreated, the Persian king ran east, managing to reach Arbela by around midnight. When he crossed a bridge over the Lykos River (now known as the Great Zab), a tributary of the Tigris, he considered destroying the bridge to slow Alexander's pursuit. However, he nobly chose to leave it intact so that his own retreating troops could get across. Indeed, Bessus and the Bactrian cavalry caught up with the fleeing king, as did Darius's royal guard and some of the Greek mercenaries that were still loyal to the Persians.

As Arrian writes, Alexander rested his cavalry until midnight, then rode in pursuit. When they reached Arbela the next day, they learned that Darius had come and gone, so Alexander halted the chase. With his head start, Darius did not stop, even to rest, cheating Alexander of the man-to-man showdown that he craved.

Just as accounts of the size of the forces that met at Gaugamela vary widely, so too do estimates of casualties. Arrian states that Alexander lost 1,000 cavalry and a mere 100 infantrymen. Diodorus lists 500 dead among the Greco-Macedonian forces, while Curtius says it was 300. Arrian reports 300,000 killed in action on the Persian side, adding that more than that number were captured. Diodorus and Curtius list somewhat more conservative casualty estimates of 90,000 and 40,000 Persians respectively.

Though Darius had survived, he had been defeated in the heart of his empire—an empire that was no longer his. As Justinus writes, Alexander's "victory was so decisive, that after it none ventured to rebel against him; and the Persians, after a supremacy of so many years, patiently submitted to the yoke of servitude." Plutarch writes that Alexander "traversed all Babylonia, which at once submitted to him."

One of the few surviving contemporary accounts of the Battle of Gaugamela is a Babylonian cuneiform tablet now in the British Museum in London. Primarily a record of astronomical observations, it tells of ill omens that appeared before the downfall of Darius and contains a brief mention of the battle itself.

Roughly translated, it reads: "Opposite each other they fought and a heavy defeat was inflicted on the troops of Darius. The king, his troops deserted him, and to their cities they fled." Speaking of Alexander, the tablet's author writes that "on the twenty-fourth of the lunar month [October 1], in the morning, the King of the World erected his flag."

CHAPTER 8

To the Victor Go the Spoils

IF NOT THE KING OF THE WORLD, ALEXANDER DID ASSUME THE TITLE of King of Asia in the autumn of 331 BC. To the people of Greece who had sent Alexander forth in their name to avenge 150 years of Persian antagonism, Alexander sent a message that Plutarch paraphrases as telling them that "all their tyrannies were abolished and they might live under their own laws."

As Plutarch writes, in the wake of Gaugamela, "the empire of the Persians was thought to be utterly dissolved, and Alexander, proclaimed King of Asia, made magnificent sacrifices to the gods and rewarded his friends with wealth, estates, and provinces."

After his decisive victory, Alexander continued his march, intending to occupy the former Persian Empire that was now his. He headed south on a good road toward the ancient city of Babylon, and sent his general, Philoxenus, to reconnoiter Susa, the great seat of Darius's imperial power—now the southwestern Iranian city of Shush—about 150 miles east of the Tigris River.

Though everyone seemed to be singing his praises now, Alexander took no chances at Babylon, approaching the city in battle order, prepared for a fight. However, as Arrian writes, "the Babylonians came out to meet him in mass, with their priests and rulers, each of whom individually brought gifts, and offered to surrender their city, citadel, and money. Entering the city, he commanded the Babylonians to rebuild all the temples which Xerxes had destroyed, and especially that of Belus [Bel Marduk], the patron deity of Babylon, whom the Babylonians venerate more than any other god."

The temple of Belus has been identified with the enormous ziggurat known in the Sumerian language as Etemenanki, meaning "the temple of the foundation of heaven and earth." Standing about 300 feet high, quite tall for a structure in antiquity, it is also thought to be the same structure described in the Bible as the "Tower of Babel," as "Babel" is seen as the Hebrew equivalent of the Greek "Babylon." The many languages mentioned in the descriptions of Babel in the Book of Genesis reflect the reality of Babylon as a cultural crossroads.

Built some time before the reign of Hammurabi in the eighteenth century BC, the temple was destroyed but rebuilt by Nebuchadnezzar the Great in the sixth century BC, and subsequently damaged under Persian rule.

A mere satrapy of Persia since Cyrus the Great captured the city two centuries earlier, Babylon saw Alexander as a liberator who promised a return to former glory. This is not to say that Babylon was anything but glorious in 331. In his particularly detailed discussion of Alexander's stay in Babylon, Curtius uses extensive superlatives when describing the city, and he mentions that Alexander visited the Hanging Gardens of Babylon, one of the Seven Wonders of the Ancient World, constructed here two centuries earlier by Nebuchadnezzar.

At Babylon, Alexander found Mazaeus, the now-former Persian satrap and the general who had performed best against the Greco-Macedonian army at Gaugamela. Had the two men met on the field at Gaugamela a few weeks earlier, one would have killed the other, but now Alexander saw value in the 50-something Persian. Mazaeus swore his allegiance to Alexander, and the young King of Asia essentially gave him back his old job as satrap of Mesopotamia. In so doing, Alexander was following a practice that would continue to serve him well as the administrator of his new empire. Rather than imposing Greco-Macedonian political leadership, Alexander went with someone who was familiar. The King of Asia understood that he presided over a multiethnic world. As he had across Asia Minor, he chose indigenous politicians to serve as his satraps.

Picturing Alexander sitting in the palace, newly his, about 50 miles south of present-day Baghdad, we see an obvious comparison to the struggle in which the United States found itself embroiled after a decisive military victory in this land in 2003. In the latter case, the battlefield victory gave way to disorder because of a power vacuum. There was no single indigenous politician who could fill the vacuum and maintain order, and society shattered into factions. Alexander had picked the most powerful man in Mesopotamia to be his satrap, and Mazaeus repaid him with loyalty; his sons served in Alexander's army. The United States could hardly have allowed Saddam Hussein to serve as Iraq's governor, but it also ruled out—probably with good cause—a pack of cards' worth of his henchmen. We'll never know what might have happened if the Americans had tried to rehabilitate someone from among the Bath Party elite. We'll never know whether Alexander succeeded because of his perceptiveness or because of his luck, although he seems to have been an exceptional judge of character when picking his satraps. There would be cases where he was double-crossed, but not many, and not in Babylon. However he structured the political organization, though, Alexander was careful to keep the military command under Macedonian control, assigning Agathon to command the citadel of Babylon with 700 Macedonians and 300 mercenary troops.

Curtius notes that Alexander bivouacked his army in Babylon for 34 days of rest and relaxation, "longer than anywhere else." It was certainly longer than they remained at that other glorious royal city, Memphis. This being the famous "fertile crescent," there was ample food and drink, and ample opportunity to restock provisions for future campaigns. The glorious city was meanwhile not without its vices, of which the victorious troops happily availed themselves. During this time, reinforcements were streaming in, and it may be argued that these vices might have served as a recruitment and retention tool. Antipater sent Amyntas, the son of Andromenes, with 6,000 Macedonian infantry and 500 cavalry, as well as 3,500 Thracian infantry and 600 cavalry. Also arriving while Alexander was in Babylon were 4,000 Peloponnesian mercenary infantry and 380 cavalry.

❖

Having escaped Alexander's dragnet, Darius had correctly assumed that Alexander would march south toward Babylon. Therefore, to avoid another run-in with the new King of Asia, he retreated through the mountains of Armenia. Accompanied by a few of his commanders, including Bessus, and a number of their surviving troops, he headed into the area known as Medes, or Media, which is now the northwestern part of Iran. Once independent, Media had been incorporated into the Achaemenid Persian Empire by Cyrus the Great.

Darius must have been more than a little despondent. Twice he had met an outnumbered Alexander in battle, and twice he had fled the battlefield in defeat and panic. The loss of his family after Issus was a crushing blow, and his having been unable to secure their release was humiliating. The guilt that he felt at having abandoned them was an especially difficult pill to swallow, especially when he learned later of their resentment toward him, and how well they were being treated in Alexander's care.

At some point before the Battle of Gaugamela, Darius had learned that his queen (and sister), Stateira, known as the most beautiful woman in the world, had died in childbirth. The stories are unclear as to how long after her death the news reached Darius, but by that time, nearly two years had passed since she was captured at Issus. Darius had to have understood that it was impossible that he was the father of the child. Many later writers have suggested that Alexander was the father, although there is nothing in the earliest accounts to either confirm or preclude this.

Plutarch writes that when he got the word of her death, Darius exclaimed "Alas for the evil genius of the Persians, if the sister and wife of their king must not only become a captive in her life, but also in her death be deprived of royal burial."

"Nay, O King," replied the man, an escaped chamberlain, who brought him the news. "As regards her receiving every fitting honor, thou hast no charge to make against the evil genius of the Persians. For neither did my mistress Stateira, while she lived, or thy mother or thy children, lack any of their former great blessings except the light of thy countenance . . . nor after her death was she deprived of any funeral adornment, nay, she was honored with the tears of enemies. For Alexander is as gentle after victory as he is terrible in battle."

Perhaps it was the cruelest blow to Darius that Alexander, not he, had been there for Stateira and gave her a royal funeral.

✠

Around the end of November 331 BC, as Darius anguished in the hills to the north, Alexander and his refreshed Greco-Macedonian army left Babylon, heading south and eastward toward Susa. As they passed though the Sittacene region, he paused to make some changes.

Alexander had spent at least part of his 34 days at Babylon planning and thinking about the organization of his command for the future of the campaign into Persia, although he waited until they were away from the city to implement the changes. At this point, we get some insight into the innovations that helped make Alexander a truly great field commander. We see a man capable of thinking outside the box, of making organizational changes to long entrenched traditions, and making them for sound operational and tactical reasons.

It had always been the practice for both the Persians and the Greeks to organize the cavalry within an army into units based on origin and nationality. It was much like the way regiments were organized within the U.S. Army during the Civil War. There were the 7th Michigan Cavalry, the 8th Ohio Infantry and so on. After the war, during the campaigns in the West, the U.S. Army was comprised of regiments, such as the famed 7th Cavalry, that consisted of troops from many states—and foreign countries. In the early days of Alexander's campaign, Thracian cavalry fought as a unit, as did the Thessalian cavalry. Alexander now discontinued this practice, eliminating ethnic distinctions and integrating his cavalry regiments.

He also reorganized the command structure, putting those men in charge who had exhibited bravery, tactical skill or other strong leadership qualities. For example, Atarrhias, who had distinguished himself at Halicarnassus in 334, was singled out among the hypaspists, or shield-bearing guards, for command. He was the foremost of eight newly assigned chiliarches (Arrian mentions that Adaeus already was a chiliarch). This rank is roughly equivalent to a battalion commander, typically a lieutenant colonel, in a modern army. The other seven were Amyntas, who had recently arrived from Greece, as well as Amyntas Lyncestes, Antigenes, Antigones, Hellanicus, Philotas (son of Parmenio), and Theodotus.

Another practical step was to substitute the use of a trumpet to sound a charge or order a decampment, replacing it in certain circumstances with the use of flags, which were less likely to alert the enemy.

❖

While on the road to Susa, Alexander was met by a messenger from Philoxenus, his advance man in that city. The news was good. Susa, though the Persian imperial administrative center since the reign of Cambyses II in the sixth century BC, was ready to welcome Alexander as its new ruler. Abulites, the satrap, sent his son to meet Alexander to confirm this promise. Curtius writes that it is uncertain whether Abulites did this on orders from Darius, now in exile, or on his own initiative to prevent Susa from being looted.

In Susa, Alexander was greeted as a hero. The wealth, the possessions and the palaces of the Persian monarchy were his. Curtius notes that Abulites himself met Alexander with "gifts of a regal opulence." Plutarch tells that at the palace, Alexander "came into possession of 40,000 talents of coined money," a total that is also mentioned by Diodorus, although he includes some bullion. Meanwhile, Arrian raises his fellow historians, placing the total figure at 50,000 talents. If the latter, the cash alone among Alexander's new-found wealth was worth more than $750 million by today's reckoning.

Like Diodorus, Curtius also mentions silver bullion, specifically valued at 5,000 talents, and colorfully observes that "a succession of kings had amassed this great wealth over a long period of time for their children and descendants, as they thought, but now a single hour brought it all into the hands of a foreign king."

In Susa, Alexander also found treasures that had been looted from Greece and Greek enclaves in Asia Minor by Persian invaders over the previous 150 years of conflict. In particular, he discovered the sixth-century statues of Harmodius and Aristogeiton. Pilfered by Xerxes, they had been seen as emblematic of Athenian democracy. These he ordered packed up and shipped back to Athens, where they remained on display on the Acropolis for several centuries until they went missing.

In the palace, Alexander naturally took a seat on the royal throne that he had won at Gaugamela. In an amusing anecdote, Curtius tells us that it was too high for him and his feet did not reach the floor. Therefore one of the royal pages placed a table beneath his feet.

"Noticing some distress on the part of a eunuch who had belonged to Darius, the king asked him why he was upset," writes Curtius. "The eunuch declared that it was from this that Darius used to eat, and he could not withhold his tears at the sight of his consecrated table put to such disrespectful use."

Alexander, fearing that he had offended the gods of hospitality, was about to have the table taken away when Parmenio's son Philotas said, "No, your majesty, don't do that. Take this as an omen . . . the table from which your foe ate his banquets has been made a stool for your feet."

With that bit of symbolism, the King of Asia probably relaxed and had a good laugh, though he did not remain in this throne room for as long as he had relaxed in Babylon. As at Babylon, he tackled the administrative chores of his office. Again, he reappointed the Persian satrap to rule as his own. Abulites was reinstated as the head of government, but again Alexander put one of his own in charge of the troops. He put Archelaus in command with a garrison of 3,000 men. According to Curtius, Xenophilus was put in command of the citadel with 1,000 veteran troops, although Arrian say that it was Mazarus, one of Alexander's Companions, who was made commander here.

Sisygambis, the mother of Darius, who had been part of Alexander's entourage for more than two years, was now home, so he let her and her young granddaughters, Stateira and Drypteis, remain at the palace in Susa. According to Curtius, he now formally adopted her as his mother, telling her, "the title due to my dear mother Olympias, I give to you."

As for Sisygambis, she had earlier renounced Darius, and said she now considered Alexander to be her only son. Of course, Sisygambis was not Alexander's only adopted mother. She shared this honor with Ada of Halicarnassus.

❖

Leaving Susa, the Greco-Macedonian army marched eastward from the administrative capital of the Achaemenid Persian Empire toward its ceremonial capital. The ancient city of Persepolis, whose name literally means "City of the Persians," was in the region of Persis, the original home of the Persian people. Located northeast of the modern Iranian city of Shiraz, Persepolis was where Darius I had built his imperial palace in the sixth century BC. It was described by Diodorus as "the richest city under the sun . . . famed throughout the whole civilized world."

Crossing the broad Pasitigris (now Karun) River, they climbed into the Zagros Mountains, the longest range in present-day Iran. Beyond these mountains lay Persis, but in the mountains Alexander encountered the mountain people whom the Greeks knew as the Uxians, and who are the ancestors of the Bakhtari people. Never fully subjugated by the Persians, the Uxians were used to receiving payoffs—even from the kings of Persia—for safe passage through the Zagros.

Alexander sent word that he would meet them the following day in the narrow pass by which the Persian royal road crossed the mountains. He promised he would make the usual payment, but he had no intention of paying tribute to his subjects. This was Asia, and he was the King of Asia.

With these arrangements settled and the Uxians believing they had the situation under control, Alexander put his plan into place. He sent a force under Craterus to seize the high ground around the intended meeting place. Then he personally led a strike force consisting of his own bodyguards and more than 8,000 others on a night march through the mountains by way of a back road that was less traveled. They succeeded in making a series of bloody predawn attacks that decimated the Uxian villages.

Alexander then returned to meet the unsuspecting army of Uxians who planned to collect the toll. When they arrived, they found Alexander already in control of the highest pass. Realizing that they had been checkmated, the Uxian army scattered, many of them picked off by the men under the command of Craterus or Alexander.

Ultimately, the Uxians are said to have begged Alexander for the right to pay him for the privilege of living in their own mountainous land. The annual payment is said to have included 100 horses, 500 hundred oxen and 30,000 sheep, which would prove useful for Alexander's occupation forces on both sides of the Zagros.

CHAPTER 9

Last Stand at Persian Gate

THE FIRST DAYS OF JANUARY 330 BC FOUND ALEXANDER AND HIS invincible Greco-Macedonian army marching through the drifting snow in the Zagros Mountains, heading toward Persepolis. Apart from the Uxians, every Persian city that Alexander had visited in the three months since Gaugamela—from small villages to the great cities of Babylon and Susa—had embraced him as either a welcome liberator or a rightful conqueror. Soon and suddenly, this would change.

Actually, there were two roads involved in the next phase of Alexander's campaign. He sent Parmenio with the main body of troops, especially the most heavily armed and armored, and the supply train toward Persepolis by way of the Persian royal road, while he cut through the mountains by a narrower route with a smaller, more mobile force. Of his total force of nearly 50,000, it is uncertain how many men Alexander had in his own contingent, but it was probably fewer than half.

Defending Persepolis was the satrap of Persis, a general named Ariobarzan who was a veteran of Gaugamela. (Known in old Persian as Ariyabrdhna, Ariobarzan's name is often spelled as Ariobarzanes in more recent translations of first- and second-century accounts of Alexander's campaigns.) A member of an old Persian family, Ariobarzan traced his lineage to Pharnabazus, who had been satrap of that part of Phrygia closest to the Hellespont about three decades earlier. Ariobarzan's own father was Artabazus, the grandson of Pharnabazus. Before being named as satrap of Persis, Ariobarzan had been a member of Darius III's court. His sister, Barsine, had been among the women captured along with the family of Darius after the Battle of Issus. As Curtius writes, Barsine had become, and remained, Alexander's mistress, although little is else is known about her.

Arrian states that Ariobarzan had 40,000 infantry and 700 cavalry, while Curtius estimates 25,000 infantry. Both are probably gross exaggerations. By most modern estimates, Ariobarzan had fewer than 1,000 men—and probably only about 700—with which to oppose Alexander. However, he had the lay of the land on his side.

As noted previously, defenders, especially outnumbered defenders, try to use terrain features as force multipliers, or as means of neutralizing the other side's larger numbers. In mountainous terrain, passes present natural chokepoints where an invader cannot advance on a broad front and must reduce his army's formation to a narrow stream of just a few abreast. By holding high ground, a defender can hit the vanguard of the invader from above as well as in front.

Ariobarzan had such a chokepoint at his disposal. His strategy is often compared to that of Themistocles, who intercepted Xerxes and his Persian invasion force at Thermopylae in April 480 BC. In so doing, Themistocles had prevented Xerxes from being able to use his vastly superior numbers, and managed to hold him off for a time with just 300 men.

Ariobarzan's Thermopylae lay on the path of Alexander's troops at a mountain pass known to history as the Persian Gates or Persian Gate, because it was literally a gateway into Persis. Now known as Tang'e Meyran or Darvazeh-ye Fars, this pass is located northeast of present day Yasuj, Iran, on the road connecting that city with Sedeh. Near the present-day village of Cheshmeh Chenar, the road narrows abruptly on a curve. Here, the modern road is barely two lanes wide and is paralleled for a long distance by vertical cliffs. In the fourth century BC, this was the ideal place to stop a major invasion force in its tracks.

One of the worst mistakes in Alexander's career was his assumption that he could transit this dangerously narrow canyon with impunity. Fresh from an easy victory over the Uxians, he had been lulled into a false sense of overconfidence.

※

Alexander led his men into this constricted space, and nothing happened—until much of the Greco-Macedonian column was between the walls. Alexander rounded a turn to discover that the Persians had blocked the narrow road with a barricade. Suddenly, the enemy struck from positions in the high ground above, using spears, arrows and large rocks.

Alexander and his men were literally between the rocks and the hard places. They could move neither forward nor sideways, and it was nearly impossible to turn around. The column was quickly paralyzed by men and horses tripping and stumbling on the bodies of the fallen.

There are no accounts of the casualties suffered by Alexander on that cold January day, but most who have studied the battle and terrain have concluded that this was the worst moment of his campaign in Persia, coming, ironically, three months after he thought he had so decisively defeated Darius. He probably thought that the worst was behind him.

In this, one is reminded that the deadliest single loss of life in U.S. Navy history occurred after three and a half years of World War II, but only two weeks before the Japanese accepted unconditional surrender terms. The USS *Indianapolis* was sunk by the Japanese submarine I–58 on July 30, 1945, with the loss of 880 men out of a complement of 1,196. As with Alexander at the Persian Gate, an unexpected and terrible loss had been inflicted upon the victorious just as they were confidently assuming the war was over.

The narrowness of the space in which Alexander's men were trapped was the catalyst for tremendous casualties, probably more than were lost in the 1945 incident, though almost certainly not two thirds of his force. Paradoxically, the confined space, which made the men within it sitting ducks, saved many others because most of the column, marching three or four abreast, had yet to reach the site of the ambush when Ariobarzan sprang his trap.

Curtius tells that some of Alexander's men actually tried to climb the steep hillsides to counterattack, but were repulsed. Alexander rallied the men from confused chaos and organized an orderly retreat, directing them to withdraw in close formation with their shields interlocked above their heads.

They pulled back a distance of 30 stades, or about three and a half miles. This gives us an indication that the length of the pass section in which Ariobarzan had fortified the high ground was probably no longer than a mile or two. The place where the Greco-Macedonians made camp was an open area short of the narrow canyon that is just north of the modern Iranian city of Yasuj. Here, Alexander pondered his next move.

In this, he demonstrated the good sense to eschew consulting his soothsayers in favor of practical intelligence assessment. He asked his staff to locate and bring him people with knowledge of the trails and passes of the Zagros Mountains, and this they did. Several alternate routes were proposed and discussed. The idea was advanced that the entire army pull back and take a completely different route, abandoning the Persian Gate entirely. However, Alexander decided that he had to return to the Persian Gate. In their speedy withdrawal, his men had left behind the bodies of those killed, and Alexander refused to leave without properly burying the dead.

This left him with the challenge of finding a route by which he could surreptitiously outflank Ariobarzan and launch a surprise attack against the rear of the Persian encampment, which was located beyond the barricade that had stopped his army's advance though the pass.

A recently captured Greek-speaking prisoner was brought to Alexander, who asked him whether there was such a route. Plutarch tells us that "the man spoke two languages, since his father was a Lycian and his mother a Persian; and it was he, they say, whom the priestess had in mind when she prophesied, Alexander being yet a boy, that a 'lycus,' or wolf, would be Alexander's guide on his march against the Persians."

As Curtius explains, this man told Alexander that "he was wasting his time trying to take an army into Persia over the mountain ridge. The paths through the woods barely afforded passage for one man at a time; everything was overgrown with brush and the inter-twining tree-branches produced one continuous forest."

When Alexander asked him how he knew this, whether it was first-hand knowledge, or something he had heard from others, the man said that he had been a shepherd in this area and knew the trails from having been on them. Alexander promised an appropriate reward to the man and ordered him to lead the way. When the man cautioned him that the trail was not for the faint of heart, the King of Asia asked the man whether "he believed that Alexander in his pursuit of glory and undying fame could not go where his sheep had taken him!"

With this, Alexander selected a strike force, including contin-gents commanded by Amyntas, Coenus, Philotas and Polyperchon. He ordered them to travel light, with just their weapons and three days' provisions, and headed out of camp under cover of darkness.

He put Craterus in charge of the base camp outside the Persian Gate with orders to perpetuate the illusion that the entire Greco-Macedonian army remained there. The Persians watching from the nearby mountains could see them, and could judge the size of the camp by the number of campfires observed each night, so Craterus would keep many extras burning while Alexander slipped away.

The plan was for Alexander to circle around and hit Ariobarzan from behind. At the sound of a trumpet call, Craterus was to mount up and lead his command back through the Persian Gate and join the fight. If Ariobarzan somehow spotted Alexander on the alternate trail and tried an interception, Craterus was to create a diversion sufficient to draw Ariobarzan away from attacking Alexander.

According to both Arrian and Curtius, the trail was every bit as arduous as promised, with the difficulty exacerbated by deep snow. Alexander and his men found themselves traveling in terrain where the trail was not only hard to follow, but hard to see beneath the drifts. To top it off, the only one who knew the route was a man whose loyalty was far from certain.

Plutarch, on the other hand, says simply that the Lydian-Persian prisoner guided Alexander "by a circuit of no great extent," dismissing the Persian Gate affair as just a minor stumbling block. Diodorus al-ludes to it only in passing, and Justinus doesn't mention it at all.

Finally, when Alexander's men reached the crest of the mountains, they could see Ariobarzan's main encampment as well as the places where his forces had blocked the road and fortified the high ground above the narrow Persian Gate. Alexander now further divided his command, deciding to assault the Persian positions with a pincer movement. Amyntas, Coenus, Philotas and Polyperchon were to lead their troops down toward the vicinity of the Persian roadblock in the Gate, while Alexander would keep going with a smaller contingent, following the original plan, and take a much longer indirect route to circle in behind Ariobarzan's camp.

The attack achieved complete surprise. As Arrian describes, they fell upon the Persian outer perimeter guards before daylight, destroyed them, and attacked Ariobarzan's camp "at the approach of dawn without being observed."

Alexander ordered the trumpet call, the signal that alerted Craterus to launch a frontal attack against the barrier in the Persian Gate. Arrian describes a complete rout, noting that Ariobarzan's troops, "being in a state of confusion from being attacked on all sides, fled without coming to close conflict; but they were hemmed in on all hands, Alexander pressing upon them in one direction and the men of Craterus running up in another. Therefore most of them were compelled to wheel round and flee into the fortifications, which were already in the hands of the Macedonians."

To this scene, Curtius adds that "at the same time further panic was instilled in the Persians by Philotas, Polyperchon, Amyntas and Coenus, who had been told to take a different route. The Persians were under attack from two directions and Macedonian arms were gleaming all around them. But they put up a memorable fight. To my mind, pressure of circumstances can turn even cowardice into courage, and desperation often provides the basis for hope. Unarmed men grappled with men who were armed, dragging them to the ground by virtue of their bodily weight and stabbing many with their own weapons."

Curtius tells that Ariobarzan fell fighting against troops under the command of Craterus, while Arrian states that Ariobarzan, "with a few horsemen, escaped into the mountains." Most scholars agree that if he got away, Alexander's troops soon caught and killed him.

There are varying estimates of how long Ariobarzan kept Alexander bottled up at the Persian Gate, but Alexander was probably stopped dead in his tracks here longer than at any other juncture except for sieges of fortified cities that he initiated himself.* For Ariobarzan, it was a heroic stand by the last Persian general to challenge the King of Asia in battle.

---

*In his 2005 article, "First Iranian National Hero," published in the *Persian Journal,* Manouchehr Saadat Noury writes that Ariobarzan was killed on the last day of January in 330 BC after 48 days of fighting. Other sources state that Ariobarzan had bottled Alexander up at the Persian Gate for about a month.

CHAPTER 10

From Persepolis to the Caspian Gates

PERSEPOLIS, THE GREAT PERSIAN METROPOLIS THAT DIODORUS described as "famed throughout the whole civilized world for being the richest city under the sun," now lay before Alexander, ripe for the taking. The winter snows were probably already beginning to melt as Alexander came down out of the mountains in the early months of 330 BC.

With Ariobarzan out of the way, there were rumors circulating in Persepolis that Darius might return to fight Alexander again, but nobody knew for sure. Nor did anyone seem to know where Darius had gone. There were rumors that he had fled deep into Central Asia, but in fact he was only about 250 miles north in Ecbatana, which corresponds with the present Iranian city of Hamadan. Despite the fact that he had retreated far from Alexander's immediate reach—or perhaps *because* of this fact—Darius was bragging to those around him that he hoped to face Alexander once again in battle, and this may have been the source of the rumors.

Inside Persepolis, Tiridates, the man in charge, sat down and wrote a letter to the King of Asia. Diodorus describes Tiridates as the governor of the city, while Curtius calls him the guardian of the treasury. In the disarray into which the Persian Empire was crumbling, it is probable that the political command structure was also falling apart, and he may have been the only bureaucrat still coming to work. Alternatively, in a city with the riches of Persepolis, the guardian of the treasury would have held quite a powerful office. Tiridates had asked himself who he feared more, Darius or Alexander, and decided to cover his bases. In his letter, he told Alexander that if he arrived in Persepolis before any of Darius's troops showed up, he "would become master of it, for Tiridates would betray it to him."

However, Darius was not coming. There were no realistic chances that he would initiate another large-scale battle with the man who had defeated and humiliated him twice. He no longer had sufficient manpower loyal to him, and it is possible, even probable, that he no longer had the nerve.

⊞

As Alexander made his way out of the Zagros Mountains toward Persepolis, poor road conditions slowed the progress of his wheeled vehicles, so he rode ahead with a cavalry contingent. As he reached the outer suburbs of the grand capital of the Persian Empire, he made an unanticipated discovery that can only be compared to what Allied troops discovered in Nazi Germany as they closed in on the major cities of the Third Reich in the spring of 1945.

Just as the Allies stumbled into the walking human skeletons of the Nazi death camps, Alexander and his men were, as Curtius describes, "met by a pitiful group of men whose misfortune has few parallels in history. . . . They looked more like outlandish phantoms than men, with no recognizably human characteristic apart from their voices. Thus they occasioned more tears than they had shed themselves."

They were, as Diodorus and Curtius describe in detail, elderly Greeks who had been in Persian captivity for many years. They had not only been starved and mistreated, but most had been the victims of mutilation and forced amputations. Curtius gives the number of such unfortunate captives at 4,000, while Diodorus mentions that there were only 800. Both report that Alexander was overcome with grief and anger. He gave them food, clothes and cash, and made arrangements for their repatriation to their homes in Greece or the Greek colonies from which they had been captured.

This grisly first impression certainly skewed Alexander's opinion of Persepolis and determined the way that he would deal with the Persians when he rode into the city. It may have been the richest city under the sun, but an angry Alexander described it as "the most hateful of the cities of Asia." Diodorus says that he "gave it over to his soldiers to plunder."

One anecdote mentioned by Diodorus says that Alexander passed by a great statue of Xerxes that had been carelessly toppled by his troops as they ransacked. As Diodurus writes, Alexander spoke poetically to this statue, as though speaking to the Persian king himself, asking "Shall I pass on and leave thee lying there, because of thine expedition against the Hellenes, or, because of thy magnanimity and virtue in other ways, shall I set thee up again?"

He let Xerxes lie.

✛

The immense wealth that Alexander had found in Babylon and Susa paled by comparison with what had been stockpiled in Persepolis since the days of Cyrus the Great two centuries earlier. He visited its sumptuous palaces as his troops looted the richly appointed homes of the Persian elite. In its citadel, Alexander found vaults "packed full of silver and gold," that Diodorus and Curtius agree were valued at 120,000 talents, or nearly $2 billion in current valuation.

Plutarch doesn't give any figures for the value, but does say that it took 10,000 pairs of mules and 5,000 camels to carry away the furniture and other property that Alexander shipped back to Greece. Alexander carried at least part of the money with him as he continued his ongoing campaign.

When Alexander finally sat beneath the golden canopy on the royal throne, Demaratus the Corinthian, an old-timer who had earlier been an aide to Philip II, is said to have shed tears for all the Greeks and Macedonians who had died before they got to see this.

Plutarch tells that "wishing to refresh his soldiers," Alexander decided to stay in Persepolis for four months, much longer than they had spent in Babylon. Reportedly, the parties were no less lavish here. Diodorus tells that Alexander entertained "bountifully."

Diodorus goes on to say that one night, as "feasting and drinking was far advanced," and a "drunken madness took possession of the minds of the intoxicated guests," an Athenian woman named Thaïs, the lover or possibly a wife of Ptolemy, rose as if to make a toast.

As Plutarch writes, she said that "for all her hardships in wandering over Asia she was being requited that day by thus reveling luxuriously in the splendid palace of the Persians; but it would be a still greater pleasure to go in revel rout and set fire to the house of the Xerxes who burned Athens, she herself kindling the fire under the eyes of Alexander, in order that a tradition might prevail among men that the women in the train of Alexander inflicted a greater punishment upon the Persians in behalf of Hellas than all her famous commanders by sea and land."

The reply from fellow revelers, according to Curtius was "why do we not avenge Greece, then, and put the city to torch?"

All of this was received with great applause. Diodorus says that they spontaneously formed a victory procession in honor of Dionysus, with Alexander and Thaïs leading the way, accompanied by people singing and carrying torches, as well as female musicians playing flutes and pipes. Alexander himself is said to have thrown the first torch, and Thaïs the second. An immense inferno was soon burning throughout the palace complex.

According to Plutarch, Alexander quickly repented and ordered the fires put out, although Curtius says that his regret did not come to him until the next day. Though much of the city was destroyed, enough remained that it would continue to be an imperial administrative center under the dominion of Alexander and his successors. Over time, Persepolis fell into ruin, but it has been preserved as an archeological site and was declared a UNESCO World Heritage Site in 1979.

With Alexander's months in Persepolis capped by the ill-considered conflagration, he made plans to continue his campaign, marching north toward Ecbatana in search of the elusive Darius.

Though the erstwhile king of Persia was just 250 miles away, he was keeping a low profile, for it seems that Alexander did not learn of his location until late spring of 330 BC. Arrian paints a picture of a man on the run and suggests that he was running scared. He writes that if Alexander "marched against him, [Darius] resolved to proceed into the interior towards Parthia [Parthava] and Hyrcania, as far as Bactria."

These regions mentioned by Arrian were not merely escape routes for Darius that summer, but the theater in which Alexander and his army would be operating for much of the next three years. Known in Old Persian as Parthava and in Latin as Parthia, this area corresponds to northeastern Iran on today's map. Hyrcania was the satrapy that forms a crescent around the southern end of the Caspian Sea, mainly in Iran, but with its eastern tip in present Turkmenistan. Farther afield, Bactria is the vast region that today includes northern Afghanistan, southern Tajikistan, and southeastern Uzbekistan.

Darius still had a significant army. Curtius reports, probably with some considerable exaggeration, that it consisted of 30,000 infantry (including 4,000 diehard Greek mercenaries), and 4,000 "slingers and archers," as well as 3,300 cavalry, mainly Bactrians led by their satrap, Bessus, who had commanded the Persian left wing at Gaugamela.

It is hard to imagine a force that large remaining in the service of a deposed monarch who was running out of money, and who had resolved not to fight. His bragging that he could beat Alexander was hollow bravado, meant to keep the rank and file within his dwindling army loyal, but his generals knew better. They were already plotting against him.

When Darius heard that Alexander was coming to Ecbatana, he left town. He took money from the treasury, but was accompanied by only 3,000 cavalry and 6,000 infantry.

Once he reached the city, Alexander mapped out the next phase of the campaign and reorganized his command. As he had done nearly a year earlier, Alexander chose to do this at a remote location rather than in a major city where his army would be distracted. In the fall of 331 BC, he had reorganized in the Sittacene, shortly after marching out of Babylon. In 330, he did so in Ecbatana, a couple of weeks after his army had pulled out of Persepolis.

❖

An important part of the Ecbatana reorganization involved downsizing. Over the coming months, Alexander would manifest his leadership skills on several occasions by allowing the weariest among his command the opportunity to leave. By doing this, Alexander accomplished two things. First, it allowed him the opportunity to be perceived as magnanimous by his troops, especially by those who returned home to tell of it. Second, it allowed him to weed out the slowest and most exhausted of his command, the men who would present more of a burden than a contribution to the coming effort. At Ecbatana, Greek forces, including the Thessalian cavalry whose enlistments were up, were paid off—with a bonus from Alexander's own pocket—and dismissed to go home. However, according to Arrian "not a few" reenlisted to continue with Alexander.

The army was now split into three major combat contingents for the pursuit of Darius. When Parmenio arrived with the money train, the cash was deposited at the citadel of Ecbatana, to be guarded by Harpalus, with 6,000 Macedonian troops. Parmenio would then lead a force of Thracians, Greek mercenaries and other cavalry into Hyrcania. Cleitus the Black, who had been recuperating from illness in Susa, now caught up with Alexander, and would lead a separate command into Parthia. Alexander himself would lead the Companion Cavalry, other mounted units and the Macedonian phalanx.

There were probably some reenlistees who questioned their decision in the ensuing days if they happened to be in Alexander's own contingent. Arrian describes a forced march, ordered by a man obsessed with catching the fleeing Darius, telling us that "many of his soldiers were left behind, worn out with fatigue, and many of the horses died."

Alexander chased Darius north through the old city of Rhagae (now the city of Rey, near the Iranian capital of Tehran), and through the Caspian Gates, a pass in the Alburz Mountains that is southeast of the Caspian Sea and about a day's ride from Rhagae. This pass is not to be confused with another Caspian Gates, located on the west side of the Caspian Sea near the border of Azerbaijan and the Russian Republic of Dagestan.

Making camp near the Caspian Gates, Alexander sent Coenus on a foraging trip to gather provisions for the coming march into the desert beyond. It was here that Alexander was approached by a group of Persians, including a son of Mazaeus, who had been traveling with

Darius. They brought some news that may or may not have surprised Alexander.

As Arrian relates, Bessus and several others said they had made good on their plot to depose Darius and had put him under arrest. A cuneiform tablet in the British Museum that is among what are called the Babylonian Chronicles dates this to July 330 BC. Bessus said that he was now in charge of Darius's army, although a few Darius loyalists had gone their own way. Sensing that a showdown with Darius was on the threshold of escaping him, Alexander acted. Without waiting for Coenus to return, he assembled a small group of Companions, and rode out immediately. He put Craterus in charge of the remaining troops with orders to follow him.

✦

Resting little and riding through the night, Alexander and a small contingent of just 60 men finally caught up to Darius, but this was an anticlimax. After the great "million-man" battles, and the four years of geopolitical confrontation represented by these two grand figures, they finally met on a dusty desert road, with a comparative handful of onlookers.

Curtius and Plutarch agree that Darius was near death. Diodorus and Arrian say that he was already dead. "They found him lying in a wagon, his body all full of javelins, at the point of death," writes Plutarch. "Nevertheless, he asked for something to drink, and when he had drunk some cold water which Polystratus gave him, he said to him: 'My man, this is the extremity of my ill-fortune, that I receive good at thy hands and am not able to return it; but Alexander will requite thee for thy good offices, and the gods will reward Alexander for his kindness to my mother, wife, and children; to him, through thee, I give this right hand.'"

Just as he had accorded Stateira, the wife of Darius, a royal funeral, Alexander was magnanimous with her widower. As Arrian writes, Alexander sent the body of Darius to Persepolis, "with orders that it should be buried in the royal sepulcher, in the same way as the other Persian kings before him had been buried."

A nineteenth century decorative frieze depicting Alexander in profile, wearing his helmet. (Author's collection)

A teenaged Alexander (left) is instructed by Aristotle in his father's palace. Alexander continued to exchange letters with the great philosopher during his later campaigns in Asia. (Author's collection)

(above) *The Macedonian phalanx triumphs over Thracian cavalry thanks to their long spears, known as sarissas. (Author's collection)*

(left) *This nineteenth century illustration of a bas-relief in Tarsus in Asia Minor depicts Alexander with horns. On coins and in sculptures that date to his time, he is often shown with ram's horns, symbolizing his relationship to the god Zeus, or in Egyptian mythology, Amun. (Author's collection)*

Alexander nearly lost his life in the Battle of Granicus. He had beaten off an attack from Rhoesaces, but Spithridates had struck him and was about to deliver the coup de grace. Luckily, Cleitus the Black dashed up and cut off the Persian's arm. (Author's collection)

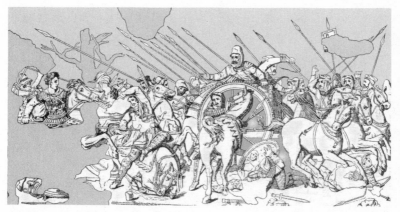

This illustration is of a second century Roman mosaic depicting the Battle of Issus that was found in the ruins of Pompeii. Alexander is on his horse at the left, while a frightened Darius is seen in his chariot on the right. (Author's collection)

Alexander and some of his officers survey the enemy defensive positions from high atop one of his siege engines during the campaign against the island fortress of Tyre in 332 BC. (Author's collection)

Defenders watch from Tyre's towering fortifications as vessels from the fleet loyal to Alexander approach one of the city's two harbors. (Author's collection)

In the spring of 331 BC, Alexander traveled through the desert to Siwa Oasis to visit the legendary Oracle of the Egyptian deity Amun, whom the Greeks called Ammon. The Oracle told Alexander that he was the son of Zeus. (Author's collection)

This 1897 magazine illustration by André Castaigne depicts Persian chariots, with scythes on their hubcaps, charging the Macedonian line at the Battle of Gaugamela. The Persians also fielded a small number of elephants in the battle. (Author's collection)

Alexander studies the dead body of his arch-rival, Darius, the king of Persia, in Bactria in the summer of 330 BC. Murdered by conspirators from within his own army, Darius received a royal funeral from Alexander. According to some accounts, Alexander may have arrived in time to hear Darius's final words. (Author's collection)

A nineteenth century illustration of Alexander's troops using flotation devices to cross a river in Central Asia, possibly the Syr Darya, known to the Greeks as the Jaxartes. Alexander, having adopted Asian customs, is conveyed across in a boat, shaded by a parasol. Note the snow-capped peaks of the Hindu Kush. (Author's collection)

As depicted in this 1899 illustration by André Castaigne, the Macedonian phalanx eventually managed to rout the elephant cavalry at the Hydaspes, but only with great difficulty. (Author's collection)

ALEXANDER

A nineteenth century illustration of a classical bust of Alexander the Great. For both the Greeks and the Romans, Alexander epitomized heroism, and both were fond of depictions of him in heroic poses. (Author's collection)

CHAPTER 11

The King of Asia

By THE FALL OF 330 BC, THE GREAT MACEDONIAN CONQUEROR HAD led his army to the fringes of geographical knowledge. He was seeing new and amazing places that Greeks and Macedonians knew existed based only on second and third hand stories told by traders and travelers, but which virtually nobody in Greece had ever actually seen. Though Darius had been defeated, and Alexander had sat on his thrones at Susa and Persepolis, the King of Asia marched on, determined to visit personally the far reaches of the former Persian Empire and to survey all of his newly conquered domain. As he continued his march toward Parthia and Hyrcania, Alexander was astounded to behold the Caspian Sea for the first time. He had now traveled farther than anyone he had known in Macedonia. The fact that he had conquered all the lands through which he had passed in making this journey truly fed the ego of the man who was the King of Asia.

Alexander was at a critical crossroads in his military career, and of his life. He had defeated the Persian Empire and had gazed on the dead eyes of Darius III. His mission had been accomplished. Four years earlier, when Alexander had last stood on European soil, a general assembly of the Greeks had voted to make an expedition against Persia with Alexander proclaimed as their leader. Now, Persia had been defeated and occupied, and Darius was dead.

Many saw this as an end as, arguably, it was. However, Alexander saw it only as a moment of transition. There were still lands beyond the horizon, and new missions to be exploited by the momentum achieved by Alexander's army thus far.

He and his army were perceived by themselves and by much of the world known to them as invincible. In Alexander's day, it was understood that the land at the farthest side of Asia was that which we know as India. This was understood by the best Greco-Macedonian minds of the day to be the end of the earth. Europeans and Persians may have been aware of Zhou Dynasty China and lands farther afield, but if so, they had little concrete information.

Alexander had reached a point of no return where he was no longer a Macedonian general, or even a Macedonian king. He was something bigger. He readily thought of himself as the King of the World.

Alexander's having styled himself as the King of Asia raised two important issues that caused discontent within his army and that would remain as a gnawing undercurrent in his relations with his troops, especially his officer corps, over the coming years of the campaign. Many did not share his sense of being called to conquer the rest of the world, and most were uncomfortable when the King of Asia began to dress the part.

Plutarch tells that it was when he reached Parthia that Alexander "first put on the barbaric dress [clothing in the Central Asia style], either from a desire to adapt himself to the native customs, believing that community of race and custom goes far towards softening the hearts of men; or else this was an attempt to introduce the obeisance among the Macedonians, by accustoming little by little to put up with changes and alterations in his mode of life."

Alexander's decision heralded a change in his own concept of his role as King of Asia. He wanted to influence the hearts and minds of his Asian subjects by demonstrating to them that he was, and considered himself to be, an Asian monarch rather than a European conqueror who was imposing his will upon Asia. Indeed, by 330 BC, most of Alexander's empire was in Asia, and most of his subjects were Asian.

At the same time, he wanted those in his mainly Greco-Macedonian army to understand that they were citizens of an empire that embraced parts of three continents—Europe, Africa and Asia. However, many of those in his army, especially among his officer corps, were critical of Alexander for having gone native, with Plutarch reporting that "the sight was offensive to the Macedonians."

Though the officers were primarily Macedonian and theoretically the most loyal of his troops, his decision to embrace Central Asian customs and culture caused growing dissension among them. Philotas, Parmenio's son, the chiliarch, or battalion commander, who headed the Companion Cavalry, was especially outspoken, though he said what was on many minds.

Bothering the troops even more than Alexander's embrace of customs and culture was his new sense of his destiny to continue the campaign to the end of the earth. After the death of Darius, many of the troops assumed that the war was over now that the stated objective had been achieved. As Diodorus points out, "the Macedonians regarded Darius's death as the end of the campaign and were impatient to go home."

Alexander was not ignorant of this discontent. He was an extraordinary judge of human character, a leader who led by inspiring his men, not by enforcing his will arbitrarily. He was the kind of leader who understood that the momentum could not be maintained within an army of men who truly believed that their job was done. Just as great conquerors are cognizant of the hearts and minds of newly conquered subjects and rule with an informed touch, great generals are attentive to the hearts and minds of their troops.

As he had demonstrated in a bit of a preview at Ecbatana, he was willing to downsize, especially if it meant weeding out dissension in the ranks. This was especially important now that he had decided to continue the campaign beyond the original mandate to rid the world of the Persian Empire. As Diodorus tells it, Alexander "assembled the allied troops from the Greek cities and praising them for their services released them from their military duty. He gave to each of the cavalry a talent and to each of the infantry ten minas [about a sixth of a talent]. Besides this he paid them their wages up to date and added more to cover the period of their march back until they should return to their homes."

After the plunder of Persepolis, Alexander was not only able to pay off the troops he discharged, but he had the cash—in the neighborhood of $100 million by today's value—to be generous with retention bonuses for those who stayed. Diodorus explains that "to those who would remain with him in the royal army, he gave a bonus of three talents each. He treated the soldiers with such lavishness in part because of his native generosity and in part because he had come into possession of very much money in the course of his pursuit of Darius."

Downsizings had probably been gradually reducing the size of the Greco-Macedonian coalition force since before Persepolis, and certainly the demobilization of the Thessalian cavalry at Ecbatana made it a smaller force than it had been in its heyday at Gaugamela. This left Alexander with a smaller army, but one in which loyalty was stronger and morale was higher that in the army that had followed him to the Caspian Gates. The phrase "leaner and meaner" comes to mind.

On a purely practical level, the downsizing may have indicated that Alexander believed a big army to be no longer necessary, now that the army of the Persian Empire—the largest in the world so far as Alexander knew—had been defeated. To put it in a modern context, he may have assumed that the era of large battles between great field armies had given war to smaller scale counterinsurgency operations, such as the brief campaign against the Uxians. Indeed, as he marched into the lands south of the Caspian, he had been involved in more counterinsurgency skirmishes where his army outfought the Amard people, known in some accounts as the Mardians.

Within his new army, Alexander thoughtfully created a cadre of volunteers, mainly Macedonians, who would constitute the core of his future army. It was much like the decision made by the United States to phase out mandatory conscription after the Vietnam War and transition to an all-volunteer force. Officers such as Craterus, Coenus and Amyntas stayed on with Alexander and his leaner army. So too did Parmenio, Alexander's veteran left wing commander, who remained in charge of the garrison at Ecbatana as Alexander led the army into Parthia and Hyrcania. Likewise remaining with Alexander were elite units such as the Companion Cavalry.

Meanwhile, he augmented his army of familiar volunteers with new blood. As Alexander's self-image changed, so too did the complexion of his army. He brought foreign troops into the ranks while at the same time holding to the weapons and tactics that had served him well all his life. Plutarch mentions that he chose 30,000 Persian boys and "gave orders that they should learn the Greek language and be trained to use Macedonian weapons."

Nor were the political dimensions of his rule as King of Asia a one-way street. Plutarch points out that as Alexander "adapted his own mode of life still more to the customs of the country," he also "tried to bring these into closer agreement with Macedonian customs, thinking that by a mixture and community of practice which produced good will, rather than by force, his authority would be kept secure while he was far away."

In that one sentence, we get a glimpse of Alexander's competence, if not brilliance, as a political administrator.

❖

Even as the King of Asia was reorganizing his life and reorienting his worldview, old issues were still festering. While he was in the city of Susia in Hyrcania (now Tus in Iran), Alexander got word that Bessus, the leader of the plot against Darius, and perhaps the man who inflicted the mortal wound, was still alive and still active. He was now back in Bactria, where he claimed to be the King of Persia under the royal name Artaxerxes V.

Alexander also soon learned that Satibarzanes, the man whom he had recently reappointed as satrap of Aria, a Central Asian satrapy between Parthia and Bactria, had joined forces with Bessus. This alliance was a good career move for neither man. Had Bessus recognized Alexander as King of Persia and as King of Asia, Alexander would probably have given him a satrapy, just as he had done for Satibarzanes. However, Bessus had thumbed his nose at Alexander, and Alexander would not now rest until Bessus was in the ground.

As he had done at the Persian Gate and during the pursuit of Darius, Alexander formed a small, fast strike force and led them ahead of the main body of troops. They included Agrianians and the troops commanded by Amyntas and Coenus. Making a forced march, they headed for the Arian capital. Located near Herat in modern Afghanistan, the city is called Artacana by Curtius and Artacoana by Arrian. If Alexander imagined a decisive battle here, he was disappointed. Satibarzanes rode away in fear as the Macedonians arrived, and the rest of his army collapsed in disarray.

Alexander sent a 2,000-man cavalry contingent under Erigyius, son of Larichus, in pursuit. Having been surrounded, Satibarzanes announced that he would meet any of the Macedonian officers in man-to-man combat. Erigyius accepted the challenge and killed Satibarzanes.

Alexander continued his campaign eastward. In November 330 BC, he marched into the part of the former Persian satrapy of Drangiana that corresponds with the modern western Afghan province of Farah. November in the Afghan mountains can be a depressing time and place, and this may have played a role in the reemergence of the festering dissention in his ranks, which Alexander thought he had put to rest.

It was in these mountains that Alexander became aware of a conspiracy against him led by Philotas, the chiliarch who was the son of Parmenio. Essentially, the idea was that Alexander should be relieved of his command, much as Bessus had earlier deposed Darius. The plot originated among elements within the officer corps and does not seem to have had much, if any, support among the troops.

Plots against Alexander's life were not a new phenomenon. There was the case of Alexander, the son of Aeropus, in 334, and Alexander's first- and second-century biographers, citing Ptolemy and Aristobulus, mention other conspiracies that were exposed in 332 when the army was in Egypt. Indeed, one of the charges that would be raised against Philotas was that he had been aware of the 332 plot—though he was not then a conspirator—but had failed to alert Alexander.

In any case, Alexander was made aware of the plot in Drangiana, and he intervened before it became an active mutiny. According to Plutarch, Alexander was alerted by Antigine, Philotas's own mistress. Curtius, meanwhile, tells that Philotas was incriminated by Dymnus, who committed suicide and died before Alexander himself could question him.

Initially, Alexander questioned Philotas and then let him go, but the following day, he had him arrested and tried at the Macedonian equivalent of a court-martial. Alexander spoke at length about betrayal, and Philotas about at length about his innocence. Ultimately, Philotas confessed. Curtius says that it was under torture, but Arrian does not mention this. Philotas and several others were executed.

During the trial, according to Curtius, a letter to Philotas from his father was introduced as evidence that Parmenio was also involved in the plot. It read in part, "take care of yourselves and of your people—that is how we shall accomplish our purpose."

The "purpose" was interpreted by the court as being the overthrow of Alexander, and it was thereby determined that Parmenio had been part of the conspiracy. Alexander then decreed that Parmenio himself, the old general who had been a trusted lieutenant of Philip II and an important field commander in all of Alexander's victories, was a condemned man.

In reflecting on the execution of Parmenio, Arrian writes that it was done "perhaps because Alexander deemed it incredible that Philotas should conspire against him and Parmenio not participate in his son's plan; or perhaps, he thought that even if he had no share in it, he would now be a dangerous man if he survived after his son had been violently removed."

To replace Philotas in command of the Companion Cavalry, Alexander named two officers, Cleitus and Hephaestion, the latter a longtime friend of Alexander, and possibly his male lover. Alexander no longer wanted to have a single man in charge of that key organization.

As 330 BC came to a close, Alexander continued into Arachotia. On the banks of the Arghandab River, near the site of the ancient city of Mundigak, he founded another of the cities that he called Alexandria. Through the centuries, the name changed several times. Today, it is Kandahar, Afghanistan's second-largest city.

From here, he led his army northeastward into Bactria, through the western mountains of the Hindu Kush range. Having dealt decisively with discord within his own ranks, he now pushed hard on a difficult winter pursuit of Bessus.

As Arrian writes, when Bessus learned that Alexander was chasing him, he crossed the Oxus River, now the Amu Darya (or Amu River), which forms the modern border between Afghanistan and Uzbekistan. He burned the pontoon bridge that he had used, then led his army to Nautaca, now the Uzbek city of Shahrisabz, which is about 110 miles north of the river as the crow flies. As he withdrew, Bessus was accompanied by Spitamenes and Oxyartes with Sogdian cavalry, although they didn't remain long. Fugitive pretenders find it hard to maintain a loyal army. As Arrian points out, "the Bactrian cavalry, perceiving that Bessus had resolved to take to flight, all dispersed in various directions to their own abodes."

However, Bessus and his dwindling army, its strength sapped by the desertions, had every reason to believe that they were now safe. It was late winter, and the cold, fast-moving Oxus was two-thirds of a mile wide. Indeed, Arrian described it as being the largest river in what was known as Asia in ancient times. This may have been an exaggeration, but the river was still a challenging terrain feature.

Though the river gave Bessus a breather, and Alexander pause, the characterization of it as insurmountable only stoked the fires of Alexander's engineering creativity. There were few trees in this cold desert from which to extract bridge-building lumber, so Alexander decided to challenge the conventional wisdom of crossing amid the spring runoff and float a contingent of troops across.

The hides that the troops used as tents had been oiled to make them water resistant, so Alexander ordered these packed with light, buoyant material such as hay, and sewn tight, turning them into flotation devices. Five days later, a specially selected portion of Alexander's command was across.

＊

In the spring of 329 BC, as he was marching north from the Oxus River, Alexander was met by emissaries from Spitamenes and Dataphernes, who had previously sided with Bessus. They conveyed a proposition to Alexander in which they said that they were ready to arrest Bessus themselves in exchange for favors from Alexander. Intrigued by the offer, Alexander sent Ptolemy ahead to negotiate. According to Arrian, Ptolemy claims to have headed a sizable force, including "three regiments of the Companion Cavalry, all the horse javelin men, and of the infantry, the brigade of Philotas, one regiment of 1,000 hypaspists, all the Agrianians, and half the archers." The chronicles do not explain why Alexander did not lead this group himself.

Expecting a surrender, Ptolemy was surprised to learn that Spitamenes and Dataphernes, ashamed of betraying Bessus, had changed their minds again. Ptolemy then pursued the fugitives with his cavalry, finally finding Bessus in a small village. As Arrian writes, Ptolemy "issued a proclamation to the barbarians in the village, that they would be allowed to depart uninjured if they surrendered Bessus to him. They accordingly admitted Ptolemy and his men."

At this point, Arrian notes a discrepancy in the accounts. Aristobulus says that Spitamenes and Dataphernes finally delivered Bessus to Ptolemy, while Ptolemy insists that he captured the man himself. In any case, when Alexander got word that Bessus was in custody, he ordered Ptolemy to "bind the prisoner naked in a wooden collar, and thus to lead him and place him on the right-hand side of the road along which [Alexander] was about to march with the army."

❖

Probably referencing Ptolemy's own first-hand account, Arrian writes that when Bessus reached the place, Alexander asked him why he had "arrested Darius, his own king, who was also his kinsman and benefactor, and then led him as a prisoner in chains, and at last killed him."

After what Philotas and the others had nearly done to him, Alexander considered regicide particularly abhorrent. Curtius mentions that he used the phrase "bestial madness" to describe what Bessus did to Darius. Bessus replied that he was not acting alone, and that they were just trying to save themselves from Alexander.

With this, the King of Asia ordered this last Persian potentate with a pretense of questioning his authority to be tortured and executed. Curtius reports that Bessus was taken back to the place where he had inflicted the mortal injuries to Darius, and crucified by Darius's brother Oxyartes, who had since transferred his loyalty to Alexander.

CHAPTER 12

The Crossroads at Syr Darya

IN THE SPRING OF 329 BC, ALEXANDER LED HIS ARMY INTO SAMARKAND, the great trading city that the ancient Greeks knew as Maracanda and that was appropriately dubbed "Crossroads of Culture" in 2001 when it was named as a UNESCO World Heritage Site. Located 50 miles north of Nautaca, where Bessus had holed up briefly, Samarkand had been an intersection of Central Asian culture for centuries, and the capital of the Persian satrapy of Sogdiana (or Sogdia) since around 700 BC. As the great Silk Road trading route between China and Europe developed in subsequent centuries, Samarkand only increased in importance as a convergence of commerce and culture. Today, it is the second largest city in Uzbekistan with a population of over half a million people.

His arrival at this city marked an important crossroads in Alexander's own career and campaign, and it was one at which he probably reflected upon the future of his strategic vision.

To the west lay the lands, stretching back to the Mediterranean, that Alexander had already conquered. To the south, all the way to the Arabian Sea, lay the remnants of the Persian Empire, which were now Alexander's. To the east lay India and the ends of the earth. This was now his long-term goal. However, if Alexander's strategic eye was on the riches of the east, his immediate concern was the northern boundary of his dominions. Alexander had conquered the Persian Empire, and it had submitted to him, but he was now at the *edge* of the Persian Empire. He was at the frontier between the lands that had been subjugated by generations, and the lands into which the Persians had chosen not to send conquering armies. This frontier, beyond which the Persian Empire never extended, was defined by the great river then known as the Jaxartes, and now known as the Syr Darya. Beyond that river were the mysterious lands of the people whom the Greeks and Romans grouped ambiguously under the master ethnic heading "Scythians"—including the Abian (Eastern) Scythians, who were also called Sacae (Saka). These terms did not describe a homogeneous ethnicity or culture, but were rather catch-all descriptions that included a myriad of greatly disparate peoples living across what is now Romania, Russia, Ukraine, and the Central Asian Republics. As such, the term "Scythian" was used by Greco-Roman writers in much the same way that modern writers use the umbrella term "Native American" to describe the descendants of that profusion of unrelated cultures that existed in pre-Columbian America. So great in number were the Scythians that Arrian describes them as the largest nation dwelling in Europe—although most of Scythia was in Asia.

At issue as Alexander led his army through Samarkand was whether it would be worthwhile to continue his campaign northward against the Scythians, across the Syr Darya and into the endless steppes of Central Asia.

❖

Alexander reached the great river at the point where it flows through modern Tajikistan, about 150 miles northeast of Samarkand. Here, the Scythians were quick to ambush the intruders. As Arrian writes, a group of Macedonians, "scattered in foraging, were cut to pieces by the barbarians," who then escaped into the mountains. Initial attempts to assault this high ground were met by a hail of rocks and Scythian arrows. Alexander himself was shot through the left leg with an arrow that fractured his fibula. Ultimately, the Macedonians prevailed. A few days after this incident, Alexander received Scythian emissaries wishing to negotiate a détente with the King of Asia. However, after the ambush, Alexander did not trust the Scythians, viewing their olive branch as a play for a temporary cease-fire rather than any desire for peaceful coexistence. As Arrian tells it, Alexander sent some of the Companion Cavalry north with them, "under the pretext indeed that they were to conclude a friendly alliance by the embassy; but the real object of the mission was rather to spy into the natural features of the Scythian land, the number of the inhabitants and their customs, as well as the armaments which they possessed for making military expeditions."

As Alexander evaluated his intelligence and considered the possibility of a campaign against the Scythians, he was at a strategic crossroads similar to that contemplated by the Roman Emperor Hadrian in the second century AD. Just as Alexander looked across the Syr Darya into the rugged, untamed and uncharted land to the north, so too had Hadrian marched across Britain to confront the hostility of the Picts of Scotland. After sparring with these savage warriors, Hadrian had made the decision to wall them out, rather than try to subjugate them. Hadrian's Wall became the northern demarcation line of the Roman Empire in Britain, and a symbol of the natural limitations of empire-building.

In fact, Cyrus the Great had made the same decision as Hadrian with regard to Scythia when he established the northern boundary of the Achaemenid Persian Empire two centuries earlier. To mark his northern boundary on the banks of the Syr Darya, and to serve as fortresses along his own version of a "Hadrian's Wall," Cyrus had established a number of Persian cities on the river. The largest of these was known as Cyropolis, or "City of Cyrus," which is now Kurkath, Tajikistan.

Alexander made the decision to do as Cyrus had done and form a bulwark along the Syr Darya. Rather than passively digging in, though, he decided on a show of force to demonstrate to the Scythians that transgressions would not be tolerated. He had learned from his patrols north of the river and his interactions with the Scythians that their idea of détente would include unremitting cross-border raids or "military expeditions," whenever it suited them, or when they perceived that Alexander had let his guard down.

Therefore, Alexander seized the initiative himself. During the summer of 329 BC, he undertook a lightning campaign to capture the cities along the Syr Darya that were now populated as much by

Scythians and other Central Asian people as by ethnic Persians. The idea was that these cities would become the fortresses on his own "Hadrian's Wall," just as they had served that purpose for Cyrus and his successors. His initial step was to send Craterus to surround the largest of them, the City of Cyrus itself.

Alexander intended to blockade Cyropolis, saving it for last, and take down the smaller outposts first. Arrian describes a series of rapid assaults on multiple forts in which infantry attacks were preceded by bombardments by slingers, archers and javelin throwers, as well as missiles "hurled from the military engines." He mentions that Alexander's men captured five such sites in the space of just two days. The message that this blitzkrieg sent to the Scythians and others was clear. However, just to underscore that a new boss was setting up to rule his border with an iron hand, Alexander brutally burned these cities, slaughtered all the men and sent the women and children into slavery.

Cyropolis, with its higher walls and larger number of defenders, presented Alexander with a tougher challenge. As Arrian points out, "the majority of the barbarians of this district, and at the same time the most warlike of them, had fled for refuge thither, and consequently it was not possible for the Macedonians to capture it so easily at the first assault."

Alexander brought up his siege engines to batter the walls of the city, allowing the defenders to believe that this was to be his tactic in attempting to subdue the city. As the defenders prepared for such a siege, Alexander prepared a surprise.

In his reconnaissance of the approaches to the city, Alexander observed that Cyropolis had been built astride the Syr Darya, which flowed beneath the walls and through the city. It was now late summer, so the river was low, and there was space between the bottom of the wall and the surface of the river. Alexander took a small contingent drawn from his bodyguard detail, along with some archers, Agrianians and others, and managed to slip through this space undetected.

Here, as they had done in other sieges such as Gaza and Tyre, Alexander's men were able to enter the city and open its gates from the inside. The rest of his army then swarmed into Cyropolis. Arrian describes a desperate enemy counterattack in which Alexander was hit in the head by a rock, which inflicted a serious concussion that sidelined him temporarily.

As he was recuperating after the successful siege of Cyropolis, Alexander began contemplating the establishment of his own fortress city on the Syr Darya. As Cyrus had built his city as a strategic statement, Alexander saw the need for an outpost of his own to anchor his northern frontier.

As Arrian described it, the city would be "a bulwark to secure the land against the incursions of the barbarians dwelling on the further side of the river. . . . He also thought it would be built in a place which would serve as a favourable basis of operations for an invasion of Scythia, if such an event should ever occur."

In fact, aside from border operations, a major Alexandrian campaign north of the Syr Darya would never materialize. Even the invincible King of Asia understood his limitations. Like Cyrus before him, Alexander had already decided on a defensive line at the Syr Darya rather than allowing his army to be sucked into an endless campaign on the endless steppes of Central Asia.

For his new city, Alexander picked a site that "seemed to him suitable and likely to cause the city to grow to large dimensions. . . . Moreover he thought that the city would become great, both by reason of the multitude of those who would join in colonizing it, and on account of the celebrity of the name [Alexander's own] conferred upon it."

The city of Alexandria Eschate, meaning "Alexandria the Farthest," would be as Alexander imagined it, an important outpost of Hellenic civilization in Central Asia for many decades after his death. Eventually it became, like Samarkand, an important stopping point along the Silk Road. Owned successively by Arabs, Persians and Mongols through the centuries, it later became known by variations on the names Khujand and Khojent. Renamed as Leninabad between 1939 and 1991 under Soviet rule, it is now Khudzhand (or Khodzhent), Tajikstan.

Arrian tells that the King of Asia fortified Alexandria Eschate in 20 days, although it is improbable, as some have suggested, that major finished construction of permanent perimeter walls had been completed in so short a time. Arrian goes on to say that Alexander populated the city with Greek mercenaries and "those of the neighboring barbarians who volunteered to take part in the settlement," as well as Macedonians from his army "who were now unfit for military service."

Alexander's brutal approach to subduing the river cities, which had been intended to send a no-nonsense message to the Scythians, had done so only for a short time. Arrian tells that the Greco-Macedonians soon saw that the Scythians were not retiring from the river's bank, "but were seen shooting arrows into the river, which was not wide here, and were uttering audacious words in their barbaric tongue to insult Alexander, to the effect that he durst not touch Scythians, or if he did, he would learn what was the difference between them and the [Persians]."

Apparently, over the two centuries since the Persians had institutionalized the Syr Darya as their northern border, this sort of taunting had become an accepted part of life on the frontier. The Scythians knew where the line had been drawn and that the north side of the river was a safe zone, much as the Yalu River demarcated a safe zone for Communist air power during the Korean War.

Alexander probably knew and understood this arrangement, but he was clearly unwilling to abide by it. As Arrian put it, "after having subdued almost the whole of Asia, [Alexander was not about to be] a laughing-stock to Scythians, as Darius [I], the father of Xerxes, had been in days of yore."

Though he had ruled out an extensive campaign north of the river, Alexander was certainly not willing to allow the opposite shore to be an inviolate sanctuary for his enemies. He developed a plan for a major cross-river operation to take place in early August 329 BC. As was his custom before launching a new offensive, Alexander offered the usual sacrifices to the gods. He usually received a positive omen, but this time, Aristander, his faithful fortune-teller, cautioned him that the signs were not so good. Danger awaited him. Indeed, things had not been going well recently. A broken leg and a concussion in the space of a couple of weeks indicated that Alexander's luck might have changed for the worse.

Alexander didn't like what he was hearing from the omens interpreted by his soothsayer, and he demanded good news. However, as Arrian writes, "Aristander refused to explain the will of the gods contrary to the revelations made by the deity simply because Alexander wished to hear the contrary." Nevertheless, Alexander decided that he was willing to accept whatever danger came his way and was ready to go ahead with the plan.

❖

As he had when crossing the Oxus, Alexander utilized skins as flotation devices, although on the Syr Darya, August was a time of relatively lower water. Thanks to Arrian, probably referencing a firsthand account by Aristobulus, we have a detailed description. The operation began with secretly prepositioning troops and matériel, including the skins, near the river. The opening salvo came from siege engines, which targeted Scythian personnel, especially cavalry, on the north bank.

Arrian describes a Scythian commander "struck right through the wicker shield and breastplate," who fell from his horse. He goes on to say that "others, being alarmed at the discharge of missiles from so great a distance, and at the death of their champion, retreated a little from the bank."

With this, Alexander signaled the trumpets to sound a cavalry charge, and he himself led the troops across the river. The archers and slingers crossed immediately, with orders to keep the Scythians pinned down so that the Greco-Macedonian infantry phalanx and remaining cavalry could cross.

Having established his bridgehead on the north bank and gotten his men across into it, Alexander launched his main attack. First to move were a regiment of the Greek auxiliary cavalry and four squadrons of infantry with sarissas. These troops served as bait for a trap.

The Scythian counterstrategy involved an encirclement of this vanguard with cavalry—a taking of the bait. Anticipating this, Alexander quickly moved to encircle the Scythian cavalry. As Arrian tells, "Alexander mixed the archers, the Agrianians, and other light troops under the command of Balacrus, with the cavalry, and then led them against the enemy."

The Scythian cavalry, used to having the upper hand in terms of mobility, now found themselves pressed between the units they had surrounded and another mobile force surrounding them. They were the innermost of two concentric circles, and they were taking fire from both sides.

Alexander then ordered three regiments of the Companion Cavalry and his full contingent of horse-javelin-men to charge, while he led a coordinated cavalry attack himself. The effect, as Arrian describes, was that "the enemy were no longer able as before to wheel their cavalry force round in circles, for at one and the same time the cavalry and the light-armed infantry mixed with the horsemen pressed upon them, and did not permit them to wheel about in safety."

The Scythians were routed and in retreat. The battle is important from the perspective of military history insofar as it is a case of a highly mobile force of horsemen from the steppes of Central Asia being defeated on their own turf by a European army. It was the type of contest that the Persians had long avoided.

The cumbersome nature of large, heavily armed armies was often a disadvantage when pitted against fast and highly mobile cavalry. As such, the Syr Darya battle was a clash similar to many that were fought by the U.S. Army against the Plains Indians in the western United States during the latter half of the nineteenth century. A good parallel is the June 1876 Battle of the Rosebud between General George Crook and the Lakota-Cheyenne force that included the tactically brilliant Oglala Lakota leader Crazy Horse. In the latter case, though, the indigenous nomadic horsemen were not defeated by European tactics.

Crook would demonstrate in later operations against the Apache that he had learned to adapt his tactics to the situation, rather than going by the book. Part of Alexander's tactical acumen as a commander was that he always seemed to be able to use his cavalry to its greatest advantage, whatever the situation, whoever the enemy.

Alexander pursued the Scythians, but he gave up the chase, partly because of the oppressive August heat, and partly because he became ill, felled by a bout of dysentery. The latter was apparently caused by tainted water, of which Alexander consumed a great deal because of the weather. In this, it is said, Aristander's prediction came true. Despite a battlefield victory, Alexander had succumbed to danger. Though most, like Alexander, recovered, a large number of the Greco-Macedonian troops were probably put out of commission by the illness.

In his account, Arrian gives the number of enemy dead as 1,000, with 150 captured, uncharacteristically small numbers for someone usually so given to exaggeration. Indeed, these figures may be close to being accurate.

✦

It is worth noting that in the summer of 329 BC there is a change in the nature of the reporting from Alexander's camp. It becomes more realistic. Not only do we have believable enemy casualty data, but there are multiple reports of Alexander's being injured or exhibiting human frailties during a short span of time. This is possibly attributable to later biographers referencing the accounts written by Callisthenes, whose affection for Alexander was waning. He was not alone. Several times since Persepolis Alexander had made a point of magnanimously discharging the tired and dispirited among his ranks, but the problem continued to grow. As Alexander reached geographic and strategic crossroads in Central Asia that summer, his army was approaching a crossroads of morale.

CHAPTER 13

On the Frontier

DURING THE SUMMER OF 329 BC, AS ALEXANDER WAS PREOCCUPIED with conquering Cyropolis and establishing his own Alexandria Eschate, he received word of trouble in Samarkand. Spitamenes, the turncoat who had delivered Bessus to Alexander, had turned again and was now besieging Alexander's garrison at the citadel in the Sogdian capital.

Alexander responded with force, ordering the Macedonian commanders Andromachus, Caranus and Menedemus to ride to the city with 60 Companion Cavalrymen, 800 mercenary cavalrymen and 1,500 mercenary infantrymen. Rather than placing one of these officers in command of this expedition, he chose to put the Lydian interpreter Pharnuches in charge because of his language skills. Meanwhile, having been, as Arrian describes, "emboldened" by an alliance with Scythian elements who had sent him 600 cavalry troops, Spitamenes rode to intercept Alexander's men. Arrian says that he was "not willing either to wait for the enemy or to attack them himself; but rode round and discharged arrows at the phalanx of infantry."

When Pharnuches led an attack, Spitamenes sidestepped, essentially running circles around Pharnuches and his command, who were exhausted from the forced march from the Syr Darya. With this in mind, Pharnuches led a tactical withdrawal to a defensive position on the Polytimetus (now Zeravshan) River, which runs parallel to, and about halfway between, the Syr Darya and the Oxus. However, during the battle, when Caranus attempted to lead his cavalry across the river to a more secure position, nobody informed the infantry as to what was going on. Erroneously thinking that a general withdrawal had been ordered, they broke ranks. When Spitamenes saw the ensuing confusion, he ordered an attack. Caranus would pay with his life. Panicked Greco-Macedonian troops sought refuge on islands in the Polytimetus, and these small groups were easily overwhelmed by the Scythian cavalry.

Pharnuches, who was not used to commanding a military operation, soon realized that he was in over his head and attempted to transfer overall command to one of the Macedonian generals. But they declined because this would effectively countermand Alexander's orders, which had put Pharnuches in charge. Arrian suggests that they were also unwilling "to take a share of the blame" for the defeat they saw coming.

And such a defeat it was. As Aristobulus wrote, more than 85 percent of the troops under Pharnuches' command—including the leaders—were killed in the battle, making it perhaps the worst defeat ever suffered by a contingent from Alexander's army. By comparison, the U.S. 7th Cavalry lost just 45 percent of its troops—including its field commander—at the Little Bighorn River in a cavalry battle of roughly the same scale and that is seen in military history as a milestone loss because of the large proportion of men killed in action. There are many such comparisons, but the Little Bighorn comes to mind as a major battle that has long been cited by military historians to illustrate an unexpectedly lopsided defeat of a cavalry force.

Whatever Pharnuches' other skills or qualifications, the decision to put an interpreter in command of a military force was to be one of the few serious errors of command pointed out by Alexander's later biographers. Arrian is specifically critical of Alexander's giving command to a man who was sent to "win the favor of the barbarians [rather] than to take the supreme command in battles."

Essentially, the defeat on the Polytimetus was the dark mirror image of Alexander's brilliant victory on the Syr Darya a few weeks earlier. It was a case of Central Asian tactics not just beating Alexander's army, but humiliating it.

❖

When Alexander learned of this calamity, he responded immediately, leading a contingent himself. Covering more than 150 miles in three days, Alexander's force marched half of his Companion Cavalry, archers, Agrianians—Alexander's biographers, especially Arrian, always seemed to single out the Agrianians when reporting his order of battle—all of his hypaspists, and the lightest infantrymen from the phalanx.

Spitamenes, who had gone back to Samarkand after the Polytimetus battle, retreated when he learned that Alexander himself was coming. Though Alexander pursued him into the deserts south of Scythia, he managed to elude capture. During the winter of 329–328 BC, Spitamenes and his men rode throughout Sogdiana and Bactria, receiving support from various insurgent tribes, including the Dahae and Massagetae, and raiding cities that were nominally part of Alexander's empire. He captured and briefly held Bactra, the capital city of Bactria and the traditional center of Zoroastrians, who knew it by the name Zariaspa. Now the Afghan city of Balkh, it is located about 50 miles south of the Oxus River near Mazar-e Sharif. Bactra was also the home base of Oxyartes, one of Spitamenes's fellow generals.

Early in 328, Alexander launched a spring offensive against Spitamenes, ordering Craterus to undertake a campaign to take and hold various oases that the renegade general needed to support his operations. It would take more than a year to run down the elusive Spitamenes, but finally, in December 328 BC, troops under the command of the Macedonian general Coenus finally cornered him in the desert among the Massagetae. It is generally believed that when they realized that they were surrounded, the guerrillas who were with Spitamenes chopped off his head and handed it to Coenus, who delivered it to Alexander. Curtius, however, tells the alternate story that Spitamenes's wife chopped off his head as he slept after a night of heavy drinking.

❖

In the meantime, the dissent within the ranks that Alexander had probably hoped to have laid to rest along with the body of Philotas was simmering once again. The two years spent fighting a war of counterinsurgency in Central Asia against tribes whose names they had never heard were taking their toll on the morale of an officer corps who had signed on to fight a war of righteous conquest against Persia. The comparisons are obvious between Alexander's long series of skirmishes in this remote and rugged terrain and those conducted in Afghanistan by British, Soviet and American troops. Indeed, the small but incessant skirmishes of a counterinsurgency can wear hard on the morale of troops who are used to large but quick and decisive battles. Having established, or rather enforced, a détente with the Scythians to the north, Alexander would spend the next two years bogged down with enforcing his rule in the region south of the Syr Darya.

Also hard on the morale of the officer corps was the culture clash caused by Alexander's continued insistence on personally adopting Central Asian manners and customs. The latter was certainly much more obvious when Alexander and his officers were in winter quarters in Samarkand than they had been in the field.

By this time, much to the consternation of the more conservative Macedonians, a sizable proportion of the courtiers and hangers-on in Alexander's entourage were Asian. The Macedonians felt that Alexander should maintain a headquarters characterized by Macedonian military discipline, rather than by the soft cushions and soft courtiers that characterized life in an oriental palace such as Darius once carried with him on his campaigns.*

This gradual alienation reached its crisis point late in 328. A year had passed since Alexander had done any serious campaigning in the field, and he had become more acclimated to his role of King of Asia than to that of military leader. As Arrian writes, there was a banquet

---

*John Clark Ridpath in *History of the World* (New York: Philips and Hunt, 1885), volume 1, chapter 47, writes that "It is clear that his ear was no longer offended with the base flatteries of the East. This gradual alienation from the severe manners of his father's court was noticed with mortification by the austere Macedonians, who still constituted the body of his friends."

on the Macedonian sacred day for Dionysus, but for some reason, Alexander had made a sacrifice that day to Castor and Pollux instead. Alexander had been binge drinking, which Arrian describes as "imitating too much the custom of foreigners."

Among those present at this dinner party was Cleitus the Black, one of the most competent Macedonian officers, a close friend of Alexander's and the man who had saved his life at Granicus. He too, had been drinking too much.*

With the booze having washed away his self-restraint, Cleitus drunkenly asserted that Alexander's achievements were not his, but those of the Macedonians who had fought with him. Arrian points out, probably citing the eyewitness account of Aristobulus, that had Cleitus not been drunk, he would simply have bitten his tongue, but he had lost his self-control. "This hand, oh Alexander, preserved thee on that occasion," Cleitus said, reminding Alexander of Granicus.

Alexander called for his guards but, realizing his state of mind, they wisely ignored him. Cleitus, pushing things, suggested that Alexander was like a Darius, impotently constrained by his own attendants. There are various versions of what happened next. Aristobulus tells that Cleitus was led away, but came back again to insult Alexander. Others say that a furious Alexander immediately grabbed a javelin and killed Cleitus. In either case, Cleitus was murdered by Alexander in a drunken fury. All accounts tell that Alexander was almost immediately overcome with regret. Arrian calls Alexander the slave of two vices, anger and drunkenness, "by neither of which is it seemly for a prudent man to be enslaved."

Of the ancient historians who were there, or nearby, Aristobulus is critical of Cleitus for pushing Alexander too far, but Callisthenes was critical of Alexander for pushing the Macedonian officers too far.

---

*Colorfully describing the scene, John Clark Ridpath in *History of the World* (New York: Philips and Hunt, 1885), volume 1, chapter 47, writes that "When all were well heated with wine, some of the fawning puppies of the East began in their usual obsequious way to flatter the king on his great achievements and divine paternity. Thereupon Cleitus . . . rebuked the sycophants with all the hot words in his vocabulary. Alexander, to his shame, interfered to stop the reproaches of Cleitus, who thereupon turned on his master a torrent of well deserved rebukes."

The issue, as it had been since Alexander first put on the barbaric dress in 330, was his letting the "King of Asia" role go to his head. The gradual alienation was exacerbated by Alexander's becoming a slave to the third vice of putting too much stock in the praise of his Asian courtiers.

The straw that broke the camel's back for Callisthenes came not long after the death of Cleitus. Anaxarchus, a Thracian philosopher who had been accompanying Alexander's campaign, asserted that, to quote Arrian, "there is no honor which Alexander is unworthy to receive." By this, he included the Persian practice of proskynesis, or prostration before a person of higher social rank. Members of Alexander's Asian court routinely prostrated themselves before him, and Callisthenes had observed that this was going to Alexander's head. To the Greco-Macedonian mind, such behavior was an anathema. According to their tradition, one bowed before gods, *not* before men. Arrian notes that Callisthenes told Anaxarchus that "men have made distinctions between those honors which are due to men, and those due to gods." Anaxarchus replied that Alexander, by nature of his accomplishments and his descent from Zeus, deserved such treatment. A number of supplicants then prostrated themselves, but Callisthenes refused to do so.

Subsequently, Callisthenes was implicated in a plot to assassinate Alexander and was arrested. As Arrian notes, the accounts of Callisthenes' demise are inconsistent. Aristobulus says that Callisthenes died of "natural" causes, but Ptolemy writes that he was hanged.

The deaths of Spitamenes, Cleitus and Callisthenes all probably occurred within the space of a month or two in the winter of 328–327, although Curtius mentions the death of Cleitus as occurring later in 327. The deaths of an elusive foe, a close friend and a commentator turned critic were long on symbolism.

The death of Spitamenes reminded Alexander of the difficulties and dangers of the counterinsurgency that he was forced to fight in Central Asia.

The death of Cleitus showed him how out of touch he was with those friends who truly mattered.

The death of Callisthenes illustrated that as he had tried to pander to the hearts and minds of his new subjects, he was losing the hearts and minds of his own people.

CHAPTER 14

Men Fly over Sogdian Rock

EARLY IN 327 BC, ALEXANDER WAS AT HIS WINTER QUARTERS IN NAUTACA in Bactria anxiously preparing to resume his march into India. Arrian writes at length about administrative changes that Alexander made in his Central Asian dominions as he prepared to leave the area indefinitely. On the military side, we learn that Amyntas was left in charge in Bactria with a force of 3,500 cavalrymen and 10,000 infantrymen.

As he was doing this, however, Alexander found that he was forced to concern himself with unfinished counterinsurgency—that is, if it is not redundant to use the adjective "unfinished" with counterinsurgency. Arrian tells that Alexander received word that "many of the Sogdians had fled for refuge into their strongholds and refused to submit" to the authority of the King of Asia.

One such stronghold was the mountain fortress atop steep cliffs near Samarkand that was known as the Sogdian Rock, the Rock of Ariamazes, or simply "The Rock." Barricaded atop the Rock were the Sogdian leader Ariamazes (or Arimazes) and a force that Curtius numbers at 30,000, with a stockpile of provisions said to be sufficient to maintain this number of personnel for two years.

Also present, according to Arrian, were the families of a number of Central Asian nobles, including Oxyartes of Zariaspa, who, like Spitamenes, had commanded troops under Bessus only to turn on him and deliver him to Alexander. Like Spitamenes, Oxyartes had sworn an allegiance to Alexander from which he later backed out. Because the Sogdian Rock was considered to be an impregnable fortress, Oxyartes felt confident that it was a good place to keep his family.

The cliffs were steep and high. Curtius estimates that the fortress was 18,000 feet up from the valley floor. This is certainly an exaggeration, but it may have appeared as such to those looking up. He goes on to say that Alexander initially rejected the idea of assaulting the Sogdian Rock but "was overcome by a desire to bring even nature to her knees."

Before he attacked, he sent his man Cophes to inform Ariamazes that if his troops surrendered, he would allow them to depart in safety.

As Arrian relates, "they burst out laughing, and in their barbaric tongue bade Alexander seek winged soldiers to capture the mountain for him, since they had no apprehension of danger from other men."

A certain number of Alexander's sieges had been resolved through the use of engineers and massive numbers of laborers constructing large earthworks, but this siege would be determined by the fortitude of individuals. Alexander solved the problem by deferring to individual creativity.

The problem was indeed a difficult one. The cliffs were high, the snow was deep and the ice was treacherous. Conversely, the men under Alexander's command were innovative and resourceful.

Curtius explains that he ordered his staff to bring him the most agile men they had, men used to climbing mountains. "My comrades!" Alexander said when 300 mountaineers with experience scaling rocks during previous sieges had been brought to him. "With you I have stormed the fortifications of cities that had remained undefeated. With you I have crossed mountain chains snow-covered throughout the year, entered the defiles of Cilicia. . . . The rock which you see is accessible by one path only and that is occupied by the barbarians, who are ignoring everything else—no guards are posted apart from those facing toward our camp. You will find a way up if you use your skill in searching for tracks that lead to the top. Nature has set nothing so high that it cannot be surmounted by courage."

Arrian writes that Alexander offered inducements to men who could also conquer the heights of the Sogdian Rock, with a 12-talent ($185,000) reward to the first man who reached the top of the cliff protecting the fortress.

Roping themselves, and using metal tent pegs as pitons, they made the difficult ascent. Arrian and Curtius write that around 30 of the climbers fell to their deaths, and their bodies were never recovered from the crevices and snow banks. However, the others were able to climb into positions on cliffs above the fortress. They rested as they could through the night, and at dawn they signaled Alexander that they were in position.

Cophes took a message to the defenders of the fortress explaining that Alexander had found the flying men, and that they were now perched on the high ground from which arrows would now rain down. The men above had positioned themselves in such a way as to make it seem as though they were more numerous than they were. The sight spelled checkmate to the Sogdian Rock's defenders and Ariamazes promptly surrendered.

◈

Though Alexander's fame and prestige were enhanced by the success of this operation, Curtius suggests that the troops in the field understood that it was the initiative and bravery of the mountaineers that made it a success. He writes that Alexander received "more notoriety than credit." Curtius writes that Alexander was particularly brutal with respect to those who surrendered, mentioning whippings, crucifixions and delivering prisoners into slavery. While this extreme treatment of a defeated population was not out of character for Alexander—he did it at Tyre, Gaza and elsewhere—other commentators do not mention it. Arrian in particular gives a completely opposite impression, painting Alexander as being quite generous, even chivalrous, in his victory at the Sogdian Rock. Among those who surrendered was Roxana (or Roxane), the daughter of Oxyartes. As Arrian writes, she was "asserted by the men who served in Alexander's army to have been the most beautiful of all the Asiatic women whom they had seen, with the single exception of the wife of Darius"—the late Stateira. This fact was not lost on Alexander, who made Roxana his first wife. Though he had often been urged by his advisers and generals to marry in order to solidify some alliance or other, Alexander had until now remained unmarried.

There are two basic versions of Alexander's motivation for marrying Roxana, and first- and second-century biographers discuss each as plausible. In one version, it is love at first sight. In the other, the marriage is an attempt to unite Alexander and the Macedonians with the Asians through marriage, an affirmation of Alexander's legitimacy as King of Asia.

Plutarch writes that the marriage "was a love affair, and yet it was thought to harmonize well with the matters which he had in hand. For the barbarians were encouraged by the partnership into which the marriage brought them, and they were beyond measure fond of Alexander."

There is also some disagreement among the sources over the question as to when Alexander first laid eyes on Roxana. Arrian seems to suggest that it was immediately after the Sogdian Rock siege, while both Plutarch and Curtius say that it was at a later banquet arranged by Oxyartes, with whom, according to them, Alexander had a amicable relationship.

"Oxyartes had arranged a banquet of typical barbaric extravagance, at which he entertained the king," writes Curtius, painting a picture of a cordial rapport between Oxyartes and Alexander. "While he conducted the festivities with warm geniality, Oxyartes had 30 young noblewomen brought in, one of whom was his own daughter Roxane, a woman of remarkable physical beauty with a dignified bearing rarely found in barbarians. Though she was one of a number chosen for their beauty, she nonetheless attracted everybody's attention, especially that of the king."

He adds that Alexander fell in love on the spot.

The wedding, celebrated in the Central Asian style, as might have been expected, displeased the conservatives among the Macedonian contingent. Left unsaid is how this turn of events was welcomed by Barsine, the Phrygian woman who had been Alexander's mistress for the past six years. She was now about 36, and Roxana was half that age. The awkwardness of this situation must have been exacerbated by the fact that it was around this time that Barsine gave birth to Alexander's son Heracles. The boy was not a legitimate heir because his mother was not married to Alexander.

✦

The story of the brilliant takedown of the Sogdian Rock has loomed large in the Alexander literature through the years, but it was only one of several such operations that unfolded during 327 BC before the Greco-Macedonian army moved south into India. Arrian mentions a Rock of Chorienes, located somewhere in what is now eastern Afghanistan, which is also called the Rock of Sisimithres, and to which a warlord named Chorienes and "many other chiefs had fled for refuge."

It was "difficult to ascend even by men in single file and when no one barred the way. . . . A deep ravine also enclosed the rock all round, so that whoever intended to lead an army up to it, must long before make a causeway of earth over this ravine in order that he might start from level ground, when he led his troops to the assault."

As he had so often, Alexander approached the assault as an engineering issue. To access the ravine, Alexander ordered tall conifers to be cut down and made into ladders. When this was done, he began to build a bridge across this ravine. A screen made of tree branches was also built to shield the construction crews from arrows fired from above.

Nervous that Alexander might actually succeed, Chorienes sent down a messenger, asking Alexander to send Oxyartes, who had previously submitted to Alexander, up to talk with him. Oxyartes was able to persuade Chorienes to "entrust himself and the place to Alexander; for he told him that there was nothing which Alexander and his army could not take by storm."

Alexander himself went to the summit to accept the surrender. Completely contrary to what Curtius tells happened at the Sogdian Rock, Alexander was overly magnanimous in victory, permitting Chorienes to keep his rock and making him satrap of the region. The actions involving Chorienes and his rock were among the last major military and political actions that Alexander would take in Central Asia.

CHAPTER 15

Into the Headwaters of the Indus

The Greco-Macedonian army of Alexander crossed the Hindu Kush range through the 3,510-foot Khyber Pass during the summer of 327 BC, trading the sweltering heat of the desert for the coolness of the mountains. This pass, which today marks the border between Afghanistan and Pakistan, had been an important trade route between Central Asia and India for centuries before Alexander, and would continue to be so for centuries to come. It was also an important invasion route for armies including those of Darius I, Tamerlane and Genghis Khan, as well as the British in the nineteenth century.

It is as an invasion route that the pass has especially earned both fame and infamy. Rudyard Kipling called it "a sword cut through the mountains," while British General George Molesworth wrote in the early twentieth century that "every stone in the Khyber has been soaked in blood." Blood of soldiers continues to be spilled on the route to this day.

Alexander and his army then made their way down into the valleys of the Indus River drainage and into what is now the Punjab region of Pakistan. One of his first encounters was with a man named Ambhi, whom the chroniclers call Taxiles. He was the ruler of a kingdom which Plutarch describes as "a realm in India as large as Egypt, with good pasturage, too, and in the highest degree productive of beautiful fruits."

Taxiles' capital was at the city of Taxila, located near the modern Pakistani city of Attock, between Peshawar and Rawalpindi, but his meeting with Alexander seems to have taken place west of this city. Plutarch says that Taxiles greeted Alexander warmly, saying "Why must we war and fight with one another, Alexander, if thou art not come to rob us of water or of necessary sustenance, the only things for which men of sense are obliged to fight obstinately? As for other wealth and possessions, so-called, if I am thy superior therein, I am ready to confer favors; but if thine inferior, I will not object to thanking you for favors conferred."

"Canst thou think, pray, that after such words of kindness our interview is to end without a battle?" Alexander replied. "Nay, thou shalt not get the better of me; for I will contend against thee and fight to the last with my favors, that thou mayest not surpass me in generosity."

The generosity flowed in both directions with regard to military matters as well. Alexander's reputation had preceded him, and Taxiles was eager to be on good terms with a powerful ally in his conflicts with his own rivals. When Taxiles died a short time later, his son and heir, Omphis (Diodorus calls him Mophis), also placed his armed forces at Alexander's disposal.

With Taxiles having contributed a token force to his new ally, Alexander now ordered Hephaestion and Perdiccas, a veteran phalanx commander, to lead a contingent, including half of the Companion Cavalry, toward the Indus. Their orders were, according to Arrian, to "capture the places on their route by force, or to bring them over on terms of capitulation." One of their first targets was a series of towns in Peukelaotis, now known as Hashtnagar and part of the Charsadda District in the North West Frontier Province of Pakistan. Arrian reports a 30-day campaign, while Curtius mentions "subduing a tribe of little account."

Alexander, meanwhile, led the other half of the Companion Cavalry, as well as his hypaspists, archers, Agrianians and other infantry into the mountains against other mountain people. Identified by Arrian as Aspasians, Guraeans and Assacenians (or Assacenii), they may be associated with or related to the people known in Sanskrit as

Aśvaka or Aśvakayana, who inhabited the region at the time. The Guraeans are probably the people in the vicinity of the Choaspes River, known to the ancient Europeans as the Guraeus and now called the Karkheh in western Iran. For Curtius, these people are perhaps included among the tribes of little account.

In these mountains, and among these tribes, Alexander found himself in a situation similar to that in which U.S. forces would find themselves more than 2,300 years later—in exactly the same mountains. Then as now, the people were an elusive foe, living in a forbidding land and unused to being governed by the laws or bureaucrats of outsiders.

Despite the passage of nearly two dozen centuries, little has changed along the ambiguous border that now separates Afghanistan from the Federally Administered Tribal Areas of Pakistan. Indeed, today this border itself exists only on maps, as the Pashtun tribes who inhabit this harsh and difficult land recognize only the sorts of turf delineations that have defined boundaries and boundary changes throughout all those centuries. The British had efficiently imposed their rule upon most of the Indian Subcontinent, but they met with repeated failure when it came to these mountains, and with Afghanistan beyond. Like the British in the nineteenth century, the Soviet Union learned the hard way in the 1980s about the nature of war in Afghanistan.

When Pakistan became independent in 1947, the new government followed with the example of the British, ceding autonomy to the peoples of the Tribal Areas. Even today, the Pakistani government exercises only nominal political control in this region, and the Supreme Court of Pakistan has no jurisdiction here.

Given that so much attention is being focussed today on this long-dismissed corner of the world, it is a pity that Alexander's biographers—other than Arrian—chose to leave us with so little information about the campaigns among the "tribes of little account."

As he had from Asia Minor to Central Asia, Alexander pursued a ruthless offensive against the cities whose people resisted him. In Arrian's descriptions of these operations, he describes the Macedonians systematically surrounding fortified mountain towns, breaching their walls with scaling ladders and killing the inhabitants. This was apparently accomplished rather easily and expeditiously, although Arrian does mention that Alexander and Ptolemy were wounded slightly in the campaign.

One of the cities, which Arrian calls by the Latin name Arigaeum, was determined to have a particularly strategic location, so Alexander ordered Craterus to establish a Greco-Macedonian garrison there. The exact location of the site is unknown today.

✦

Alexander's offensive operations in these mountains culminated in the large ancient city of Massaga, in what is now Pakistan's Swat Valley, probably somewhere near modern Chakdara. This siege proved more difficult than the others. Alexander's initial plan was to lure the defenders, said to number 7,000, into a fight in open ground near Massaga, so he set up a camp to bait his trap. When he saw the enemy coming out of the gates to attack his camp, Alexander ordered a retreat to high ground nearly a mile from the city, the idea being to get the men as far away from Massaga as he could.

Seeing the Macedonians on the run, the enemy, running as fast as they could, lost order in their pursuit. Alexander then turned on this disorganized mass, charging with his sarissa-armed phalanx, and flanking them with horse-javelin-men, Agrianians and archers. Hand-to-hand combat devolved into a desperate retreat back toward Massaga, which Alexander surrounded.

Based on his experience over the previous few weeks, Alexander might have expected a quick finish to the Massaga siege, but his foe was more tenacious than he expected. On the second day, he brought in siege engines, which succeeded easily in battering down a section of the wall, but the resistance within compelled him to disengage. A renewed infantry assault on the third day, supported by archers in a siege tower, also failed. So too did an attempt to throw a bridge across from one of the mobile towers. When the bridge collapsed under the weight of the troops atop it, the defenders cheered and poured arrows and rocks into the mass of fallen Macedonians.

On the fourth day of the Massaga siege, Alexander again sent a tower with a portable bridge against the wall, deciding that this tactic had the best chance of success. During this attack, a Macedonian arrow chanced to hit the commander of the defenders. With this, and with the mounting casualties, Massaga sent an emissary to Alexander to discuss surrender. Alexander was so impressed with these men that his surrender terms amounted to his sparing them if they would join his army. This they agreed to do, and they marched out of the city and camped nearby.

However, that night Alexander received word that they planned to defect and sneak back to the hills. Alexander promptly surrounded them, and in Arrian's words, "cut them to pieces." He then captured the defenseless Massaga.

❖

A similar siege awaited Coenus at another Swat Valley city known then as Bazira. Today, the city corresponds to the Pakistani city of Barikot. A nearby archeological site known as Barikot-Ghwandai is thought to contain fortifications that date to the time of the siege.

As at Massaga, the defenders at Bazira had a defensible high ground position and no inclination to surrender. When Alexander learned that Coenus had run into a stumbling block, he promised to bring the contingent under his own direct command into action at Bazira. However, while en route, he became bogged down in an unanticipated battle and sent word to Coenus to come to him.

The plan was for Coenus to, in Arrian's words, "fortify a certain strong position to serve as a basis of operations against the city of Bazira, and then to come to him with the rest of his army, after leaving in that place a sufficient garrison to restrain the men in the city."

This action had unexpected results. When Bazira's defenders saw Coenus leaving, they thought that it was a retreat, so they hurried out to attack him. A vicious battle ensued without a decisive outcome. Though the disciplined Macedonians gained the upper hand in the fight, the defenders were able to fight their way back inside their walls, where they were able to keep the Macedonians at bay. When news of Alexander's impending arrival reached them, though, the fighters realized that he would tip the balance in the standoff. They then abandoned the city, sneaking away under cover of darkness, taking a large number of troops and weapons

Today, American forces in these same mountains continue to be schooled in the same lesson that the Macedonians learned so long ago. They have discovered that the people of these mountains can be defeated in specific battles, but so long as they can melt back into the rugged mountains themselves, the tribes will never lose a war.

Initially, Alexander followed the same doctrine the Soviets and Americans would follow more than two millennia later—one that had served him well in Asia Minor, and reasonably well in Central Asia— that of taking and holding major cities and population centers. Unlike his successors in more recent centuries, however, Alexander did not linger long in these mountains. Perhaps he had learned the lesson of not allowing himself to get bogged down in a counterinsurgency campaign when his strategic vision called for bigger objectives.

CHAPTER 16

Siege at Aornos

IN CONSIDERING THE MILITARY HISTORY OF ALEXANDER'S CAMPAIGNS, one returns again and again to the tactical brilliance of his siege operations. In considering the political career of the King of Asia, the word "audacity" is also quite appropriate. Perhaps nowhere did these two threads of tactical virtuosity and fearless daring cross more dramatically than during the winter of 327–326 BC, at a place classical writers call the Rock of Aornos, overlooking a narrow gorge of the Indus River.

Unlike the sites of other sieges, such as that of the Sogdian Rock, the site of the Rock of Aornos is known to us. Thanks to Sir Aurel Stein, who pinpointed it in 1926, and to subsequent archeological excavations that have confirmed it, we know that the steep mountain now known as Pir-Sar is Aornos. Located about 60 miles north of Islamabad, and a dozen miles from Besham Qala in the North West Frontier Province of Pakistan, Pir-Sar rises to an elevation of just over a mile.

Diodorus writes that after Alexander had "taken a number of other cities by storm and had slaughtered their defenders, he came to the 'rock' called Aornos. Here the surviving natives had taken refuge because of its great strength. It is said that Heracles of old thought to lay siege to this 'rock' but refrained because of the occurrence of certain sharp earthquake shocks and other divine signs, and this made Alexander even more eager to capture the stronghold when he heard it, and so to rival the god's reputation."

The story of the rock and the earthquakes reminded Alexander of the story in the Twelve Labors of Heracles in which the hero descends into the Underworld, tasked with capturing the multi-headed hell-hound, Cerberus. While en route, Heracles attempted to free both Theseus and Pirithous, who had been chained to a stone by Hades. He managed to free Theseus, but he failed to liberate Pirithous because of an earthquake.

Insofar as earthquakes are concerned, northwest Pakistan is quite prone to tremors. For instance, the one in 2005 killed tens of thousands of people. Their effects are mentioned in accounts of Alexander's travels through the region, and it is possible that Alexander himself felt some rumbling.

Aornos is the pinnacle of audacity because the myth holds that the siege was undertaken in large part because Alexander wanted to do what Heracles had *failed* to do. While the Heracles connection was probably discussed at the time, Arrian is correct when he dismisses this as Alexander's reason for assaulting Pir-Sar. He writes, "I am inclined to think, that in regard to this rock the name of Heracles was mentioned simply to add to the marvelousness of the tale."

◈

Leaving Craterus in charge of the bulk of the army, Alexander selected a strike force consisting of archers, Agrianians, Companion Cavalry and troops from the phalanx. With these, he established an advance base camp near Pir-Sar and undertook a survey of possible routes up the steep mountain.

The mountaintop consists of two summits, with the western summit being higher, and the eastern summit being broader. It was on the latter, which classical writers refer to specifically as the Rock of Aornos, that the enemy stronghold was located.

While conducting his reconnaissance, Alexander met an old man who lived in a cave on the side of the mountain with two of his sons. As Diodorus explains, "he told his story and offered to guide the king through the hills and bring him to a point [on the western summit] where he would be above the people who occupied the rock."

No doubt recalling the tactic that had worked at the Sogdian Rock, Alexander ordered Ptolemy to lead a contingent up by this route. With the highest ground on the west thus captured, the position of the defenders would be compromised. At the Sogdian Rock, this had checkmated the defenders.

With great difficulty, Ptolemy and his men did manage to climb to the high ground without alerting the defenders and established a fortified position on the western summit. This done, Ptolemy signaled Alexander with a torch. Alexander saw this and began to assault the Rock of Aornos from below. Unfortunately, the defenders had also seen Ptolemy's signal, and they moved quickly to blunt Alexander's attack.

Attacking uphill on ground that the enemy knows is always difficult, and so it was for Alexander and his troops. Curtius gives a particularly graphic account of the trials of the Aornos Rock climb, noting that many troops were "overtaken by a pitiful fate. Slipping from the sheer cliff-face, they were swallowed up by the river flowing past it. This was a painful spectacle even to those not in danger but, when another's death demonstrated to them what they had to fear themselves. . . . As they climbed, the barbarians rolled huge boulders on to them, and those who were hit fell headlong from their unsure and slippery footholds."

Stymied both by terrain and by enemy action, Alexander ordered a withdrawal. Seeing that Alexander had been repulsed, the defenders turned on Ptolemy. Alexander was repelled because the defenders had the advantage of higher ground, but the defenders had the disadvantage as they attacked Ptolemy from beneath. A vicious battle ensued, but as night fell on the first day of the Siege of Aornos, Ptolemy's men were still in place.

Overnight, Alexander sent a courier up the mountain with a message containing the battle plan for the next day. Ptolemy was to go over from defense to offense and attack downward in an assault coordinated with Alexander's own renewed assault upward. Alexander's hope was to link up the two forces.

Alexander jumped off at daybreak, following the same route up the hill that Ptolemy had taken previously. The defenders did not make it easy for either Greco-Macedonian contingent. As Arrian writes, "until midday, a smart battle was kept up between the Indians and the Macedonians, the latter striving to force a way of approach, and the former hurling missiles at them as they ascended."

After a day of difficult climbing and fighting, Alexander did manage to link up with Ptolemy on the western summit of the mountain, but the enemy position on the eastern summit remained intact, separated from Alexander by a broad, easily defensible chasm.

At this point, Alexander turned, as he usually did during a difficult siege, to engineering. As he had built a causeway to the island fortress of Tyre, Alexander would build a bridge across the canyon. "At the approach of the dawn, he issued an order that each soldier individually should cut 100 stakes," Arrian writes. "When these had been cut he heaped up a great mound towards the rock, beginning from the top of the hill where they had encamped."

Curtius tells that Alexander was himself the first to throw a log into the chasm, and that "the shout that followed from the troops revealed their enthusiasm, for none refused a job the king had undertaken before him."

Alexander also attacked the enemy stronghold using siege engines. This meant that they would have been faced with the arduous task of moving heavy artillery up trails that had previously been described as being difficult for a man to climb. Conversely, if they had not dragged them up, Alexander's men would have had to construct siege engines on-site atop the mountain. Either way, deploying siege engines at such a location is an amazing feat.

While Curtius says that the gully had been filled within seven days, Arrian states that the construction work continued without interruption for three days, and that a handful of Macedonian troops were now in positions level with the Rock of Aornos. Perhaps Curtius is including the overall duration of the entire siege operation.

Diodorus tells that "the dart-throwing catapults and other engines were emplaced, and the king also made it evident that he would not break off the siege."

However, Curtius asserts that "Alexander had now decided to abandon the project—there was apparently no hope of gaining the rock—but he nonetheless made a show of persevering with the siege, ordering roads to be blocked, siege-towers moved up, and exhausted troops replaced by others."

Curtius also leaves us an account of Alexander's being severely wounded in the battle, something not mentioned by Arrian, Diodorus or Plutarch. Indeed, Plutarch has almost nothing to say about the siege. Curtius describes hand-to-hand combat, saying that Alexander, "bearing in mind both his name and his promise [to outdo Heracles], fought with more vigor than caution and finally fell, pierced by weapons from every side."

There are also some other discrepancies in the accounts related by the biographers, although all agree on the outcome of the battle. Arrian tells that the defenders were "alarmed at the indescribable audacity" of the Macedonians "who had forced their way to [the Rock of Aornos], and seeing that the mound was already united with it, desisted from attempting any longer to resist."

All accounts state that the defenders of the Rock of Aornos eventually gave up and abandoned the rock. In Arrian's version, an emissary was sent to Alexander to discus surrender terms, with back-and-forth haggling going on all day. The defenders wanted to stall until nightfall, hoping that they could slip away during the night. Alexander figured this out and let them get way with it.

Diodorus tells a similar story, stating that Alexander, "craftily anticipating what would happen, removed the guard which had been left in the path, allowing those who wished to withdraw from the rock. In fear of the Macedonian fighting qualities and the king's determination, the Indians left the rock under cover of darkness."

Curtius tells that they got away after fighting the Greco-Macedonian assault force to a standstill. He says that the defenders "spent two days and nights feasting and beating drums in their usual manner, ostentatiously demonstrating not only their confidence but their belief that they had won. On the third night, however, drumbeats were no longer heard. Torches blazed all over the rocky hill, lit by the barbarians to make their flight safer when they would, in the darkness of night, be running over crags impossible to negotiate."

Arrian and Curtius both say that Alexander himself was the first to scale the eastern summit, doing so after it was abandoned by the enemy. Says Curtius, "it was at first decided that the king should not take part in the hazardous undertaking himself; but as soon as the trumpet signal was given, this resolute man of action turned to his bodyguards, told them to follow him, and was the first to clamber up the rock."

Both Arrian and Curtius also agree that Alexander's troops caught up with and slaughtered the retreating defenders. Arrian tells that Alexander's men "killed many of them in their flight. Others retreating with panic terror perished by leaping down the precipices."

Curtius, with more of a flair for the dramatic, says that Alexander struck "terror into the Indians in their disordered flight. Many thought the enemy were upon them and hurled themselves to their deaths down the slippery crags and impassable rocks."

Plutarch, who barely mentions the battle, is quite critical of Alexander's ambush in its final act, noting that "after he had made a truce with them in a certain city and allowed them to depart, he fell upon them as they marched and slew them all. And this act adheres like a stain to his military career; in all other instances he waged war according to usage and like a king."

His successful siege of the Rock of Aornos in the late winter of 326 BC was not Alexander's greatest moment, nor even his greatest siege. As Curtius correctly points out, it was a victory "over the terrain rather than the enemy."

CHAPTER 17

Triumph at Hydaspes

Having crossed the Indus, and having humbled the Rock of Aornos, one of India's greatest citadels, in the spring of 326 BC Alexander moved on to the next milepost in his campaign, the river the Greco-Macedonians called Hydaspes, which was known to the Hindus, and mentioned in their ancient scriptures, as the Vitasta. Now called the Jhelum, the river is a tributary of the Indus, with its headwaters in what is now India, but with most of its course in present Pakistan.

Across the Hydaspes lay the kingdom of Paurava, ruled by a king named Porus, who was an enemy of Omphis, son of Taxiles. No doubt this enmity was an ulterior motive behind Omphis's willingness to meld his army with that of Alexander. Indeed, he contributed 5,000 troops to Alexander's Hydaspes operation against Porus.

Porus was an enigmatic individual about whom little is known apart from what was written by the European chroniclers of Alexander's exploits. They say that he was a large man. According to Plutarch, "most historians agree that Porus was four cubits and a span high." In fact, there are several disagreeing estimates of his height, but all of them are over six feet, and some over seven. Plutarch is probably right when he adds that "the size and majesty of his body made his elephant seem as fitting a mount for him as a horse for the horseman."

Alexander waited until late spring 326 BC to make his crossing of the Hydaspes. Knowing that fording the broad river was out of the question, Alexander ordered Coenus back to the place where they had crossed the Indus to collect all of the boats—including triacontors, or 30-oared galleys—they had used. Having disassembled these vessels, he trucked them forward in wagons.

Porus certainly knew that Alexander was coming, so he positioned his army on the eastern shore of the Hydaspes, ready to counter Alexander's attempt to cross. Obviously, Alexander's troops would be at their most vulnerable while crossing, and Porus wanted to take advantage of this.

What Porus did not know about Alexander's impending crossing was when and where. Alexander intended to keep it that way. As to the issue of *when,* Alexander deliberately planted the story, probably with one of the civilian travelers or merchants who routinely crossed the river, that he would wait until the lowest ebb of the river in the fall. He backed up this obfuscation by stockpiling provisions sufficient to sustain an army camp for several months. Waiting until lower water was a logical strategic assumption that Porus was inclined to believe, although the Indian monarch did not slacken his vigil.

As for *where* the Greco-Macedonian army would cross, Alexander deliberately shifted his troops, marching various units up and down the western shore within sight of Porus's observers. This compelled him to cover any number of possible crossing points. Accounts of the days preceding the battle tell of cavalry contingents on each side following one another up and down the river.

The two armies camped directly across the Hydaspes from one another, watching and waiting. The coming battle was shaping up to be Alexander's largest battle involving field armies since his decisive defeat of Darius at Gaugamela five years earlier.

Estimates of the strength of the two sides vary, as such figures usually do throughout the annals of Alexander's campaigns. Alexander's army, including its Taxilan allies, probably numbered fewer than the approximately 40,000 infantry and 7,000 cavalry that Alexander fielded in his great battles against Darius.

Arrian estimates that the contingent led personally by Alexander, which would make the initial contact with Porus, consisted of 6,000 infantry and 5,000 cavalry. It included the units that Alexander always liked to have in his strike forces, specifically archers, his Companion Cavalry and the Agrianians, the expert javelin-throwers who Alexander valued so highly in his order of battle. Also included were Greco-Macedonian cavalry regiments led by Hephaestion, Perdiccas and Demetrius, as well as Bactrian, Dahae, Sogdian and Scythian cavalry units. From the infantry phalanx, Alexander brought brigades led by Coenus and Cleitus the White, a Macedonian officer so named to distinguish him from the late Cleitus the Black.

As for the opposing side, both Arrian and Curtius agree that Porus fielded 30,000 infantrymen and 300 chariots, and Arrian adds that he had 4,000 cavalry and around 200 elephants. Other estimates range from Plutarch's claim of an infantry force of 20,000, plus 2,000 cavalry, to Diodorus's 50,000 infantry and 3,000 cavalry. Diodorus adds more than a thousand chariots, and all agree that there was a sizable elephant contingent.

The latter were problematic for Alexander. As Arrian points out, these immense animals would spook Alexander's horses, who would "refuse even to mount the opposite bank, because the elephants would at once fall upon them and frighten them both by their aspect and trumpeting."

For this reason, among many obvious others, Alexander ruled out a direct assault across the Hydaspes toward the main enemy camp as the initial gambit of the operation. Instead, he chose a place around a bend in the river approximately 20 miles upstream from his own primary encampment.

Alexander's object was to achieve a sufficient measure of surprise so that he could establish a bridgehead before Porus could stop his crossing. To disguise the move, Alexander ordered preparations for river crossings at several other locations, accompanied by plenty of noise and clamor.

It was much like the elaborate obfuscation undertaken by the Anglo-American Allies in the spring of 1944 to convince the Germans that they intended to make the cross-Channel invasion in the Pas de Calais (the Strait of Dover) rather than at Normandy. Indeed, Adolf Hitler continued to believe that the true invasion would take place near Calais long after the Allies landed in Normandy on June 6. Like Hitler, Porus was duped.

When Porus became engaged in battle with Alexander, Craterus was to lead a crossing into the area of the enemy encampment. If Porus had in fact moved to meet Alexander with the full strength of his army, his encampment would now be the Indian rear, and Porus would be outflanked.

In Craterus's order of battle, Arrian lists "his own division of cavalry, and the horsemen from the Arachotians and Parapamisadians, as well as the brigades of Alcetas and Polyperchon from the phalanx of the Macedonian infantry, together with the chiefs of the Indians dwelling this side of the Hydaspes [Omphis and his 5,000 men]."

In between these two positions, Alexander posted infantry and cavalry units under the command of Attalus (son of Andromenes) and of Gorgias and Meleager, with orders to cross in increments as they saw the battle being joined on the opposite side.

The exact locations are the subject of many theories, but they are unknown today. The course of the river has changed so often over the ensuing centuries that the original sites were probably washed away long ago.

❖

The date of Alexander's operation is given as being as early as May 326 BC, or as late as July, after the summer solstice. Arrian says that it took place in the month of Munychion, which runs from mid-April to mid-May.

Alexander made his move from the camp to the crossing point during the night before his D-Day for added stealth, but his troops were caught in a tropical downpour as they made their way overland. The bad news involved troops getting soaked while hiking though mud. The good news was that Porus's men never noticed the mass movement of more than 11,000 men.

The storm abated at daybreak as the troops reached the intended crossing point. Here they were able to board the boats and triacontors, which had been secretly reassembled and prepositioned here.

To stories of military operations, corollary tales of reconnaissance screw-ups are often added. With the June 1944 Normandy operations, Allied photo-reconnaissance analysts failed to realize that the "hedgerows" in Normandy were actually impenetrable masses of tall trees that proved to be a very difficult obstacle. With Alexander's Hydaspes operation, the "opposite shore" on which Alexander landed his troops was not actually that, but rather a long island parallel to the opposite shore.

When the troops had crossed the main part of the river, they were still separated from their objective by a fast-flowing channel that was swollen by the overnight storm. As with the Allies in Normandy, this slowed but did not stop Alexander and his troops. Arrian writes that Alexander "led his men through it with much difficulty; for where the water was deepest, it reached higher than the breasts of the infantry; and of the horses only the heads rose above the river."

Despite the mistake, the crossing achieved its initial tactical surprise, but once under way, the movement of so many troops was impossible to hide from the enemy sentries. Alexander quickly arranged them in battle order, knowing that Porus could counterattack at any moment.

As usual, Alexander picked his Companions and the best cavalry units to operate under his personal command on the right wing. In the center, along with his hypaspists, or shield-bearing infantry, and on the left, he placed Agrianians and archers. Arrian notes too that "in front of all the cavalry he posted the horse-archers." As he had a much larger proportion of cavalry to infantry than was typically seen in orders of battle during this era, it is clear that Alexander planned to emphasize tactics of mobility and maneuver.

Arrian writes that Alexander had decided "if Porus should engage him with all his forces, he would easily be able to overcome him by attacking with his cavalry, or to stand on the defensive until his infantry arrived in the course of the action; but if the Indians should be alarmed at his extraordinary audacity in making the passage of the river and take to flight, he would be able to keep close to them in their flight."

According to Aristobulus, Porus had sent his son with a recon force of 60 chariots to investigate the landing zone. They arrived even as the Macedonians were struggling ashore, but they chose not to engage them. As Arrian correctly points out, "he could have hindered Alexander's crossing (for he made the passage with difficulty even when no one opposed him), if the Indians had leaped down from their chariots and assaulted those who first emerged from the water."

However, Arrian goes on to question Aristobulus on the size of this force, observing that 60 was "too many to be sent out as a reconnoitering party . . . but they were by no means a sufficient force to keep back those of the enemy who had not yet got across, as well as to attack those who had already landed."

He goes on to quote Ptolemy's account that the son of Porus arrived *after* Alexander had already made the last passage from the island, and that he arrived "at the head of 2,000 cavalry and 120 chariots."

In his account, Curtius states that Porus initially sent 4,000 cavalry troops, agreeing with Ptolemy that this contingent arrived *after* the "brightening daylight" revealed Alexander's battle line.

In any event, Porus sent a smaller force than he would have had he known the true scale of Alexander's now successful crossing. As with Hitler's reaction to the Normandy landings, Porus probably listened to the initial report but downplayed Alexander's crossing as a mere diversion, not the main assault.

Conversely, Alexander initially thought that the first wave of chariots and cavalry that attacked him were the vanguard of the entire Indian army. However, when he discovered that this was a self-contained unit, he surrounded them with his cavalry and routed them, killing 400, including the son of Porus. The chariots, slipping, sliding and getting stuck in the mud that resulted from the storm, proved easy prey for Alexander's men.

It was not until he heard the reports of the troops retreating from this fight that Porus realized that Alexander himself had crossed with an army, not just a small diversionary force.

Leaving a small contingent of men and elephants to guard against a possible move by Craterus, Porus organized his army for battle. As Darius had done at Gaugamela, Porus picked the battle site, finding a place that was level and relatively free of mud, terrain that favored the chariots, which he placed on his left and right wings ahead of his cavalry.

In his center, as Arrian describes, Porus placed his elephants at intervals "before the whole of the phalanx of infantry, [to] produce terror everywhere among Alexander's cavalry. Besides, he thought that none of the enemy would have the boldness to push themselves into the spaces between the elephants, the cavalry being deterred by the fright of their horses."

Curtius says that the "Macedonians were momentarily checked by the appearance not only of the elephants but also of the Indian king himself. Set at intervals among the troops, the elephants looked like towers from a distance, while Porus himself was of almost super-human size. The elephant which he was riding seemed to increase that size, for it stood above the other animals by as much as Porus towered over the other Indians."

He adds that Alexander was not intimidated.

"When you see me in the thick of the fight, set our right wing in motion and attack the enemy while they are in confusion," Alexander is said to have ordered, speaking specifically to Antigenes, Leonnatus and Tauron, who led the phalanx. "Our [sarissas] are long and sturdy; they can never serve us better than against these elephants and their drivers. Dislodge the riders and stab the beasts. They are a military force of dubious value."

In the opening skirmish, Alexander had raced his cavalry ahead of his phalanx to rout a smaller force. Now he paused to permit his pha-lanx an opportunity to catch up, then catch their breath.

❖

As he studied the enemy battle line, Alexander could see that an attack on the Indian center would be difficult, so he proceeded with cavalry attacks against both wings of Porus's formation. While Alexander and Hephaestion, supported by mounted archers, attacked the Indian left, the cavalry regiments of Coenus and Demetrius would cross the field behind their own phalanx and hit the Indian right. Alexander's pha-lanx would not attack until they saw that the Indians had been dis-rupted by the cavalry charge.

Alexander led the opening attack, hitting the Indian left wing so hard and so fast that they were quickly on the defensive.

Porus, probably seeing Alexander's cavalry in an extended posi-tion relative to his line, ordered his own right wing cavalry to cross ahead of his phalanx to intercept and cut off Alexander's cavalry. This was a huge tactical error because it disrupted his line in the critical first moments of the engagement.

As the Indian cavalry moved left, Coenus arrived in the void they vacated, almost as though out of nowhere, to outflank Porus's right. As Arrian describes it, Coenus "appeared with his men in their rear, according to his instructions. The Indians, observing this, were compelled to make the line of their cavalry face both ways; the largest and best part against Alexander, while the rest wheeled round against Coenus and his forces. This therefore at once threw the ranks as well as the decisions of the Indians into confusion."

Porus's cavalry wheeled and turned, dashing in opposite directions, and Alexander seized the opportunity to strike the confused mass. The Indians attempted to react, but their line was now so disorganized that they couldn't coordinate a counterattack. They broke under Alexander's disciplined onslaught and retreated to the elephant line ahead of their phalanx for a measure of safety.

With this, Porus ordered his elephant line forward.

Alexander's phalanx, having been ordered to move out when they saw confusion in the Indian lines, was now in motion. So too was Porus's phalanx, marching behind the elephants on a collision course with Alexander's infantry.

As Arrian describes, when the two sides smashed into one another, it was an action "unlike any of the previous contests; for wherever the beasts [elephants] could wheel round, they rushed forth against the ranks of infantry and demolished the phalanx of the Macedonians, dense as it was."

The elephants were trained for combat and were an effective weapon—at least at first. Though they were greeted by a hail of arrows and the jabs of the sarissas, they thundered forward, trampling infantrymen, or goring and tossing them with their tusks.

"A particularly terrifying sight was when elephants would snatch up men in armor in their trunks and pass them over their heads to the drivers," Curtius mentions in a colorfully graphic anecdote.

Seeing Alexander's phalanx starting to crumble, the Indian cavalry rallied and counterattacked against Alexander and Coenus. This was probably Porus's best moment of the battle, the moment when the fortunes of war tipped in his favor.

As for Porus personally, Diodorus writes that he was "outstanding in bodily strength beyond any of his followers. . . . His javelins were flung with such force that they were little inferior to the darts of the catapults. The Macedonians who opposed him were amazed at his fighting ability."

It was Porus's moment of glory. He stopped Alexander's phalanx cold, but he never fully grasped the initiative. Curtius reports that the bloody battle involving the phalanxes of both sides see-sawed back and forth until late in the day.

As Arrian writes, Alexander's men, "who far excelled both in strength and military discipline, got the mastery over [the Indian cavalry] the second time, they were again repulsed towards the elephants and cooped up among them."

Curtius tells that Alexander sent the Agrianians and the Thracians against the elephants, "for they were better at skirmishing than at fighting at close quarters," and they hurled a massive volley of arrows against both elephants and drivers. When Alexander's cavalry finally routed the Indian cavalry for the second time and they retreated among the elephants a second time, the Indian position irrevocably unraveled.

"Alexander himself surrounded the whole line with his cavalry, and gave the signal that the infantry should link their shields together so as to form a very densely closed body, and thus advance in phalanx," Arrian says of the moment when Alexander's army seized the initiative. "By this means the Indian cavalry, with the exception of a few men, was quite cut up in the action; as was also the infantry, since the Macedonians were now pressing upon them from all sides. Upon this, all who could do so turned to flight through the spaces which intervened between the parts of Alexander's cavalry."

Though the elephants had been trained for battle, they were subject to fear and confusion, as are well-trained human soldiers. Sometimes at the end of a long day of adrenaline-pumping, hand-to-hand combat, there comes a moment of panic, and panic is contagious. Surrounded by a confused mass of horses, the elephants found it hard to move. "Being a ponderous, practically immobile animal, the elephant was no match for the swift Macedonian horses," says Curtius.

As the big animals found it hard to move, their line broke and they moved in opposite directions, trampling Indians as well as Macedonians. Many had been wounded, and many had lost their drivers to arrows or sarissas. Curtius mentions soldiers attacking the legs of the elephants with axes, and hacking their trunks with swords.

"Frantic with pain, rushing forward at friends and foes alike, they pushed about, trampled down and killed them in every kind of way," writes Arrian of the collapse of the elephant line. "Indians retreating among them were now receiving greater injury from them. But when the beasts were tired out, and were no longer able to charge with any vigour, they began to retire slowly."

Describing the break in the cohesion of Porus's human warriors, Curtius reports "they ignored the king's orders, as commonly happens when men are in confusion and fear usurps the leader's authority, and there were as many commanders-in-chief as there were groups of men wandering about. One was giving orders to form a united line, another to split into companies. Some called for making a stand, others for encircling the enemy rear. There was no common plan of action."

With the battle tipping sharply in Alexander's favor, Craterus undertook his own crossing of the Hydaspes, arriving as the Indian line was in collapse and as Porus's troops began their retreat. They were able to chase down the retreating Indians as Alexander's previously engaged command wrapped up the battle.

Arrian says that Porus's command lost 20,000 infantrymen and 3,000 cavalrymen, while Diodorus gives the more conservative estimate of 12,000 deaths and 9,000 captured. Among those killed were both sons of Porus. Arrian says that all of the chariots were destroyed and all of the elephants not killed were captured.

Arrian goes on to say that Alexander lost 80 infantrymen, 10 mounted archers and 220 cavalrymen, including 20 Companions. Diodorus gives a similar number of cavalry casualties, 280, but says that Alexander lost 700 infantrymen.

Unlike Darius at Issus or Gaugamela, Porus himself never retreated. He remained on the battlefield even after most of those around him died or ran. Diodorus tells that Alexander ordered his archers to concentrate their fire on Porus, but he continued to fight heroically, despite multiple wounds and serious loss of blood. Curtius adds that Porus's elephant was unwounded through most of the battle, though this steed also attacked repeatedly.

Though Curtius does not mention it, Arrian writes that Alexander was wounded by the son of Porus in the opening skirmishes of the battle, but apparently not in a way that slowed him down. Arrian also goes on to say that Alexander's favorite horse, Bucephalas, was mortally wounded. If true, Bucephalas would have been around 18 years old, quite up in years for a warhorse.

At last, as most Indians who were still ambulatory fled the field and only pockets of resistance remained, Porus was approached by an emissary from Alexander, the brother of Taxiles, to suggest that it was time to surrender. Alexander himself was en route, but was delayed by having to change horses when Bucephalas collapsed.

"I know you," Porus said, according to Curtius. "Brother of Taxiles, traitor to his empire and his throne."

With this, the injured Porus hurled a javelin, which penetrated the envoy's chest, killing him.

As Alexander rode up, the injured Porus was starting to fall off his elephant. The driver, who thought his king was consciously trying to dismount, spurred the animal to its knees. Porus fell to the ground, apparently lifeless.

When Alexander ordered Porus stripped, his elephant moved to protect and lift him. The Macedonians troops cut loose with a fusillade of arrows and spears, killing the gallant animal.

As Porus was being placed into a chariot, Alexander saw his eyelids flicker open.

"What folly forced you, knowing as you did the fame of my achievements, to try the fortunes of war, when Taxiles served as an example of my clemency towards those who surrender, an example so close to you?" Alexander asked, according to Curtius.

"Since you ask," replied Porus. "I shall answer you with the frankness your inquiry has granted me. I did not think there was anyone stronger than I. Though I knew my own strength, I had not yet tested yours, and now the outcome of the war has shown you to be the stronger. Even so, being second to you brings me no little satisfaction."

Both Arrian and Plutarch tell that Alexander asked Porus how he expected to be treated by his victor, and that Porus replied that he wanted to be treated as a king.

According to Curtius, Porus added to his earlier comments that Alexander should have discovered by the events of the day "how transitory good fortune is."

CHAPTER 18

Ever Eastward

ALEXANDER COULD BE AS MAGNANIMOUS IN VICTORY AS HE WAS ruthless in combat, and Porus was a beneficiary of this generosity. As Curtius tells, "contrary to everyone's expectations, Alexander made him one of his friends and shortly afterwards, bestowed on him an empire larger than he had formerly held. . . . No trait of Alexander's was more firmly held or enduring than his admiration for genuine excellence and brilliant achievement."

The "empire" to which Curtius refers was actually a satrapy. As he had so often, for example with Mazaeus at Babylon, Alexander frequently handed conquered kingdoms back to their kings as satrapies within his own empire. Paurava became a satrapy, but Porus continued as its ruler. When Alexander found a satrap whom he liked, meaning a powerful leader whom he could trust, he was generous. In this case, he incorporated other lands that he conquered into Porus's satrapy, and the Indian leader actually came out ahead after his defeat at the Hydaspes.

Of course, the more Alexander elevated Porus's importance and emphasized his brilliance as a great leader, the more brilliant Alexander's victory over him became.

Alexander's magnanimity toward Porus extended to asking him to lead troops under Alexander's command in future operations, an invitation that Porus accepted. One might ask whether Porus thought he had a choice.

The Battle of the Hydaspes was an important milestone in Alexander's campaign. It was his first victory in a major battle against a large field army other than a Persian army, and it was sufficiently decisive to give him the same aura of invincibility in India that he had enjoyed elsewhere. It was an important milestone in world history because it marked the extension of a European empire across western and Central Asia and into the Indian Subcontinent.

Alexander himself was in a good mood. He understood the importance of Hydaspes and saw it as the beginning in yet another phase of his campaign that would take him to the edge of the earth. As Curtius puts it, he "was delighted to have won so memorable a victory which, he believed, opened up to him the limits of the East."

To his men, he declared that "any strength the Indians had possessed had been shattered," and he stressed the riches that awaited them in India. As Alexander put it, "the spoils from the Persians were cheap and paltry in comparison."

In the summer of 326 BC, before continuing his campaign, Alexander founded two cities in the vicinity, Nicaea and Bucephala. Also called Alexandria Bucephalas, the latter was named for his horse, who had died at the Hydaspes. The city is thought to have been near the modern Pakistani city of Jhelum. Leaving Craterus to garrison these cities, Alexander continued eastward around the end of June with a force consisting of half of his Companion Cavalry, the Agrianians, archers and selected infantrymen.

❖

As in Asia Minor after the victory at Granicus and in Persia after Gaugamela, Alexander found few to challenge his authority. Arrian writes that the people of the cities and minor kingdoms through which Alexander passed, "came over to him on terms of capitulation; and he thus took thirty-seven cities, the inhabitants of which, where they were fewest, amounted to no less then 5,000, and those of many numbered above 10,000. He also took many villages, which were no less populous than the cities."

Some of these territories were given to Porus to rule. In others, such as the dominion of the king whom Arrian calls Abisares, and whom Diodorus calls Embisaris, Alexander generously allowed the current king to remain in power as his satrap.

Alexander, with a brigade led by Porus, crossed the Acesines River, now known as the Chenab, which like the Hydaspes flows into the Indus. Here Alexander left a contingent of troops commanded by Coenus. According to Arrian, it was also while he was near the Acesines that Alexander received word that the Malhi (known to the Greeks as Malli) people and some of their allies, the Cathaeans and Oxydracians, planned to resist his advance at the city of Sangala, now Sialkot in Pakistan. Alexander reached the city after a three-day march. When Arrian mentions "Oxydracians," whom Curtius calls "Sudracae," the people referenced may be the Kshatriyas, the ancient military order, or warrior caste, in Hinduism. Curtius adds that the Malhi-Sudracae alliance could muster 100,000 troops.

Arrian describes Sangala as being a large city, with a population of around 80,000 at the time. It was located near a shallow lake and built on a low hill, around which the defenders had literally circled their wagons, arranging a "triple palisade of wagons." In his brief mention of this incident, Curtius says they were chariots, not wagons.

Initially, Alexander planned a cavalry assault against the point in the circular enemy line where there seemed to be the fewest wagons, expecting that the enemy would come out to do battle. When the defenders instead returned fire from their defensive positions among the wagons, Alexander dismounted and personally led the phalanx against them.

When the phalanx forced its way through the middle palisade, the enemy retreated within the city walls. Alexander surrounded as much of the city wall as possible and positioned his cavalry around the shallow lake, correctly surmising that the defenders might make an attempt to escape from the city that night by wading across the lake. The first to break out were "cut to pieces" by the cavalry, frightening others, who raced back to the safety of the city. Over the course of several ensuing nights, similar escape attempts were similarly thwarted.

Alexander ordered scaling ladders to be built and miners to begin digging under the walls. As the miners broke through, Alexander's troops and some allies from Porus's army hit the walls with the ladders. According to Arrian, 7,000 defenders were killed, and the rest of the population captured. He adds that fewer than 100 of Alexander's men were killed during the entire siege. When Alexander demolished Sangala to make a statement to those who would defy him, Arrian says that the people of nearby potentates abandoned their cities and fled.

⊞

From Sangala, Alexander marched eastward again, crossing the Hydraotes River (now the Ravi) and passing from present-day Pakistan into what is now India. As in accounts of the march from the Hydaspes to Sangala, his biographers mention that Alexander both besieged and accepted the capitulation of various cities, but they don't go into a great deal of detail. This was probably because such small skirmishes were now considered routine. Diodorus also mentions in passing that Hephaestion undertook a simultaneous campaign elsewhere in which he "conquered a big piece of India."

One local ruler to greet Alexander openly as his conqueror was a man whom the biographers call "Phegeus" after a minor monarch from Greek mythology. After two days of feasting, courtesy of Phegeus, Alexander led his army to the Hyphasis River, now known as the Beas. Beyond the Hyphasis lay the great Ganges River, the widest and deepest of the rivers of India.

It was from Phegeus that Alexander learned the details of what and who lay ahead, between the Ganges and what was perceived as the end of the earth. Here lay two great nations, the Nanda Empire (the Prasii or Tabraesian people) of the Magadha region, corresponding roughly to parts of the modern Indian states of Uttar Pradesh and Bihar; and the Gangaridai Empire (Gandaridae or Ganderite people), corresponding roughly to parts of the modern Indian state of West Bengal and the nation of Bangladesh. The latter lies on the body of water we know as the Bay of Bengal, but that Greco-Macedonian conventional wisdom held to be the Great Outer Sea, or Ocean, that encircled the land mass of the entire world, which lay on a flat plane. Therefore, Gangaridai was the end of the earth.

Alexander's biographers note that the Nanda alone could muster an infantry force of 200,000 men. Diodorus and Curtius mention that they could field 20,000 cavalry and 2,000 chariots, while Plutarch uses much larger figures of 80,000 and 8,000 respectively. The number of trained war elephants varies among these chroniclers—from Curtius' 3,000 to Plutarch's 6,000. When told of the immense army that awaited him, Alexander asked Porus whether these numbers were possible. Porus said he thought them to be correct.

From the banks of the Hyphasis, Alexander looked eastward, pondering the campaign past and the campaign that still lay ahead. He had come 10,000 miles from Macedonia, but he was still 1,000 miles from the Bay of Bengal. Although he had come just a quarter of the distance from the Khyber Pass to the Bay of Bengal, he had, as Arrian calculated, "conquered seven nations in all, containing more than 2,000 cities," since coming to India. The end of the earth seemed tantalizingly close.

He believed, and stated in a speech attributed to him by Arrian, that once he reached the Bay of Bengal, he could sail westward into the Persian Gulf, and around Africa, which he imagined as being about a quarter of its actual size, and therefore easily subjugated. This would take him through the Pillars of Heracles (the Straits of Gibraltar) at the western end of the Mediterranean. From there, Alexander imagined sailing back to Greece, having conquered all of Africa, and all of Asia save for Scythia north of the Syr Darya.

By 325 BC, Alexander's empire was already the largest the world had yet seen, he was still undefeated in battle, and the oracles of both Delphi and Amun had told him that he would conquer the whole world.

CHAPTER 19

The End of the Road

LATE IN THE SUMMER OF 326 BC, ALEXANDER REACHED A CROSSROADS similar to the one he had faced five years earlier after the capture of Persepolis and the death of Darius. Back then, men within his army believed that the mission had been accomplished and thought it was time to go home. Others, who had signed on to beat the Persians, stayed on for the sake of plunder and adventure—or out of loyalty to Alexander. Now these men had reached the point where they too had had enough.

"Alexander observed that his soldiers were exhausted with their constant campaigns," writes Diodorus. "They had spent almost eight years among toils and dangers, and it was necessary to raise their spirits by an effective appeal if they were to undertake the expedition against the Gandaridae. There had been many losses among the soldiers, and no relief from fighting was in sight. The hooves of the horses had been worn thin by steady marching. The arms and armor were wearing out, and Greek clothing was quite gone. They had to clothe themselves in foreign materials, recutting the garments of the Indians. This was the season also, as luck would have it, of the heavy rains. These had been going on for seventy days, to the accompaniment of continuous thunder and lightning."

As Arrian writes, "the spirit of the Macedonians now began to flag, when they saw the king raising one labor after another, and incurring one danger after another."

He goes on to say that "conferences were held throughout the camp, in which those who were the most moderate bewailed their lot, while others respectfully declared that they would not follow Alexander any farther, even if he should lead the way."

It was more of a sit-down strike than a mutiny, but it was not merely a handful of malcontents. It appears to have been virtually universal. They had been fighting, not for Macedonia, or even Greece, but for a polyglot empire with which many could no longer identify.

Plutarch tells of Alexander's reaction—which was to pout. "Alexander shut himself up in his tent from displeasure and wrath and lay there," he writes. "Feeling no gratitude for what he had already achieved unless he should cross the Ganges, nay, counting retreat a confession of defeat."

Curtius and Arrian both recount him calling together his officer corps and addressing them with his point of view.

"Seeing that you no longer follow me into dangerous enterprises with a resolution equal to that which formerly animated you, I have collected you together into the same spot, so that I may either persuade you to march forward with me, or may be persuaded by you to return," Alexander said, according to Arrian. "If indeed the labors which you have already undergone up to our present position seem to you worthy of disapprobation, and if you do not approve of my leading you into them, there can be no advantage in my speaking any further."

Alexander said he believed "to a brave man there is no end to labors except the labors themselves, provided they lead to glorious achievements."

He went on to name all of the places between the Hellespont and the Hyphasis that they had conquered and asked why they wanted to stop now, of all places, and asked rhetorically what they feared.

He then explained what *he* feared. He said that if they gave up now, "many warlike nations are left unconquered beyond the Hyphasis as far as the Eastern Sea, and many besides between these and Hyrcania in the direction of the north wind, and not far from these the Scythian races. Wherefore, if we go back, there is reason to fear that the races which are now held in subjection, not being firm in their allegiance, may be excited to revolt by those who are not yet subdued. Then our many labors will prove to have been in vain; or it will be necessary for us to incur over again fresh labors and dangers, as at the beginning."

He told them that if he was asking them to take risks on his behalf that he was unwilling to take, he could understand their "growing faint in spirit and resolution," but they all understood that he shared the risks of battle, and led his men from the front. Indeed, that fact probably played a major role in why they had followed him as far as they already had.

He invited anyone who wished to do so to speak in rebuttal, but for a long time, there was only silence, with the officers hanging their heads.

Finally, Coenus broke the awkward hush, saying that he would speak on behalf, not of himself, but of all his fellow officers. He observed that he and the others had willingly taken chances and had fought as hard as the situation demanded, facts that were undisputed. He said that the officers and men had followed him thus far, and would continue to follow him, but no longer wholeheartedly.

"Thou thyself see how many Macedonians and Greeks started with thee, and how few of us have been left," Coenus told Alexander, according to Arrian. "All those whose parents still survive, feel a great yearning to see them once more; they feel a yearning after their wives and children, and a yearning for their native land itself; which it is surely pardonable for them to yearn to see again with the honor and dignity they have acquired from thee, returning as great men, whereas they departed small, and as rich men instead of being poor. Do not lead us now against our will; for thou wilt no longer find us the same men in regard to dangers, since free will will be wanting to us in the contests. But, rather, if it seem good to thee, return of thy own accord to thy own land, see thy mother, regulate the affairs of the Greeks, and carry to the home of thy fathers, these victories so many and great."

Most important in Coenus's remarks was that he did not belittle Alexander's strategic vision, nor intimate that it was not worth aspiring to. He specifically told Alexander that he was welcome to resume his empire building.

"Macedonians and Greeks will follow thee, young men in place of old, fresh men in place of exhausted ones, and men to whom warfare has no terrors, because up to the present time they have had no experience of it," Arrian said, suggesting that Alexander refresh, rearm and begin anew. "They will be eager to set out, from hope of future reward. The probability also is, that they will accompany thee with still more zeal on this account, when they see that those who in the earlier expedition shared thy labors and dangers have returned to their own abodes as rich men instead of being poor, and renowned instead of being obscure as they were before. Self control in the midst of success is the noblest of all virtues, oh king, for thou hast nothing to fear from enemies, while thou art commanding and leading such an army as this."

Coenus's remarks drew applause from his fellow officers, but scorn from Alexander, who angrily adjourned the meeting.

The following day, Alexander told them that he intended to continue, but would force no Macedonian to accompany him against his will. Quoting Ptolemy, Arrian writes that Alexander shut himself up in his tent for two days, then offered a sacrifice for passage of the Hyphasis—the omens were not positive. At this point, he called in the Companions closest to him and said sadly that "as all things indicated the advisability of his returning, he made known to the army that he had resolved to march back again."

Arrian describes general rejoicing among the officers, and that "most of them shed tears of joy."

As he often did upon reaching milestone events during his campaign, Alexander staged a celebration and a feast. He then ordered the construction of a dozen towering altars to mark the greatest extent of his empire, and turned about to march back to the Hydaspes, where he had won his greatest victory in the Indian subcontinent.

It was here that Coenus died, stricken by an illness, perhaps a tropical disease endemic to the region.

Alexander arranged a magnificent funeral befitting a general of Coenus's accomplishments. Eulogizing the loyal phalanx commander who had been instrumental in convincing him to withdraw from India, Alexander noted the irony of this death. If any one man deserved to see Macedonia again, Alexander observed, it was Coenus.

CHAPTER 20

A Macedonian against the Malhi

IT IS IMPORTANT TO NOTE THAT ALEXANDER APPROACHED THE NEXT phase of his campaign as exactly that, not as a retreat. Far from having given up empire building, Alexander demonstrated that a major part of his tactical doctrine in 325 BC still involved besieging enemy cities and destroying their armies. In this regard, he seems to have been especially and intensely interested in defeating and subjugating the Malhi, the people with whom he had done battle at Sangala.

Instead of resolving to march back to Greece by way of the route that he had taken coming east, Alexander decided to travel to the Great Outer Sea and visit the lands that bordered it. Rather than turning about 180 degrees, he made a turn of 90 degrees and headed south, by way of the great Indian rivers, to explore them, and to crush the Malhi and others on the way.

At the Hydaspes, Alexander took advantage of the ample availability of lumber in the surrounding forests to undertake a massive shipbuilding program. He still had the vessels, including his 80 triacontors, and to these, he added large transport barges for hauling horses and equipment, as well as troops and camp followers. Though not all of Alexander's army would travel by water, this was probably seen as an efficient way to move sizable amounts of matériel.

To crew these ships and oversee their design and construction, Alexander was able to turn to the Cypriots, Egyptians and Phoenicians, all people from seagoing cultures, who had been part of his army. To command the fleet, he picked Nearchus, an old fiend of Cretan background who had served as Alexander's satrap in Lycia and Pamphylia in 334–333, but who had later rejoined Alexander in Bactria with a contingent of new troops.

Naming Porus as his satrap in the parts of India that he had subdued, Alexander organized his troops for the next phase of the campaign. Craterus was placed in command of a mixed column of infantry and cavalry that would march along the west bank of the Hydaspes, while Hephaestion would command a column of similar composition, along with 200 elephants, on the east bank. Alexander himself would travel on the river, taking his personal bodyguard cavalry, as well as the archers, the Agrianians and the hypaspists.

Thus organized, Alexander departed in the late autumn of 326. Ptolemy's account, as referenced by Arrian, states that the total number of vessels "fell not far short of 2,000." The sight of this fleet on the rivers was to be a source of amazement to the people who watched in pass. Arrian causally mentions that wherever the fleet put ashore, Alexander "received some of the Indians dwelling near into allegiance by surrender on terms of agreement, while he reduced by force those who came into a trial of strength with him."

Five days into the voyage, Alexander faced his first serious adversary in the form of the whitewater rapids below the confluence of the Hydaspes and Acesines rivers. Having lost some of his ships here, Alexander put ashore and rested before sailing south into the area controlled by the Malhi.

Here he linked up with Craterus and Hephaestion and reconfigured the force for offensive action against the Malhi. Alexander had concluded, probably based on intelligence reports and his own earlier experience at Sangala, that the Malhi were predisposed to abandoning their cities rather than defending them. Therefore he developed a plan to cut them off from escape, one that would be only marginally successful.

In advance of the others, Alexander gave Hephaestion's brigade a five-day head start overland with another unit under Ptolemy following in three days. They would intercept any enemy that fled from the bulk of the army, which was led by Alexander himself. Meanwhile, Nearchus would take the fleet downstream ahead of the army. All would rendezvous at the confluence of the Acesines and the Hydraotes.

Taking a brigade that included archers, Agrianians, hypaspists and half the Companion Cavalry, Alexander planned a series of fast attacks against fortified cities. To achieve a measure of surprise at the start of his campaign, Alexander conducted an all-day, all-night forced march through a desert area in order to surprise attack the first city from an unexpected direction.

As he assaulted this city, he sent cavalry under Perdiccas and Cleitus ahead to the next city. Their orders were to blockade this city to prevent anyone from getting out to warn other Malhi cities of Alexander's approach.

Alexander captured the first city, forcing the defenders into the citadel, which he stormed, wiping them out to the last man. Perdiccas, meanwhile, found that the Malhi had abandoned the second city, but he caught up with some of them as they took refuge in the swamps near the Hydraotes. Many of the refugees managed to get across the river, but when Alexander arrived on the scene the following day, he caught a large group in the process of crossing and killed them in the midst of the ford.

On the other side of the Hydraotes, Alexander and his army undertook a lightning operation against Malhi cities that is reminiscent of that four years earlier in the summer of 329 BC against the Scythian cities on the Syr Darya. As Alexander rode to attack one city, he sent Peithon or Demetrius against another.

As Alexander had surmised, most Malhi cities had been abandoned, so the campaign became one of pursuit. Eventually, the retreating Malhi coalesced into a force that Arrian estimates at 50,000, greatly outnumbering Alexander's contingent.

This army took refuge in a city that many scholars have identified as Multan, now the sixth largest city in Pakistan, whose name is derived from the term for "City of the Malhi." A fifteenth-century Flemish manuscript illustration in the collection of the Getty Museum that depicts a scene from this battle is entitled "Alexander Fights in the Town of the Sudracae," suggesting a confusion of the Malhi and Oxydracians, or that their alliance was so close that the names could be used interchangeably.*

❖

Alexander proceeded to seal off the city until the infantry phalanx arrived to surround the walls completely. This done, he was able to camp, to rest his exhausted men and horses, and to plan the siege.

Undertaken the following morning, this operation consisted of simultaneous attacks on opposite walls led by Perdiccas on one side and Alexander on the other. The enemy reaction followed a familiar course. As Alexander's men besieged the walls, the defenders fell back, retreating to their fortified citadel.

Perdiccas was delayed in making his initial assault, but Alexander's contingent forced their way through a gate and began digging to undermine a tower on the citadel.

At this point, Alexander made a critical decision. As Arrian describes, he decided that "the men who carried the [scaling] ladders were too slow, [so he] snatched one from a man who was carrying it, placed it against the wall himself, and began to mount it, crouching under his shield."

Arrian writes that Alexander, followed by Habreas, Leonnatus and Peucestas, got atop the citadel wall and found themselves in close-range sword fights with the defenders. Plutarch says only two accompanied Alexander, not mentioning Habreas. Both biographers do agree that in an effort to get up the wall quickly, some hypaspists overloaded and broke the ladder, momentarily stranding Alexander and the others.

The Malhi apparently figured out that it was Alexander himself, and he became a magnet for a hailstorm of arrows from the adjacent

---

*The specific illustration in the collection of the Getty Museum in Los Angeles depicting Alexander fighting the Malhi is in a Flemish manuscript designated as the Ludwig Manuscript XV 8, Folio 204.

towers. As Arrian describes, "he therefore perceived that if he remained where he was, he would be incurring danger without being able to perform anything at all worthy of consideration; but if he leaped down within the fort he might perhaps by this very act strike the Indians with terror."

The others followed but they immediately found themselves in combat with the enemy in close quarters. Even as they managed to keep swordsmen at bay, they were barraged by arrows. Habreas took one in the forehead and went down.

Alexander was hit in the chest, but as Arrian describes, although he was faint with exhaustion and loss of blood, he defended himself. Leonnatus and Peucestas fell in beside him, defending him even as they were wounded themselves.

Diodorus is alone in reporting that Alexander got back at his assailant, writing that "the Indian who had shot him, thinking that he was helpless, ran up and struck at him; Alexander thrust his sword up into the man's side, inflicting a mortal wound."

Diodorus is also alone in mentioning that Demophon, one of his soothsayers, had warned him not to attack this city because of "numerous portents of a great danger which would come to the king from a wound," but that Alexander had consciously disregarded this advice.

Meanwhile, outside the citadel wall, the other Macedonians were unaware of what was happening. They had seen the men fighting on top of the wall, and had seen them jump off the wall and into the citadel. Apparently the ladder that had broken was the only one available because the troops were forced to scale the wall using makeshift pitons pounded into the adobe wall itself. The first men up alerted the others that Alexander was down and that Leonnatus and Peucestas were in a desperate fight. They intervened as they could and took turns shielding the wounded Alexander.

Elsewhere, efforts to break through one of the citadel gates had succeeded, and troops were able to squeeze through that way. Once in, they massacred the defenders, sparing not even the women and children.

As for Alexander, this was the most serious wound that he ever suffered in battle, and it was one that very nearly killed him. Arrian quotes Ptolemy that "air was breathed out from the wound together with the blood . . . streaming out copiously and without ceasing at every expiration of breath," a condition that modern trauma doctors refer to as an open chest wound or sucking chest wound.

Arrian mentions reports that the arrow was removed either by Perdiccas, at Alexander's bidding, or by the physician Kritodemos of Kos, but does not say which one he believes did so. Plutarch mentions neither, but does say that the arrow head was buried in one of his ribs, was "three fingers broad and four long," and its removal "threw the king into swoons and brought him to death's door."

Kritodemos is widely credited with having saved Alexander's life, doing so by applying some of the same methods as those used by a modern trauma surgeon. These included cutting off the arrow-head and removing it carefully and applying pressure to control the bleeding.[*]

<hr>

Arrian reports that Alexander was sitting up a week later, although Curtius says that the wound was still far from healed. Meanwhile, rumors spread among the various contingents of his army, spread out on either bank and up and down the Acesines, that Alexander was dead. To quell the rumors, Alexander ordered that he be taken by boat to the main encampment at the nexus of the Acesines and Hydraotes, where Hephaestion commanded the army headquarters, and Nearchus that of the fleet.

As Arrian writes, the troops were "still incredulous, thinking, forsooth, that Alexander's corpse was being conveyed on the vessel; until at length he stretched out his hand to the multitude, when the ship was nearing the bank."

<hr>

[*]Dr. Jim Ryan, a former professor of military surgery at Britain's Royal Army Medical College, who served as a surgeon during the Falklands War, analyzed the incident for the British public service television broadcaster, Channel 4. "Kritodemos ordered Alexander stripped naked and the shaft of the arrow cut off," Dr. Ryan says. "The doctor decided that the only way to extract it without the barbs doing greater damage was to enlarge the wound. He was extraordinarily skilful . . . applying his basic good first principles, Kritodemos would have covered the wound, probably to control the hemorrhage. But in so doing, he stopped the open chest wound sucking further—and saved Alexander's life."

When a stretcher was brought to him, he insisted on walking and asked for his horse. "When he was seen again mounting his horse, the whole army re-echoed with loud clapping of hands," Arrian reports, "so that the banks of the river and the groves near them reverberated with the sound."

In turn, Alexander entertained emissaries from the Malhi and Oxydracians who had survived the bloody campaign. According to Arrian, their "leaders of the cities" and "governors of the provinces," also came, bringing gifts and now offering to submit to Alexander's rule, to pay whatever tribute he decreed and to give him hostages. He asked for and received 1,000 hostages, but gave them back in a gesture of largesse. He kept the gifts.

CHAPTER 21

From Great Rivers
to Waterless Wilderness

In the spring of 325 BC, with the Malhi at last subjugated, Alexander, who was still recuperating, resumed his voyage down the Acesines and into the Indus. At their junction, he founded the city known as Alexandria on the Indus, the site of which is thought to be near the modern Pakistani city of Uch. As in other cities across Asia, he left behind colonists, with troops to provide security. Philip, son of Machatas, was made satrap and tasked with constructing the metropolis.

As he traveled downriver, Alexander had continued good luck with most of the local potentates, who offered him tribute and at least paid lip service to their acceptance of him as their sovereign. Those who resisted were quickly and efficiently brought to heel.

Arrian mentions a king called Musicanus, the ruler of the kingdom of the Mushika, who had not sent "the gifts which were suitable for a great king," but who later was "so greatly alarmed that he went as fast as he could to meet him, bringing with him the gifts valued most highly among the Indians, and taking all his elephants."

He apologized for his error of omission, and Alexander pardoned him. As Alexander had so often done, he allowed him to continue ruling his kingdom—but as Alexander's satrap. Craterus was ordered to establish a garrison here, for use as a base of operations for maintaining Alexander's rule in the region.

Having done this, Craterus was ordered to take a sizable portion of the army westward across Arachotia and Carmania, the southern parts of the former Persian Empire, and to rendezvous with Alexander near the mouth of the Persian Gulf. As part of his command, Craterus had the brigades led by Antigenes and Attalus, as well as by the veteran phalanx division commander Meleager. Alexander's elephant herd was also sent overland with Craterus.

Arachotia corresponds to the southern part of modern Afghanistan, south of the area Alexander knew as Drangiana. Now considered to be the equivalent of the southeast Iranian province of Kermān, Carmania was actually much larger, encompassing some or all of adjacent provinces such as Sistān and Baluchistan, as well as the parts of Baluchistan that are within modern Pakistan.

After Alexander had departed downriver and Craterus had headed west across the mountains, Musicanus reportedly revolted. Alexander dispatched Peithon to lead an expedition against the rebel satrap and the cities that had been placed under his satrapy. Many of the latter were captured and destroyed, and Musicanus was arrested and executed along with his coconspirators.

Both Curtius and Plutarch mention Musicanus and, along with Arrian, discuss Alexander's dealing harshly with kings known as Sambus and Porticanus, although Arrian calls the latter Oxycanus. Arrian and Curtius also tell of Alexander's sending Peithon to deal harshly with the ruler—Curtius calls him Moeris—of the place in the northern Indus delta region called Patala (also seen as Patalia or Patalla). Arrian adds that Hephaestion was assigned to fortify the citadel there.

<hr>

By the summer of 325 BC, Alexander and his expedition were working their way though the western part of the Indus delta and beginning to experience signs of their being near the Great Outer Sea. When at last they reached the open waters of the Indian Ocean, Alexander put ashore to offer the appropriate sacrifices to the gods, especially Poseidon, the god of the sea. He then proceeded to conduct an extensive reconnaissance of the various mouths of the Indus, making note of the two largest, possibly thinking of future military operations.

Alexander then divided his forces at Patala, sending the larger part of his army toward Babylon aboard the fleet with Nearchus, first along the shore of the Great Outer Sea, then upriver on the Tigris or Euphrates. Meanwhile, he personally led a contingent overland, heading toward Babylon by way of Persepolis on a route parallel to, but several hundred miles south of, the overland route that Craterus was then taking. This route would take him through the ancient region known as Gedrosia, which includes what is now southern Baluchistan and much of the Iranian coastal province of Hormozgan. This area is characterized by several hundred miles of arid desert, then called the Gedrosian Desert, and now the Makran Desert.

Alexander departed Patala in the late summer of 325, but Nearchus remained until fall, waiting for a change in the prevailing wind, which would make sailing easier. Having gone ahead, part of the time of Alexander's contingent was taken up with digging wells so that the fleet could put ashore for fresh water. This was ironic, given that Alexander himself was heading into the longest stretch of waterless wasteland he had yet experienced.

As had been the case as they made their way down the rivers, Alexander's troops passed through the dominions of various kings and tribal leaders, some of whom were subjugated by force, others of whom paid tribute to Alexander in order to avoid the sting of that force. As in the earlier accounts of his travels and campaigns farther upriver, Alexander's biographers mention little or nothing in the way of details other than naming tribes such as the Arabitians and Oritians.

❖

Given Alexander's passion for intelligence, he should have known what awaited them in the Gedrosian Desert. Perhaps he thought his oracle-confirmed invincibility applied to natural phenomena, or perhaps he thought that after a dozen years in the field he had seen it all.

As Arrian writes, "most of the historians of Alexander's reign assert that all the hardships which his army suffered in Asia were not worthy of comparison with the labours undergone here."

The experience was terrible. Despite the fact that it was a month or more past the hottest part of the summer, Arrian describes "scorching heat and lack of water [that] destroyed a great part of the army, and especially the beasts of burden; most of which perished from thirst and some of them even from the depth and heat of the sand, because it had been thoroughly scorched by the sun."

Plutarch adds that "grievous diseases, wretched food, parching heats, and, worst of all, famine, destroyed them, since they traversed an untilled country of men who dragged out a miserable existence, who possessed but few sheep and those of a miserable sort, since the sea-fish which they ate made their flesh unsavory and rank."

Along the way, Alexander learned from the people living in the area that this same route had been taken by two centuries earlier by Cyrus the Great when he attempted to invade India, and that he gave up and escaped the desert with just seven men. With this in mind, Arrian can't help but mention "Alexander pursued this route, not from ignorance of the difficulty of the journey [although Nearchus claims that he was], but because he heard that no one had ever hitherto passed that way with an army and emerged in safety."

After 60 days in the desert, the army finally reached the relative security of Pura, the Gedrosian capital, possibly located in the vicinity of the modern Iranian cities of Bampur or Fahraj. Here Plutarch reports that they "had all things in abundance."

Alexander had emerged with more than seven men, but with a badly depleted and exhausted force. By all accounts, most of the livestock was lost. The exact human death toll is not known, but Plutarch says "not even the fourth part of his fighting force" survived the ordeal.

Alexander rested his weary army for a time in Pura, where they reveled in the excess of wine, food, singing and dancing after two months of privation. Afterward, their spirits somewhat restored, they marched onward into Carmania. Here, in about December 325 BC, Alexander linked up with Craterus and his command, with whom he had apparently been in communication via courier.

Traveling on a far northerly route out of the Indus valley, Craterus had been in contact with Alexander's Central Asia dominions across what is now Afghanistan and northern Iran. He had also brought with him to the rendezvous with Alexander several of the satraps from these dominions. These included Stasanor, then the satrap of Aria and Zarangia, and Pharismanes, then the satrap of Parthia and Hyrcania. Having heard that Alexander was coming by way of Gedrosia, they had correctly predicted his loss of livestock and brought him herds of horses and camels. Also accompanying Craterus were military leaders posted in the region, who came with contingents of troops.

⬛

In the first weeks of 324 BC, Alexander and Craterus, together with the combined and refreshed army, marched eastward, where they met Nearchus and the fleet on the coast of the Strait of Hormuz, at a place that Diodorus calls Salmus, near the modern Iranian port of Bandar Abbas.

A very trying year had passed since Alexander had begun his voyage down the Hydaspes River and undertaken the long march that his men hoped would eventually take them back to Greece and Macedonia.

Plutarch relates that Alexander was pleased to see Nearchus and that he eagerly discussed his frequently mentioned desire to sail around Arabia and Africa and into the Mediterranean.

However, as Plutarch adds, "the increasing difficulties of his march back, his wound among the Malhi, and the losses in his army, which were reported to be heavy, led men to doubt his safe return [by such an endeavor]. . . . In a word, restlessness and a desire for change spread everywhere."

The troops were marching homeward, and most had little interest in Alexander's dream of circumnavigating the known world.

CHAPTER 22

Back to Persis

AFTER COMING ASHORE IN THE EARLY WEEKS OF 324 BC FOR HIS conference with Alexander at Salmus on the shores of the Strait of Hormuz, Nearchus departed with the fleet, heading in a northwesterly direction through the Persian Gulf, bound for the mouth of the Tigris. Alexander and the army went roughly in the same direction, marching overland toward Persepolis. The two would meet again in Susa before continuing to Babylon. Hephaestion headed the larger part of the army, leading the supply train and the elephants along the coastal road, while Alexander took a lighter mobile force by a parallel inland route.

A few weeks later, as he approached Persepolis, Alexander paused at nearby Pasargadae to pay his respects at the tomb of Cyrus the Great. Since Alexander considered himself to be the king of Persia, he thought of Cyrus as his predecessor. The mausoleum, as Arrian described it, was a small stone building, with a golden coffin containing the body of Cyrus, and a couch with feet of wrought gold on a "carpet of Babylonian tapestry with purple rugs."

Alexander was in for a shock. According to Aristobulus, as quoted by Arrian, "he found it dug through and pillaged. . . . everything else had been carried off except the coffin and couch. They had even maltreated the king's body; for they had torn off the lid of the coffin and cast out the corpse."

Plutarch tells that Alexander "put to death the perpetrator of the deed, although the culprit was a prominent Macedonian native of Pella, by name Polymachus."

Alexander then ordered that the inscription on the tomb, rendered in Persian, be repeated in Greek. According to Plutarch, it read "Oh man, whosoever thou art and whencesoever thou comest, for I know that thou wilt come, I am Cyrus, and I won for the Persians their empire. Do not, therefore, begrudge me this little earth which covers my body."

Arrian tells that the inscription made reference to the kingship of Asia, reading "Oh man, I am Cyrus, son of Cambyses, who founded the empire of the Persians, and was king of Asia. Do not therefore grudge me this monument."

In any case, as Plutarch says, Alexander was "deeply affected" by these words, which reminded him of "the uncertainty and mutability of life."

Aristobulus tells that it was he himself commissioned by Alexander to restore the tomb, to "put into the coffin the parts of the body still preserved, to put the lid on."

Little is said in the chronicles of Alexander's second visit to Persepolis and his uneventful east-to-west passage though the Persian Gates, although this certainly must have brought back memories.

Mixed with the memories were his plans for the immediate future when he returned to the great city of Susa. He arrived there less than two months after his rendezvous with Nearchus at Salmus, realizing that he was soon to leave the heart of the former Persian Empire, perhaps for the last time.

Alexander had decided that the best way to fully integrate his empire was for his Macedonian officers to marry into the Persian nobility. Curtius reports that Alexander himself said that he wanted to erase the line between conqueror and conquered in order to integrate the blood lines of his entire empire. He imagined that the empire would one day be populated by a single, amalgamated ethnicity. This plan must have raised some eyebrows among the more conservative Macedonians.

Nevertheless, Arrian notes that more than 10,000 such weddings occurred in Susa in the spring of 324 BC. He goes on to list a number of the weddings, most notably those of the two daughters of Darius, who were now in their mid-teens. The youngest daughter, Drypteis, was wed to Alexander's lifelong friend Hephaestion, said also to have been Alexander's longtime male lover. Alexander himself married the eldest daughter, the girl known as Stateira, but whom Arrian calls Barsine. By this time, Alexander had been married for three years to the Bactrian princess, Roxana, who was in her early twenties. His mistress, the other Barsine, who was the mother of his illegitimate son Heracles, had not been mentioned in the chronicles for some time. She would have been in her late thirties. Alexander was 31 at the time he took his second wife.

Arrian states that "the weddings were celebrated after the Persian manner," while Plutarch reports that 9,000 guests—including perhaps Roxana—attended Alexander's own wedding. He adds that the affair was "amazingly splendid, and the host paid himself the debts which his guests owed, the whole outlay amounting to 9,870 talents," or more than $150 million.

Meanwhile, Arrian states that Alexander also "thought it a favorable opportunity to liquidate the debts of all the soldiers who had incurred them," and goes on to say that this amounted to 20,000 talents. If he had hoped this would offset the prejudice the Macedonian troops continued to feel against Alexander's having embraced Persian customs, he was wrong.

As can be expected, the weddings accentuated the long-simmering displeasure with Alexander's adoption of Asian manners. These feelings seem to have been exacerbated by the Persian-style ceremonies, and the fact that Persian families—still considered barbarians by the most conservative Macedonians—were now relatives of Macedonians. The weddings exposed that longstanding rift in Alexander's officer corps like a bare nerve.

Alexander was well aware of these feelings when he ordered the army to pull out of Susa and continue its march through Mesopotamia toward Babylon in the late spring of 324.

As Hephaestion took most of the army overland, Alexander traveled by boat, going down the Eulaeus River (now called Dez), which flows into Karun River, and eventually into the Shatt al-Arab (in Persian, Arvand), which is formed by the confluence of the Tigris with the Euphrates, near to the modern Iran-Iraq border. Here, the two linked up again for the last leg of the trip up the Tigris. Shortly thereafter, the entire army camped at a place called Opis, thought to be near the Diyala River in the modern Iraqi province of the same name.

As he had done in the fall of 331 BC in the Sittacene, and in 330 at Ecbatana, Alexander chose this place away from the distractions of a major city to reorganize his command. As before, the reorganization was timed to head off what Alexander recognized as discontent in the ranks.

Even before the reorganization, everyone recognized that the army was an international one that had long since ceased to be Greco-Macedonian. Arrian mentions Arachotian, Arian, Bactrian, Parthian, Sogdian, Zarangian, and even Persian cavalry having been integrated into the ranks. Arrian adds that this integration was never fully accepted by many of the Greco-Macedonian troops, and this may have played a role in the unhappiness of the Macedonian core of the army.

If another potential mutiny was actually brewing, Alexander boldly nipped it in the bud by simply disbanding the Macedonian core of his onetime Greco-Macedonian army, dismissing all who wished to go home.

Craterus, described by Arrian as "the man most faithful to him, and whom he valued equally with himself," was then tasked with leading the discharged troops back to Macedonia, where he would assume command of all Greco-Macedonian forces west of the Hellespont.

Alexander then began to reorganize his remaining officer corps, bringing more Persians and others into the higher ranks. Diodorus adds that "Alexander secured replacements from the Persians equal to the number of these soldiers whom he had released, and . . . in all respects he showed the same confidence in them as in the Macedonians."

Curtius surmises that Alexander could now afford to further downsize his field army because he was in an occupation mode, not fighting a war of conquest. Meanwhile, he had already established garrisons all across Asia to take care of the military requirements in the various corners of his empire.

⊞

In about October of 324 BC, Alexander led his reconfigured army eastward from Opis to spend a few weeks in the wealthy city of Ecbatana before continuing to Babylon. The catalyst for this trip may simply have been Alexander's desire to pay an official visit to another of the major Persian cities, as he had just done in Persepolis and Susa. However, mention is made by his biographers of Alexander's having visited a place en route where there were many thousands of horses. Perhaps the trip involved logistical planning for future military campaigns.

In any case, the visit to Ecbatana was characterized by a party atmosphere, with great festivity, sporting events and much drinking and eating. In the course of this, Hephaestion fell ill. A week later, as Plutarch writes, he "sat down to breakfast, ate a boiled fowl, drank a huge cooler of wine, fell sick, and in a little while died."

All of the chronicles tell of Alexander's having taken the death of his friend and lover quite hard, and plans were put in motion for a lavish funeral to be held in Babylon.

Both Plutarch and Arrian mention that after Alexander and his army left Ecbatana, they undertook a brief, but bloody, winter counterinsurgency campaign against a nomadic people living in the Zagros Mountains.

Called Kossaeans by Ptolemy (using the Greek spelling), and Cossaeans in the later biographies published in Rome, these people may have been descendants of the Kassites, who had controlled remnants of the old Babylonian Empire for a time around the fifteenth century BC. These people, like the Uxians, whom Alexander subdued in these same mountains in 331, were a tribal federation that had never been fully subjugated by the Persians, and this inspired Alexander to accomplish what they could not. As Diodorus puts it, they "had remained unconquered throughout the whole period of the Persian kingdom, and now they were too proudly self confident to be terrified of the Macedonian arms."

It is not known whether this had been planned before the march to Ecbatana, or whether it came up suddenly. It is only known that the Kossaeans were soundly defeated. Diodorus tells that Alexander "seized the routes of access into their country before they were aware of it, lay waste most of Cossaea, was superior in every engagement, and both slew many of the Cossaeans and captured many times more." As with other defeated armies, some Kossaean troops wound up serving in Alexander's own army.

This campaign would hardly warrant a mention in the long annals of Alexander's counterinsurgency skirmishing, but for the fact that it was his last battle, capping more than a decade of nonstop victories. As Arrian said of the Kossaean campaign, "no military enterprise which Alexander undertook was ever unsuccessful."

CHAPTER 23

Final Days in Babylon

ALEXANDER HAD FIRST VISITED BABYLON AFTER GAUGAMELA IN 331 BC and had been described in Babylonian cuneiform as the King of the World. When he returned in the spring of 323, he had become accustomed to proskynesis and other forms of idolization that many—especially the Macedonians—considered fit only for gods. Alexander was still about 30 miles from Babylon when he was met by Nearchus, who had just arrived from the Persian Gulf by way of the Euphrates with, according to Arrian, "two Phoenician quinqueremes, three quadriremes, 12 triremes, and 30 triacontors."

Nearchus explained that he had been approached by group of Chaldean scholars who Diodorus describes as having a "great reputation in astrology and [who were] accustomed to predict future events by a method based on age-long observations."

Diodorus goes on to say that their leader, "whose name was Belephantes, was not bold enough to address the king directly but secured a private audience with Nearchus."

All of the accounts agree that the Chaldeans urged Nearchus to warn Alexander not to enter the city, because great danger, even death, awaited him there. Apparently, Nearchus took them to see Alexander. Diodorus tells that Alexander was alarmed and disturbed, as he understood the "high reputation of these people," but Plutarch says that Alexander paid them no heed. While Alexander had traditionally placed a great deal of stock in the prognostications of his own soothsayers, he was apparently quite dismissive of the Chaldeans. Arrian tells that he replied by quoting Euripides, who said "The best of seers is he who guesses well."

According to Aristobulus, as quoted in other accounts, Belephantes told Alexander that if he must enter the city, he should do so from the west, rather than from the east. Figuring this to be a simple compromise, Alexander changed direction. However, he found this approach to be through swamps, so he reverted to the original plan. Plutarch tells that when Alexander reached the city, "he saw many ravens flying about and clawing one another, and some of them fell dead at his feet."

Despite these omens, Alexander was welcomed into the city graciously. As Diodorus writes, "as on the previous occasion [in 331] the population received [Alexander's] troops hospitably, and all turned their attention to relaxation and pleasure, since everything necessary was available in profusion."

Alexander held court at the royal palace of Nebuchadnezzar, where he received a stream of official visits from delegations representing the satraps from throughout his dominions, as well as emissaries from Greece. There was even some talk of his mother coming out to Babylon. Alexander had been in touch with Olympias by letter throughout his campaigns, but the two would never see one another again.

Meanwhile, Alexander also undertook infrastructure projects. Belephantes had told Alexander that he could reverse the bad omens by rebuilding the temple of Belus, which was probably the great ziggurat known as Etemenanki. He had ordered this to be done on his earlier visit to Babylon, but it had not been accomplished. Arrian mentions that the Chaldeans had been embezzling the money appropriated for the project and that Alexander came to think this had something to do with why they wanted him to stay out of Babylon.

In any case, Alexander now made the project a high priority. The site was in such disrepair that Alexander ordered everything cleared away and a new temple constructed from the ground up. It never happened.

Another major engineering project was the dredging of a great harbor and the building of a dockyard facility on the Euphrates so that the river city could be turned into a major seaport that would be to the Persian Gulf what Phoenicia had been to the Mediterranean.

Alexander also undertook a major shipbuilding project in anticipation of future military campaigns in Arabia and Africa. As Arrian points out, he "made these preparations of the fleet to attack the main body of the Arabs, under the pretext that they were the only barbarians of this region who had not sent an embassy to him or done anything else becoming their position and showing respect to him." He had been told that Arabia was abundant in spices and herbs, that myrrh and frankincense grew on trees, and cinnamon was cut from the shrubs.

<hr />

When he was last in Babylon, Alexander had given his troops several weeks of R&R, but this time, he was anxious to resume his campaign. Shortly after his arrival in about April 323 BC, he began organizing his army for the renewed campaign. Arrian tells in great detail that each company was led by three Macedonian officers of descending rank, commanding 12 Persians and another Macedonian. He says that the Macedonians were "armed in their hereditary manner," with swords and spears, but that the Persians included both archers and javelin throwers.

As part of an initial reconnaissance in preparation for the campaign, Alexander sent tricantors captained by Archias and Androsthenes on separate expeditions to follow the Arabian coastline (modern Kuwait and Saudi Arabia) for some distance. Alexander himself explored the tributaries of the Euphrates, as well as ancient canals that intersect it.

His coming and going from Babylon without incident throughout April and May of 323 BC convinced Alexander that the predictions of Belephantes were without merit. However, dark omens were still gathering on his roof, like the ravens described by Plutarch.

There are many accounts of a mysterious man who slipped quietly into Alexander's throne room while he was away exercising or getting a drink. The man dressed himself in Alexander's robe and diadem and seated himself on Alexander's throne. When asked who he was, he paused a long time, then told Alexander and his entourage that his name was Dionysus, and that he was sent by the deity Serapis, a Greek equivalent of one aspect of the Egyptian Osiris, the god of the afterlife. This greatly unnerved Alexander.

Most accounts say that Alexander simply sent him away, but Arrian says that he tortured the man and then offered sacrifices to offset the bad omen.

Apparently however, Alexander was sufficiently assured that the omens were in check, because he picked a date around the end of May for the beginning of the Arabian campaign. The infantry would march one day before Alexander himself led the rest of the army downriver aboard the fleet. It seems counterintuitive that he would have begun a major military operation on the Arabian Peninsula in May, when temperatures were rising from unbearable to deadly, but this is what Arrian reports.

⬧

A few days after the incident of the strange man, and four days before the infantry was to march, Alexander sat down for a relaxing evening of eating and drinking with his friends, possibly at a party given in honor of Nearchus. As often happened, the drinking continued late into the night.

Diodorus tells the story that "he drank much unmixed wine in commemoration of the death of Heracles, and finally, filling a huge beaker, downed it at a gulp. Instantly he shrieked aloud as if smitten by a violent blow and was conducted by his Friends, who led him by the hand back to his apartments."

Plutarch disputes this, stating that "this did not come upon him after he had quaffed a 'bowl of Heracles,' nor after he had been seized with a sudden pain in the back as though smitten with a spear; these particulars certain writers felt obliged to give, and so, as it were, invented in tragic fashion a moving finale for a great action."

Arrian reports that Alexander may have been on his way to bed on his own when he happened on Medius, a Companion Cavalry commander, who invited him to yet another party. According to Arrian, he apparently passed out or fell asleep at Medius's home, woke up, took a bath and then slept through the day. After supper that night, he again started drinking and stayed up most of a second night of his binge.

The following morning, after 30 hours spent either drinking or sleeping off hangovers, Alexander reportedly felt feverish. He was carried on a couch to make his daily sacrifices, and as Arrian puts it, then "lay down in the banqueting hall until dusk."

The narratives of Ptolemy and Aristobulus upon which later accounts are based, tell that over the coming days Alexander grew gradually more feverish and slept most of the time when he was neither bathing nor offering his daily sacrifices. Aristobulus says that "he had a raging fever, and that when he got very thirsty he drank wine, whereupon he became delirious."

Periodically, he did make time to call his officers to his bedside to discuss the departures for the upcoming Arabian operation. When the date finally arrived, and he was still very ill, he ordered the troops to remain at the gates.

Arrian reports that when his soldiers passed him, "he was unable to speak; yet he greeted each of them with his right hand, raising his head with difficulty and making a sign with his eyes."

Gradually he became despondent, certain that he was doomed. Another story retold by Arrian has it that Alexander tried to throw himself into the Euphrates, "so that he might disappear from men's sight, and leave among the men of aftertimes a more firmly-rooted opinion that he owed his birth to a god, and had departed to the gods."

It was Roxana who stopped him from this.

Ultimately, though, he could not be saved.

❖

As Plutarch writes, Alexander III of Macedonia died toward evening on the 28th of the month of Daesius, which corresponds to the tenth or eleventh of June in 323 BC, having lingered for about 14 days from when he first started feeling the symptoms. He was a month short of his 33rd birthday.

The cause was not that he had drunk himself to death, although it appears that he was prone binge drinking, as it is mentioned on a number of occasions. Indeed, the murder of Cleitus the Black is a notable example of a drunken excess gone too far.

In fact, the exact cause of death will probably never be known, although there has been much speculation. As so often happens in our own day when celebrities die young, there were a number of conspiracy theories involving his being poisoned. Cassander, the son of Antipater, Alexander's regent in Macedonia, who had just arrived in Babylon, is a leading suspect because both father and son now coveted Alexander's power. All of Alexander's biographers report the possibility of his having been poisoned, but most discount this, and there is no substantial proof. Indeed, poison victims usually don't take two weeks to die.

Some have suggested that his death might have been traceable to residual effects of the injuries suffered in the fight with the Malhi, but the two weeks of fever and other symptoms suggest disease. Indeed, the swamps around Babylon would have been a breeding ground for many such possibilities. Writing in the *New England Journal of Medicine* in June 1998, Dr. David Oldach of the University of Maryland School of Medicine studies the symptoms in detail, and suggests a parasite-borne disease such as malaria or typhoid fever.

In the December 2003 issue of *Emerging Infectious Diseases*, published by the Centers for Disease Control and Prevention, John Marr of the Virginia Department of Health and Charles Calisher of Colorado State University propose West Nile Virus as the culprit. They mention that this disease "was not considered by previous authors as the cause of Alexander's death, possibly because it has only recently emerged globally . . . [but] West Nile virus infections in vertebrates may have been occurring in the Middle East for centuries."

Having recalled Plutarch's mention of the raven falling dead at Alexander's feet, they remark that "amplification occurs in mosquitoes and birds several months before the virus spills over into [humans]. . . . We now know that unexplained bird die-offs can presage human cases of disease caused by West Nile virus. In 323, a similar event might have been considered an omen of Alexander the Great's death. In this instance, the oracles would have been correct."

Alexander left no details of where he wished to be buried, but when his body was placed in a multilayered gold sarcophagus, it was taken to Egypt by Ptolemy. It arrived in Alexandria by way of a few years in Memphis, where it remained on public display until about the third century AD. Here it is said to have been visited by Julius Caesar and a number of Roman emperors, including Augustus and Caligula. The location of the tomb in Alexandria and the present whereabouts of the sarcophagus are the subject of ongoing speculation.

CHAPTER 24

What Was and What Might Have Been

By the time Philip II of Macedonia died in 336 BC, he had assembled an empire in Greece and adjoining lands that was unprecedented in scope. With that as his starting point, Philip's young heir, Alexander, built an empire that was more than a dozen times larger. Alexander spent his last days and hours as a military man planning a campaign into Arabia that never materialized. The expansion of his empire through Arabia and Africa to the Pillars of Hercules never happened. When Alexander died, there was no similar ambitious young man to carry on his work. His first wife, Roxana, was pregnant at the time of his death, and his first legitimate heir, Alexander IV, was born two months later.

The power struggle began almost immediately.

Diodorus says that when asked, "To whom do you leave the kingdom?" Alexander had replied, "to the strongest." However, it has been pointed out that the Greek phrase meaning "to the strongest" is *toi kratistoi* while Alexander might actually have said *toi Krateroi* meaning "to Craterus." In fact, neither Craterus, nor strength—as Alexander would have defined it—played much of a role in the matter of succession.

Diodorus writes that when Alexander "despaired of life, he took off his ring and handed it to Perdiccas," who had once saved his life in battle. He headed a list of many candidates who would come and go in discussions of succession.

Plutarch reports that Roxana, being jealous of Alexander's second wife, Stateira, summoned her from Susa with a forged letter and killed her with the help of Perdiccas. It is possible she was also pregnant with an heir that would be a rival to Roxana's son.

Alexander IV had clear title to the throne, but being underage, power was wielded by a regency. Initially, Perdiccas shared this power with Alexander's half-brother Arrhidaeus, who took the name Philip III after their joint father. However, Perdiccas was assassinated shortly thereafter and Philip III was considered feeble-minded, so the power struggle dragged on—with an increasing cast of successors, known as the Diadochi, who eventually divided up his empire.

Among the Diadochi, Cassander is notable because in the course of consolidating his power in Greece and Macedonia, he killed Alexander's mother, Olympias, in 316, as well as both Roxana and young Alexander IV, in about 309.

The others who emerged from the power struggle with important slices of the empire were former generals. Ptolemy became sovereign of Egypt, where he took the title pharaoh, founded the long-lived Ptolemaic Dynasty and ruled until 283. Ptolemy's lover, Thaïs, who had been responsible for the big fire in Persepolis in 330, was still with him as one of his wives. Cleopatra, the legendary queen of the Nile, and the lover of Julius Caesar and Marc Antony, was Ptolemy's descendant.

Lysimachus, one of Alexander's bodyguards, ended up with Asia Minor as well as Thrace. Seleucus, named as satrap of Babylon in 323, went on to found the Seleucid Empire, which included Alexander's Persian and Central Asian dominions. He allied himself with Chandragupta Maurya, the first king to successfully unite most of the Indian subcontinent into one empire.

Much has been written about the wars of the Diadochi and of their kingdoms. Less has been written about might have happened had Alexander lived.

Alexander's career of conquest spanned a dozen years. Had he continued campaigning for that same period of time, he would have been just 44, still a relatively young man. Would he have continued?

He certainly would have campaigned in Arabia as planned, and he probably would have gone beyond. As Arrian writes, "it seems to me that Alexander was insatiably ambitious of ever acquiring fresh territory."

After Arabia, Africa would probably have been next. He had often mentioned sailing around the southern shore of the continent, which was then believed to be a latitude only slightly south of that of the Arabia peninsula. He would have been in for a big surprise and enormous challenges as the true scale of the continent was revealed. If he had tried a shortcut across the continent at the latitude of southern Arabia, it would have put him into the Sahara Desert, which would have made the Gedrosian Desert seem like a stroll through the palace.

Following Africa's coastline, he would have reached the jungles of equatorial Africa, and would have found it hard to move ashore with an army, so he might have defaulted to using only his fleet. A circumnavigation of Africa by Europeans 2,000 years before the Portuguese at the end of the fifteenth century, especially by someone as interested in local culture as Alexander, would have changed the course of history.

Other potential campaigns might also have been possible. In 327 BC, Arrian reports that Alexander had said "when Asia was in his power he would return to Greece, and thence make an expedition with all his naval and military forces to the eastern part of the Euxine [Black] Sea through the Hellespont."

In his last months, Alexander had sent Heraclides, along with a company of shipwrights, to begin cutting timber from the Hyrcanian mountains to construct ships of war because, as Arrian writes, "he was very desirous of discovering with what sea the one called the Hyrcanian or Caspian unites; whether it communicates with the water of the Euxine Sea . . . just as he had discovered that the Persian Sea, which was called the Red Sea, is really a gulf of the Great Sea."

During his final days in Babylon, Alexander was actively considering expeditions far beyond Asia, Arabia and Africa. Many were countries that, like so many before, were willing to submit as a matter of course, but this only whetted his appetite for more. Diodorus writes, "from practically all the inhabited world came envoys on various missions, some congratulating Alexander on his victories, some bringing him crowns, other concluding treaties of friendship and alliance, many bringing handsome presents, and some prepared to defend themselves against accusations."

Arrian names the Bruttii, Lucanians and Tyrrhenians from Italy, and Diodorus tells of Alexander's receiving emissaries from across North Africa, as well as Europeans, including the Gauls, "whose people became known then first in the Greek world."

Arrian mentions Alexander's interest in the ancient city of Gadeira, or Gades, now Cadiz in Spain. He says that Alexander intended to go to Sicily and the Iapygian Cape (Apulia, or the heel of Italy), "for the fame of the Romans spreading far and wide was now exciting his jealousy."

Arrian recalls that both Aristus and Asclepiades wrote of the Roman Republic's having "sent an embassy" to Alexander, although he disagrees. Arrian does not think it likely that the Romans would have reached out to Alexander "when they were not compelled to do so by fear or any hope of advantage, being possessed as they were beyond any other people by hatred to the very name and race of despots."

Had Alexander lived, would he have found himself engaged in combat with the Romans in Italy? Had his unbroken string of victories brought him victory in such a contest, history would certainly have followed a different course.

Lasting Legacy

ALEXANDER ACHIEVED IMMORTALITY. WITHIN THE WORLD KNOWN TO him, much of which he had conquered, he became a legend in his own time. With the passing years, this legend only grew. In succeeding centuries, his name continued to come up each time great generals were discussed. The Romans had a great fascination with him. More than 400 years after his death, Arrian wrote that there was "no race of men, no city, nor even a single individual to whom Alexander's name and fame had not penetrated."

Even today, war colleges throughout the world study Alexander's campaigns, and few top-ten lists of great generals omit his name. Among the generals of classical antiquity, only Julius Caesar is mentioned as often, although Caesar considered himself pale in comparison. In his biography of Caesar, contained within his *Lives of Noble Greeks and Romans,* Plutarch writes that "when he was at leisure and was reading from the history of Alexander, he was lost in thought for a long time, and then burst into tears."

When asked by his friends why he was crying, Caesar replied, "Do you not think it is matter for sorrow that while Alexander, at my age, was already king of so many peoples, I have as yet achieved no brilliant success?"

Caesar still had much to accomplish, but he would have a quarter of a century longer life than Alexander in which to do it!

When speaking of his impact on Western cultural history, a fact often cited is that Socrates taught Plato, who taught Aristotle, who taught Alexander. The implication is that the three founding fathers of Western philosophical thought led directly to Alexander. He is mentioned in the Qur'an, as well as in the Bible. For example, the First Book of the Maccabees, a deuterocanonical book written toward the end of the second century BC and included in the Bible used by some Christian denominations, explicitly includes Alexander.

In winning his impressive dozen-year string of victories, Alexander exhibited the best traits of a tactician. He studied the terrain and he studied his enemy. He not only used his enemy's weaknesses to his advantage, he exploited his enemy's strengths. He developed winning tactics, especially involving fast, mobile cavalry, to literally ride circles around his enemy. He kept an open mind, allowing the circumstances to dictate actions, rather than staying with a fixed plan after it was superseded by events. As Arrian writes, he was "very clever in getting the start of his enemies, and snatching from them their advantages by secretly forestalling them, before any one even feared what was about to happen."

He also exhibited the best traits of a battlefield leader. He was audacious, aggressive and fearless. He led from the front, in the vanguard of the opening cavalry charge, or as the first man up a scaling ladder. His indisputable charisma made him a man whom his men wanted to follow into a fight. Arrian observes that he was "renowned for rousing the courage of his soldiers, filling them with hopes of success, and dispelling their fear in the midst of danger by his own freedom from fear."

Alexander's skill as a combat commander was matched by his skill as a military engineer. His daring use of engineering surprised foes across the known world. In terms of his physical legacy, we may not know the location of his sarcophagus, but we can pull up Google Earth today and look at the remnant of the causeway he built during his defeat of Tyre.

As brilliant as he was in the field, he is best remembered for his strategic vision. No one since Cyrus the Great thought as big and followed through on it, and Alexander built a much larger empire than

Cyrus did. Alexander's empire was larger than any the world had yet seen. He almost made it to the place he understood to be the ends of the earth.

Alexander was also a visionary political leader. He built an infrastructure, created a political structure to administer his empire, and established cities, some of which survive to this day. His vision of an integrated society strengthened and helped to unify his empire. Though he was criticized during his lifetime for too readily embracing local customs, his fusion of disparate cultures ran both ways. The influence of Greek cultural ideals touched the far corners of Alexander's empire, and the resulting Hellenistic civilization defined the course of cultural history in important parts of three continents.

His farsighted view of an ethnically integrated society was millennia ahead of its time. It is hard to underestimate the grand vision embodied by what he did at Susa in 324 BC. He saw a world in which all people would have a common blood line and share common ideals. He arranged 10,000 marriages between Macedonian officers and Asian women, and at the same time, he brought 30,000 Persians boys into his army, giving them Macedonian arms and training them in the Macedonian military doctrine that had defeated armies across the world.

Paraphrasing firsthand accounts, Quintus Curtius Rufus tells in his *History of Alexander the Great* how Alexander outlined this vision to Macedonians, Greeks and Asians of many ethnicities.

"My intention [is] that by this sacred union I might erase all distinction between conquered and conqueror," he told them. "Asia and Europe are now one and the same kingdom. I give you Macedonian arms. Foreign newcomers though you are, I have made you established members of my force. You are both my fellow citizens and my soldiers. Everything is taking on the same hue. It is no disgrace for the Persians to copy Macedonian customs nor for the Macedonians to imitate the Persians. Those who are to live under the same king should enjoy the same rights."

Though Alexander's empire did not survive his death intact, the influence of Hellenistic civilization on those parts of the world remained for centuries.

The greed of his successors may have broken his empire into parts, but it is a great posthumous testament to Alexander's organizational and political skill that the major fragments survived intact for so long. Both the Seleucid Empire and Ptolemaic Dynasty lasted until Roman times.

Perhaps greater testaments to Alexander are that the Diadochi fought over the remains of his empire for longer than it took him to amass it, that none made any significant additions and that no single successor ever ruled over the entire empire of Alexander the Great.

Note on Sources

In the centuries immediately following his death in 323 BC, Alexander's life and triumphs were universally known, part of the fabric of human knowledge. He was a legend in his own time across parts of three continents, and his influence on the course of cultural and political history was felt long past his death.

While no first comprehensive accounts of Alexander's life exist from his own times, such accounts were still available to be used as references by five important Roman-era biographers whose work does survive. The Romans were deeply fascinated by Alexander, perhaps because of his imperial aspirations. Much of what we know about him is the result of the far-reaching preoccupation with him by writers who wrote of him during the Roman period.

The works that have since been lost to history include *The Deeds of Alexander*, written by Callisthenes of Olynthus, who traveled with Alexander. Other early accounts that were still available to the Romans were those written by Aristobulus of Cassandreia, a Greek historian and engineer who accompanied Alexander on his campaigns, and by Ptolemy, a boyhood friend who became one of Alexander's most trusted and longest-serving officers—as well as the founder of Egypt's Ptolemaic Dynasty. There was also a ten-volume history of Alexander's exploits written by Chares of Mytilene, a Greek bureaucrat who was a member of Alexander's court.

The first of the five earliest surviving biographies of Alexander is that by the Greek historian Diodorus Siculus (Diodorus of Sicily), who was born in the first century BC at Agyrium (now Agira) on the island of Sicily. Little is known of his life, but 15 volumes of his 40-volume *Bibliotheca Historica* or *Historical Library* remain as his legacy. Among the content of these works is his complete account of Alexander.

Probably the most comprehensive of the surviving Alexander biographies are the three that were penned in the first and second centuries AD. The Roman historian Quintus Curtius Rufus wrote the first of these in Latin. Little else is known is known of Curtius, although he may have served as a Roman military officer and senator early in the first century. Much of his work as a historian is lost, although the final eight books of his very detailed ten-volume *Historiae Alexandri Magni*, or *History of Alexander the Great*, do exist.

One of the most prolific writers of his age was the Greek historian Plutarch, whose Roman name was Lucius Mestrius Plutarchus (c. AD 46–120). A naturalized Roman citizen, he is best known for his *Parallel Lives,* also called *Lives of Noble Greeks and Romans,* a collection of biographies of more than four dozen notable individuals, including Alexander and Julius Caesar.

The most detailed of the Alexander biographies is *Anabasis Alexandri* or *The Campaigns of Alexander,* by Arrian of Nicomedia (Lucius Flavius Arrianus; c. AD 86–146). Like Plutarch, Arrian was a Greek who became a naturalized Roman citizen. Born in Nicomedia (now Izmit), near Istanbul in what is now northern Turkey, he studied philosophy at Epirus and served as an officer in the Roman army during campaigns from Gaul to Armenia. As governor of the Roman province of Achaea on the Peloponnesian Peninsula in Greece, he became acquainted with Hadrian, who later became emperor and Arrian's patron. Arrian's practical field experience as a military man brought a very important perspective to his work when he later embarked on a career as a historian. His *Anabasis Alexandri* is indispensable to understanding the sieges and battles in which Alexander was involved, fleshing out particular facts and nuances that are glossed over by the others.

From the third century, the last of the five principal biographies of Alexander is that contained within two books of the 44-volume *Epitoma Historiarum Philippicarum* or *Epitome of Philippic History* written in Latin by Marcus Junianius Justinus, known as Justin. Virtually nothing is known of him apart from his name on the title page of his ambitious history of the world.

In writing his book, various editions and translations of the works of the five biographers were referenced. For Diodorus, it was the edition of *Bibliotheca Historica* translated by C. Bradford Welles for the Loeb Classical Library and published in Cambridge by Harvard University Press in 1963. For Curtius, we referenced the translation of *Historiae Alexandri Magni* translated by John Yardley and published in New York by Penguin in 1984. For Plutarch, we used editions of *Parallel Lives* translated by Frank Cole Babbitt and by Bernadotte Perrin for the Loeb Classical Library, both published in Cambridge by Harvard University Press, in 1919 and 1936 respectively. For Arrian, it was the edition of *Anabasis Alexandri* translated by E. J. Chinnock and published in London by Henry G. Bohn in 1893. For Justinus, it was the edition of *Epitoma Historiarum Philippicarum* translated John Selby Watson and published in London by Henry G. Bohn in 1853.

Over time, Alexander's five biographers have become so entwined in the Alexander legend that they emerge as characters in his story. Not all of the biographers choose to describe exactly the same events in his life, and each places a different emphasis on various aspects of his life and career, giving us the opportunity to view Alexander from several points of view. It is from these varying perspectives we are able to shape a full, multidimensional picture of the man known to history as Alexander the Great.

Index

battles
See Artemisium; Chaeronea;
    Gaugamela; Granicus River;
    Hydaspes; Issus; Jaxartes;
    Leuctra;
    Mantinea;Marathon; Persian
    Gate; Salamis; Thermopylae
Bay of Bengal, 158–9
Bazira, siege of (327 BC), 136–7
Beauregard, P. G. T., 33
Belephantes, 183–5
Bessus, 71, 74, 76–7, 79, 84,
    100, 102, 107–12, 121, 128
Bible, 195
Bibliotheca Alexandrina, 65
Bibliotheca Historica, or
    Historical Library, 32, 78
Brison, 74
Britain, 114
    See Great Britain
British Museum, 4, 80, 102
Bronze Age, 60
Bosporus, 6, 18
Botsford, George Willis, 17, 49,
    59
Bucephala, 156
Bucephalas the horse, 17, 31, 38,
    74, 153–4, 156
Bulgaria, 6
Bull Run, First Battle of (1861),
    28, 33
Byblos, 52, 55
Byzantine Empire, 18
Byzantium, 18–19
Caesar, Julius, vii, 189, 191,
    194–5, 200
Caligula, 189
Callisthenes, 46, 48, 53, 71, 78,
    120, 125–6, 199
Cambyses II, 86
Canaanite settlements, 60
Cappadocian cavalry, 71, 74
Caranus (half-brother), 22
Caria, 35
Caspian Gates, 101–2, 106
Caspian Sea, 103
Cassander, 188, 191
Central Asia, 18, 41, 96, 104–5,
    107, 112–16, 119–20,
    123–4, 126, 127–8, 130–1,
    132, 134, 137, 156, 175,
    191
Chaeronea, battle of (338 BC),
    3, 19–20, 25
Chandragupta Maurya, 191
character (Alexander the Great)
    ambition, 160–4
    audacity, 138–9, 142
    binge drinking, 125, 186–8
    confidence, viii, 2, 3, 16–17,
        34, 73
    creativity, 34, 128
    curiosity, 18–19
    gentleness, 84–5
    inspirational, 42

judge of character, 83, 105
    magnanimity, 85, 102, 155–6
    thinking "outside the box," 34,
        42, 85
    treatment of women and
        children, 49–50, 63, 84–5,
        115
Chios, 37, 48
chiliarches, 85–6, 105, 108
China, 104, 112
Chorienes, rock of, 131
Cilician Gates, 43–4
City of Cyrus, See Cyropolis
Civil War, 28, 33, 85
Cleander, 73–4
Cleitus the Black, 26, 31–2, 101,
    109, 125–6, 188
Cleitus the White, 146, 167
Cleombrotus I, 11
Cleopatra Eurydice of Macedon
    (stepmother), 21, 22
Cleopatra of Macedon (sister),
    21–2
Cleopatra VII Philopator, 43,
    191
Coenus, 26, 46, 57, 93–4,
    101–2, 106–8, 123, 136,
    145–6, 150–1, 157, 162–4
    death of, 163–4
    on going home, 162–4
Cold War, 9, 42
Companion Cavalry, 12–13,
    19–20, 30–1, 46–7, 57–8,
    62, 72, 74, 87, 101–2, 105,
    107, 109–10, 114, 119,
    121, 123, 133, 139, 146,
    148, 153, 156, 163, 167,
    186–7
Confederate Army, 33
Cophes, 128–9
Corinth, 7–8, 10–11
Corinthian War, 10
counterinsurgency, 106–8,
    123–4, 127, 132–7, 181–2
Craterus, 26, 46, 88, 93–4, 102,
    106, 115, 123, 135, 139,
    147, 149, 153, 156, 166,
    173–6, 180, 190–1
Crazy Horse, 119
Cretan archers, 46
Crook, George, 119
Curtius (Quintus Curtius Rufus)
    (first century AD), 1, 59,
    62–3, 70–1, 78–80, 82–3,
    86–7, 90, 92–4, 97–100,
    102, 108–9, 111, 123,
    126–31, 133–4, 140–3,
    146, 149–57, 159, 161,
    170, 173, 178, 180–1, 196,
    199–200
Custer, George Armstrong, 45
Cypriots, 56, 166
Cyprus, 52, 55
Cyropolis ("City of Cyrus"),
    114–16, 121

Cyrus the Great, 6, 40, 82, 84,
    98, 114, 175, 177–8, 195
    tomb of, 177–8
Dahae, 123, 146
Damascus, 50
Danube River, 6, 24
Dardanelles
    See Hellespont
Darius I (Darius the Great), 6–7,
    88, 117, 132
Darius II, 25
Darius III, 1–2, 3–4, 25, 27–9,
    37, 40–51, 54, 63, 68–73,
    84, 90–1, 96–7, 99, 100–2,
    103–8, 111, 124–5, 130,
    145, 149, 153, 160, 179
    appeals for family back,
        49–51
    and Battle of Issus, 44–9
    death of, 102, 104, 105, 160
    guilt of, 84
Dataphernes, 110–11
Delbrück, Hans, 71
Delian League, 9
Delphi, 2, 13, 25, 39, 66, 159
Demophon, 169
Demaratus the Corinthian, 98
Demetrius, 146, 150, 167
democracy, 6, 9, 86
Diadochi, 191, 197
Diodorus Siculus (Diodorus of
    Sicily), 22, 32, 58, 71, 78,
    80, 86, 88, 93, 96–9, 102,
    105–6, 133, 138–9, 141–2,
    146, 151, 153, 157–60,
    169, 176, 180–4, 186,
    190–1, 193, 199–200
Dionysus, 14, 124–5, 186
Doloaspis, 64
Drangiana, 108, 173
Drypteis, 41, 87, 179
Dymnus, 108
Ecbatana, 96, 99–101, 105–7,
    180–1
Egypt, 52–4, 58, 60, 63–6, 68,
    70, 74, 108, 132–3, 166,
    186, 188–9, 191, 199
elephants, 71, 74, 76, 144, 146,
    149–54, 159, 166, 172–3,
    177
Epaminondas of Thebes, 10–13
Ephesian Artemis, 16–17
Ephesus, 16–17, 33, 38
Epirus, 12
Epitoma Historiarum
    Philippicarum, or Epitome of
    Philippic History, 18
Eretria, 6–7
Erigyius, 108
Europa (half-brother), 22
Euphrates, 48, 68–9, 72, 174,
    180, 183, 185, 187
Eurydice I of Macedon
    (grandmother), 11–12
Fall of Rome, 13

Massagetae, 123
Mazaces, 63
Mazaeus, 69, 72, 74, 76–9,
   82–3, 101, 155
McDowell, Irvin, 33
Media, 84
Medius, 186–7
Meleager, 147, 173
Memnon of Rhodes, 29, 32,
   35–8
Menedemus, 121
Menidas, 74–7
Mesopotamia, 69, 82–3, 179
Midas, 38–9
Miletus, 34–5
military
   See Greco-Macedonian army;
      Persian army
military engineering, 26, 32, 35,
   55, 59, 60–1, 64, 69, 73,
   110, 115, 118, 128, 131,
   141, 185, 195
   See Cyropolis; Tyre causeway
military leadership
   and dissent, 124–5, 160–4,
      179–80
   style of, 41–2, 100–1, 104–7
   and attire, 74, 104–5, 124–5,
      179
   inspirational, 42, 105
   and organizational changes,
      85–6
   up-front, viii, ix, 24–5, 30, 56,
      58, 70, 157, 162, 195
military reporting, 32–3, 49, 90,
   100, 110, 120
military strategy, 52–6
   counterinsurgency, 106–8,
      123–4
   downsizing, 100–1, 105–8,
      119, 180–1
   and marriage, 178–9, 196
   obfuscation, 146
   organizational changes, 85–6
   and recruitment, 83–4
   and vision, 3, 112, 195–6
   See governance
military tactics, 195
   maneuver, viii-ix, 3–4, 57, 75,
      147
   shock and awe, 25
   siege tactics, 35–6, 138
Miltiades the Younger, 7
Mithridates, 29–31, 40
Molesworth, George, 132
Mongols, 116
Mosul, Iraq, 1, 71
Multan, 167–8
Musicanus, 172–3
Myriandros, 44–5
Mytilene, 37
Nanda Empire, 158–9
Napoleon I of France, 8, 13
Nautaca, 110, 112, 127
Nazi concentration camps, 97

Nearchus, 166–7, 170, 174–6,
   177–8, 183–4, 186
Nebuchadnezzar II, 53, 82, 184
Nectanebo II, 63
Neoptolemus, 62
Neoptolemus of Epirus, 14
Nicanor, 34, 46
Nicaea, 156
Nicesipolis of Thessaly, 14
Nile Delta, 63–4
North American Treaty
   Organization (NATO), 9,
   42
Noury, Manouchehr Saadat, 95
Oldach, David, 188
Olympias (mother), 14, 15,
   20–1, 54, 66, 87, 184, 191
Olympic Games, 15, 16
omens, 1, 14, 30, 38–9, 54, 57,
   61–2, 64–6, 70, 80, 87, 92,
   117–18, 138–9, 163,
   184–6, 188
Omphis, 133, 144, 147
oracles, 2, 13, 25, 39, 65–7, 159,
   174, 188
   See Amun; Delphi
Orontobates, 35–6
Oxus River, 110, 118, 122–3
Oxyartes, 110–11, 123, 128–31
Oxydracians, 157, 168, 171
Pakistan, 132–6, 138–9, 144,
   156–8, 167–8, 172–3
Pamphylia, 38, 166
Parmenio, 13, 15, 21, 26, 30–1,
   34–5, 38, 44, 46–7, 72–4,
   76–9, 86–7, 89, 101,
   105–6, 108–9
Parthia, 71–2, 100–1, 103–4,
   106–7, 175–6, 180
Patala, 173–4
Paurava, 144, 155
Pausanias of Orestis, 22
Peithon, 167, 173
Peloponnesus, 8–10
Peloponnesian League, 9
Peloponnesian mercenary
   infantry, 84
Peloponnesian War (431 BC),
   9–10
Perdiccas, 133, 146, 167–8, 170,
   191
Perdiccas of Macedon (paternal
   uncle), 11–12
Pericles, 9
Persepolis, 88, 89, 96–100,
   102–3, 106, 120, 160, 174,
   177–8, 181, 191
   burning of, 99
Perseus, 66
Persian army, 29–30, 40–1,
   71–9, 85, 100, 106
   multiethnicity of, 71–9
   organization of, 85
   size of, 71–2, 100
   See Greek mercenaries

Persian Empire (550–330 BC),
   1–4, 5–6, 25, 38–9, 50–1,
   52, 59, 67, 68, 80–1, 84,
   87–8, 97–8, 103, 105–6,
   112–14, 124, 173, 178–9
   conquest of, 2, 3, 59, 67, 80,
      113, 124
   elderly Greek captives 97–8
   and intermarriage, 178–9
   opulence of, 50
   See satrapies
Persian Gate, battle of the (330
   BC), 89–95
Persian Gulf, 159, 173, 177,
   183, 185
Persian Invasions of Greece
   (map), xi
Persian Royal Road, 89
Peter I of Russia, 12
Peucestas, 64, 168–9
phalanxes, 4, 11–13, 31, 35,
   45–8, 62, 74, 76–7, 101,
   118, 121, 123, 133, 135,
   139, 146–7, 149–52, 157,
   164, 168, 173
Pharnuches, 121–3
Pharos of Alexandria, 65
Phegeus, 158
Phila of Elimiotis, 14
Philip (son of Machatas), 172
Philip II of Macedonia (father),
   vii, 3, 10, 11–14, 15–23,
   24–5, 54, 66, 98, 109, 190
   assassination of, 21–2
   on birth of Alexander, 15–16
   campaign against Persia, 21–2
   empire of, 17–18, 24–5
   king of Greece, 20–3
   marriages, 14, 20–1
   cavalry as shock force, 12–13
   repudiation of Alexander,
      20–1
   subordinate commanders, 13
Philip III of Macedonia, 191
Philoneicus. 17
Philotas, 74, 86–7, 93–4, 105,
   108–9, 111, 124
Philoxenus, 81, 86
Phocians, 17
Phocis, 13
Phoenicia, 48, 52–3, 55–6, 58,
   74, 166, 183, 185
Phrygia, 38, 90, 130
Picts of Scotland, 114
Pillars of Heracles, 159
Pinarus River, 44–6
Pindar, 25
Pir-Sar, See Aornos
Plato, 9, 12, 195
Plutarch (46–120 AD), 1–2, 14,
   15–18, 20–1, 24, 26, 30–2,
   37–9, 41, 44, 50, 52–4, 57,
   61, 63–7, 71–5, 77–8, 80,
   81, 84, 86, 92–3, 98–9,
   102, 104–5, 107–8, 130,